# Giant City State Park

*and the*

# Civilian Conservation Corps

# GIANT CITY STATE PARK
## and the
# CIVILIAN
# CONSERVATION
# CORPS

A History in Words and Pictures

Kay Rippelmeyer

Southern Illinois University Press
*Carbondale and Edwardsville*

Printed in the United States of America
13  12  11  10    4  3  2
Library of Congress Cataloging-in-Publication Data
Rippelmeyer, Kay, 1953–
Giant City State Park and the Civilian Conservation Corps : a
history in words and pictures / Kay Rippelmeyer-Tippy.
   p.  cm. — (Shawnee books)
Includes bibliographical references and index.
ISBN 13: 978-0-8093-2921-2 (cloth : alk. paper)
ISBN 13: 978-0-8093-2922-9 (pbk. : alk. paper)
ISBN 10: 0-8093-2921-2 (cloth : alk. paper)
ISBN 10: 0-8093-2922-0 (pbk. : alk. paper)
eISBN: 978-0-8093-8563-8
eISBN: 0-8093-8563-5
1. Civilian Conservation Corps (U.S.)—Illinois—Giant City
State Park—History. 2. Giant City State Park (Ill.)—History—
20th century. I. Title.
F547.J2 R56 2010
977.3′994 dc—22                                    2009018011

Printed on recycled paper.♻
The paper used in this publication meets the minimum
requirements of American National Standard for Information
Sciences—Permanence of Paper for Printed Library
Materials, ANSI Z39.48-1992. ⊚

*T*his book is dedicated to all the CCC men who shared their memories and photographs with me over the last thirty years, most of whom have died before seeing their words in print. I'm sorry that this work, inspired by you, took so long to reach publication, but I am forever grateful for having met each of you. You are the classiest group of men I've ever known.

I'm grateful as well to all my teachers, mentors, and friends, some also deceased, who encouraged me to research and to write: Barbara Burr Hubbs, David V. Koch, Howard Webb, Earle Stibitz, Betty Fladeland, John Y. Simon, Richard Peterson, Wanda Oakey, Herb Meyer, Max Hutchison, and Jenny Skufca.

At the SIU Press, Karl Kageff, Wayne Larsen, and Barb Martin kindly helped this first-time author improve the manuscript, as did Julie Bush, a most careful and considerate copy editor.

# Contents

# Illustrations

# Timeline Relevant to the Establishment of Giant City State Park

|  |  |
|---|---|
| **1903** | Fort Massac State Park established |
| **1911** | Starved Rock State Park established |
| **1925** | Illinois law directs the development of a system of state parks to preserve historic sites and natural features |
| **1927** | Black Hawk State Park established |
| | White Pines Forest established |
| | Giant City State Park established |
| **September 1927** | First tract of land purchased for Giant City State Park |
| **July 1929** | Ralph Corzine appointed as first park custodian |
| **November 1929** | Cedar rust controversy |
| **January 1930** | Road graveled from State Route 2 into Makanda |
| **November 1932** | Franklin Delano Roosevelt wins in a Democratic landslide election |
| **March 1933** | FDR is inaugurated and authorized to establish a conservation work force |
| **April 1933** | The first Civilian Conservation Corps enrollee signs up |
| **June 1933** | Giant City CCC camp established at Giant City State Park by Company #696 |
| | Company #1657 organized near Chatham |
| **December 5, 1933** | Repeal of Prohibition |
| **December 10, 1933** | Company #1657 moves into Stone Fort CCC camp at Giant City State Park |
| **1934** | Subway project at Giant City |
| **May 1934** | Company #1657 leaves Giant City for LeRoy, Illinois |
| **June 1934** | Construction begins on Giant City lodge |
| **July 1934** | Kent Keller campaigns and entertains CCC boys at Camp Giant City |
| **August 1934** | Arrival at Giant City State Park of CCC Company #692 |
| **Fall–Winter 1934** | Archaeological relic Stone Fort is reconstructed by CCC men |
| **November 1934** | Massive central oak columns raised in Giant City lodge |
| **March 1935** | Stonework on lodge completed |
| **March 10–11, 1935** | Drury Creek floods |
| **October 20, 1935** | Barbecue picnic at Giant City State Park draws a crowd of 8,000 |
| **November 1935** | Company #692 departs Giant City for Copper Falls State Park, Wisconsin |
| **Winter 1935–36** | Coldest winter on record in Midwest |
| **March 1936** | Construction of overnight cabins completed |
| **August 30, 1936** | Giant City State Park lodge dedication |
| **January 1937** | Flood relief work |
| **December 8, 1941** | United States declares war on Japan |
| **1942** | Giant City CCC camp closes |

# Giant City State Park
*and the*
# Civilian Conservation Corps

GIANT CITY STATE PARK

# Introduction

The dramatic landscape of Giant City State Park has always been described in recorded histories of southern Illinois as beautiful, strange, and beloved grounds. Located at the juncture of Jackson, Union, and Williamson counties, the land defied straight line demarcation by surveyors and road builders. Melting glaciers and eroding sandstone created the natural phenomena—towering cliffs, rock shelters, balancing boulders, and pathways through sheer wall "skyscrapers"— that gave the area its "Giant City" name, its unique geological renown, and its designation as a National Natural Landmark.

Soaring tulip poplars and sassafras trees grow straight skyward from the narrow "street" floors. Thick green mosses and delicate ferns cover the moist vertical stone walls. Referred to as "Fern Rocks" by the famous biologist George Hazen French in 1870, the area has been for over a century and a half a favorite study and collection area for naturalists and

A road leading to wonder in Giant City State Park. State of Illinois Department of Conservation, print #1212-2.

herb collectors. A few years apart, Professor French and scientist Stephen A. Forbes discovered previously unknown plants within one hundred feet of each other—French's Shooting Star and the Forbes Saxifrage.[1]

Renowned botanist Robert Mohlenbrock, in his *Giant City State Park: An Illustrated Handbook*, lists more than thirty species of ferns, over eight hundred flowering plants, more than two hundred kinds of birds, and dozens of mammals, amphibians, and reptiles that make the park their home. Twenty-seven percent of the entire state's species of ferns and flowering plants can be found in the park because it encompasses such a great diversity of habitats. Fern Rocks Nature Preserve, a 170-acre area near the park's Makanda entrance, has been dedicated as one of Illinois's pristine areas, unique for its large array of spring wildflowers and rare plants.[2]

Archaeological evidence reveals that Native Americans were well acquainted with the area for many centuries. Though they did not build any large settlements within the park boundaries, they did construct a stone enclosure and camped under rock shelters in the park. Native American hunting parties would have found the area rich in plant and animal resources, as did the first Europeans and Americans who ventured there.

In the past two centuries, the rugged terrain of Giant City, like much of the land in southern Illinois's Ozark Hills and Shawnee Hills, has been described in written accounts as an excellent place to hunt wildlife. The area long remained a hard-to-get-to, untamed place where wild animals—and certain people—could hunker down and hide. Some of the last bear and native elk seen in southern Illinois were reportedly killed there in the 1830s.[3] Theodore W. Thompson wrote that prior to the 1890s, a large catamount (mountain lion) was killed with a tree limb by the fourteen-year-old son of Daniel McConnell, Makanda's postmaster, while walking from the old Rendleman School

between Giant City and Stone Fort.[4] In addition, the area's hollows and caves were rumored to have been hiding places for Civil War deserters.[5] In the late 1920s, a newspaper published an article documenting the belief that famous Western writer Zane Grey chose the secluded Giant City State Park as a place to camp for a couple of weeks.[6]

The first recorded permanent settlers on the site of the park, the Colemans and Vancils, arrived during the years 1800 to 1806, camping first but later returning to stay because of the abundance of wildlife. The Vancils opened the Wylie farm, located in section 35, Makanda Township.[7] Even though the acres of what is now the park had been privately owned since the early 1800s, there is ample evidence that it was enjoyed throughout the nineteenth century as a "commons," a place open to visitors and neighboring locals, generation after generation. Like other unique natural areas in southern Illinois, such as Bell Smith Springs, Lusk Creek, Fern Clyffe, Fountain Bluff, and Pomona Natural Bridge, Giant City was a favorite place for holiday picnics and reunion gatherings. Even more popular than Giant City for many years was the more accessible ancient archaeological wonder Stone Fort, eastward up the hill from Makanda. In the 1880s, hundreds, perhaps thousands, climbed the hill for the annual Fourth of July celebration there.[8]

Throughout the latter half of the nineteenth century, because of their natural beauty and mystery, Giant City and Stone Fort were two of the most often visited treasures in the interior landscape of southern Illinois. The establishment of the railroad through Makanda in February 1854 did much to open the area to outsiders' appreciation.[9] Perhaps, too, the area became more famous than other natural attractions in southern Illinois because it contrasts so sharply, so suddenly, with all of the relatively flat prairie land lying to its north.

Although Giant City's landscape is unique and exceptional, its natural history is generally

A giant playground for adults. State of Illinois Department of Conservation, print #1219-1.

A Giant City street to an alley or "squeeze." State of Illinois Department of Conservation, print #1060-6.

representative of much of the land in the Shawnee National Forest of southern Illinois. This land between the rivers at the southern tip of the state (referred to by recent tourism boosters as "southernmost Illinois") lies south of the glaciation line. The Illinoian mountain of ice scraped and dumped debris, stopping just short of this southernmost region. Giant City State Park also parallels the history of the Shawnee National Forest in that both were established in the 1920s and 1930s through the efforts of farsighted, tenacious southern Illinoisans who loved this rugged land and wanted to preserve the best of it for future generations to study and enjoy. Although Giant City was established as a state park in 1927, it wasn't until the roadwork of the Civilian Conservation Corps in the 1930s

that visitors could travel in any season through Giant City as well as to many of southern Illinois's lesser-known scenic and natural wonders in the national forest.

During the years immediately preceding the advent of the CCC, the building of access roads to Giant City State Park was a slow and arduous local effort in sometimes-difficult cooperation with the State of Illinois Department of Public Works and Buildings. There was little public money for land acquisition or for road- and bridge-building. Between 1927 and 1933, southern Illinois was in a deep and, for many people, a seemingly hopeless economic depression. It is a remarkable testament to the human need for wonder and public recreation space that parks were established during these Depression-era

**Devil's Stand Table.** Hedrich-Blessing photograph, Division of Parks, Springfield, IL, #10680W.

years. A few have argued that it was precisely the dire economic situation of southern Illinois landowners that forced them to sell their land to the government, saying that "the government got them when they were down." During the economic depressions of the 1870s, 1890s, and the 1930s, many small farmers felt compelled to sell to moneyed landowners. However, research shows that the 1930s Depression-era lands sold to the state of Illinois and to the federal government were most often severely eroded, abused, and cutover lands offered by willing sellers. Some landowners liked the short-term promise of local jobs at expected work camps, while others saw the long-term altruistic benefits of large public spaces to grow trees, recreate, and hunt.

Between 1927 and 1933 at Giant City State Park, a narrow eight-hundred- to nine-hundred-acre strip constituted the newly bought public land. Wedged between orchards and bluffs cleared of their usable timber, the park straddled the Jackson-Union county line. In the park's early history, officials from the two counties who represented opposing political parties competed for equal shares of patronage jobs and funds. In 1933, when the CCC established its first camps throughout southern Illinois in its efforts to create a national forest, it also placed two camps within the boundaries of the newly designated Giant City State Park, one in Jackson County and one in Union County.

A well-known street intersection in Giant City. Division of Parks, Springfield, IL.

INTRODUCTION

Deer had become extinct in southern Illinois until the Civilian Conservation Corps era of the 1930s. Wildlife populations have multiplied in the park and nearby Shawnee National Forest since their reintroduction and habitat restoration in the 1930s.
Courtesy Giant City Visitor Center.

Camp Giant City and Camp Stone Fort were manned primarily by southern and south-central Illinois men in the CCC companies #696, #1657, and #692. Their work in the park and their lives in the CCC camps from 1933 to 1942 are central to the history of the Depression era in southern Illinois. These CCC men felt a strong attachment to the park even four or five decades after having lived there. They related their stories for this book with pride in their work and with great affection for fellow CCC enrollees. They spoke of having been transformed by their CCC years, enrolling as hungry, underweight, insecure, nearly defeated boys and becoming strong, proud, hopeful, skilled men who had learned to live and work together. Their legacy remains not only in the roads, trails, bridges, and lodge they helped build but also in the kind of men the CCC let them become.

The most striking and memorable of the creations of southern Illinois's CCC men is the Giant City lodge, which was described in the 1937 official annual of the Jefferson Barracks CCC District as "the outstanding piece of CCC construction in the United States."[10] In 1984, when the Illinois Department of Conservation applied to the National Register of Historic

On a high wall above one of the most prominent of Giant City's streets is engraved

(Of. Ill.)

ALBERT S. THOMPSON

FREMONT. BODY. GUARD.

FEB. 22ND. 1862. A.D.

Albert S. Thompson was brother to Theodore W. Thompson. They lived outside Makanda and, in defiance of the southern sympathizers in the area, raised the Union flag on a sixty-foot tulip poplar after Lincoln's inauguration. Albert was indeed in Company D of John Charles Fremont's cavalry bodyguard unit, which searched out army deserters in Missouri. The Thompsons were the owners of much of the land around Makanda and later Carbondale's SIUC campus. The woods and campus lake bear the Thompson name.

Photo by Jenny Skufca.

A portion of a 1938 aerial photograph showing Camp Giant City, the site of Camp Stone Fort, and the Union-Jackson county line between the two.

Source: Iowa Aerial Surveys, 1938, BGQ-4-30, 10-21-38, 9 x 9 inches; scale 1:20,000. Washington, D.C., U.S. Department of Agriculture, 1938.

Lodge interior under construction. Courtesy of Matthew Skertich.

Places to establish historic status for all of Illinois's Depression-era state park lodges, the department described Giant City State Park's lodge as a "disproportionately strong architectural statement," reflecting the 1930s "political clout of southern Illinoisans for whom the park has always had great sentimental value."[11]

Today, Giant City State Park encompasses over four thousand acres and is still a home and sanctuary for rare plants, birds, and animals. Visited by 1.1 million people in 2007, the park now has many miles of trails (including some for equestrians and others that are accessible to the disabled), picnic areas, camp-sites, cabins, and a horse stable as well as a visitor center featuring natural history, CCC exhibits, and an ever-growing list of the CCC enrollees who were stationed at Giant City State Park.[12]

Engendered in the vision of a few imaginative and persistent Makanda citizens, the park's establishment is credited to the state of Illinois. The dream was carried to fruition through the ideals of President Franklin Delano Roosevelt's Civilian Conservation Corps and built with wheelbarrows and shovels in the hands of everyday heroes, primarily Illinois men who agreed to work for a living.

# 1 The Land and Its People

An explanation attributed to "Indian lore" in southern Illinois is that Giant City was a battleground between the fire god and the water god. If the sun is the fire and rain the water, this is not a bad metaphor for the geological processes that took place there. Whereas Stone Fort still begs questions about its human origins, the story of Giant City's creation is laid wide open in the rocks and can be read by scientists and those with sufficient imagination.

Southern Illinois was covered for over 200 million years—from 570 to 345 million years ago—by a warm, shallow sea that extended over much of the midcontinent. What was essentially the Gulf of Mexico extended this far north. What we see today in the rock structures of Giant City and throughout the southernmost region of Illinois are the layers of limestone and sandstone that formed on top of each other at the edges of the water as the sea's shorelines fluctuated northward

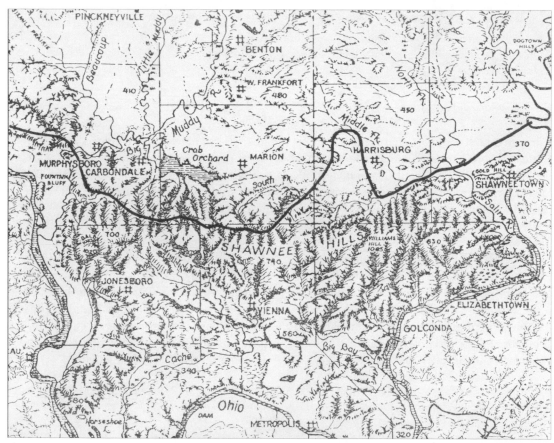

The southernmost quarter of an Illinois landforms map on which a line has been drawn showing the approximate southern extent of glaciation just north of Giant City State Park. Source: "Landforms of Illinois" by James A. Bier, 1956, publ. by Illinois State Geological Survey, Urbana, Illinois.

and southward hundreds of miles for millions of years.

Then, from 1 to 2 million years ago, as the climate cooled, an extensive polar ice cap developed in the northern hemisphere. This ice advanced southward and then retreated, repeating the cycle over hundreds of thousands of years. Four major glacial advances occurred over the land we now call Illinois. The third of these, appropriately named the Illinoian, came some 200,000 years ago and ultimately covered almost the entire state—reaching farther south than any glaciation in North America.

In southern Illinois, the southernmost reach of the Illinoian created a glacial limit line, a geological-geographic line that runs approximately from the mouth of the Wabash River on the east to the vicinity of Harrisburg, then southwest near Creal Springs and west along Cedar Creek valley, then northwest paralleling the Mississippi River. In Jackson County, this glacial line runs just north of Makanda and crosses Devil's Kitchen and Little Grassy lakes. Little if any glacial ice reached what is now Giant City State Park.

North of this line, the land has been scraped and covered over by extensive glacial deposits that formed soil sometimes a mile thick. But south of this line, the ancient rocks created under the shallow sea are in many places still visible on the surface of the land. They escaped being covered by the windblown loess that blanketed most of the land to the north. In these rocks may be found fossils of the simple animal and plant life that existed along the shores of the old sea and in coal beds that formed under the sea—evidence of the life in southern Illinois before the glaciers.[1]

Meltwater from receding glaciations created the great river valleys that form the southern boundaries of Illinois. These, together with the glacial limit line of the Illinoian ice, frame a distinct geographic and cultural region of Illinois that encompasses the present-day counties of Alexander, Pulaski, Massac, Union, Johnson, Pope, Hardin, Jackson, Williamson, Saline, and Gallatin—a region known by some historians as "Egypt." Rather than the prairie grasslands that eventually grew up in the deeper soil of central Illinois, southern Illinois grew tall trees on its ridges, in its deep hollows, and along its canyoned streams and waterfalls. A tremendous deciduous forest, primarily of oaks and hickories, extended river-to-river and was home to great herds of animals and eventually to Native Americans who thrived there for over ten thousand years.

Southern Illinois's cultural history parallels that of much of the Midwest in each phase: prehistory, European American settlement, Civil War turmoil, and eras of resource exploitation, industrialization, depressions, and recovery. But some areas of southern Illinois, because of their peculiar geography, have not been easy to change from their natural state. Geographically, as in the Appalachian regions, some ground was too steep, full of canyons and waterfalls, useless for cultivation, or too difficult for the loggers' reach. Some of extreme southern Illinois was too swampy and malaria-ridden for easy habitation, so some lands were left alone.

Fortunately as well, some southern Illinoisans recognized with uncommon good sense that parts of this remote land were too geologically or biologically instructive, or simply too beautiful, to be owned and exploited individually. The first owners of Giant City and the Stone Fort bluff had little agricultural use for the acreage, anyway. Perhaps these grounds had traditionally been shared spaces—for the Native Americans and others—secluded between the great Mississippi and Ohio river thoroughfares. Archaeologists have wondered if the stone forts found throughout southern Illinois may have been demarcations of sacred spaces, places to contemplate, places where strands of meaning could be gathered between humans, land, and spirit, strands that reach far back in time.[2]

Stone Fort and Giant City are among the most accessible of southern Illinois's special natural places because they are situated just south of the glaciation line and at the northernmost edge of the rugged ridges now called the Shawnee Hills. In 1854, when the Illinois Central Railroad came through Drury Creek valley, these wondrous places became relatively easy to reach. Drury Creek cuts a valley north and south in Jackson and Union counties. When the railroad surveyors laid out the line, their most practical choice was to follow this valley. Edmund Newsome wrote in 1882, "This lovely and dramatic valley has the appearance of a great crack or fissure in the hills, with mostly precipitous sides, and through this runs the Drury. A person can almost imagine a convulsion of nature that opened a crack running north and south for miles, making ragged edges and broken rocks tumbling down the steep sides, then afterward the gap gradually partly filled up with soil washed from the hills."[3]

By 1855, railroads ruled the land and required bridges across the larger creeks and wide rivers that were suddenly seen as obstacles to progress, no longer the sole corridors of commerce. Along Drury Creek, quarries provided much of the stone for bridges and for building construction in growing towns like Carbondale, Springfield, and Chicago.[4] Before the towns of Makanda and Cobden were laid out, they were known by their railroad names, North Pass and South Pass.[5] Makanda's railroad depot was built in 1856; its post office was established in 1857. The first building lots were not platted until 1863.[6]

Railroad land developers gambled fortunes on the railroads. Many profited might-

Makanda, ca. 1880–90. Courtesy of Jackson County Historical Society, photo #740, file #1500A.

THE LAND AND ITS PEOPLE

ily, including Lewis Ashley, chief engineer of the Southern Division of the Illinois Central Railroad, as well as John Buck and David Neal, land speculators who knew in 1852 that the railroad would go along Drury Creek and so bought property there.[7] But the railroad companies themselves became the largest landowners in southern Illinois when they were given land by the federal government in order to use the sale profits to build the rail lines.

Life changed dramatically in southern Illinois's interior with the arrival of the railroad, as new markets for wheat, lumber, fruit, and vegetables were opened. Between 1860 and 1880, Makanda's economy thrived thanks to these markets and the railroad. Along the new tracks running through Jackson and Union counties, the countryside was truly transformed. As Jane Adams explains in *The Transformation of Rural Life: Southern Illinois, 1890–1990*, now towns had a direct connection to Chicago and eventually to the St. Louis markets and attracted "commercially minded farmers and developers," among them many New Englanders with different political and cultural views than their upland southern neighbors.[8] Towns were organized at approximately five-mile intervals along the Illinois Central track, with Anna and Dongola to the south of Makanda and Boskeydell to the north. Seven miles north of Makanda, Carbondale was thriving.

Fortunes were made by some around Makanda between 1860 and the 1880s, landowners who profited from the wheat crops, the peach boom, and the success of other fruit crops, as well as from asparagus, sweet potatoes, and spring-blooming flowers. The

Makanda depot, ca. 1900. Built in 1856, this depot was destroyed by fire, as reported in the *Carbondale Free Press*, March 1, 1934. Courtesy of Jackson County Historical Society, photo #2525, file #1500C.

Map showing the property ownership of the Makanda area in 1907–8 with 1943 park boundaries outlined. The two county maps were joined at the Union-Jackson county lines, resulting in some natural discrepancies. The park boundaries are derived from the U.S. Geological Survey 15 Minute Carbondale Quadrangle (Edition 1922–43). Map work by Herb Meyer. Sources: 1907 Jackson County Atlas and 1908 Union County Atlas. U.S. Department of the Interior Geological Survey, Carbondale Quadrangle, 1943.

peach crop had seldom failed, according to one source, because "heavily timbered hills afforded protection and insect enemies were few." In the month of August alone in 1867, ninety-five carloads of fruit were shipped from Makanda Station, including three carloads per day of grapes. During the strawberry harvest season of 1870, as many as three train cars of that fruit were shipped each day from Makanda northward or to eastern cities. In the summer of 1874, Makanda workers loaded as many as six train cars with fruit each day, for a season total number of 220 cars from that station. Makanda continued to thrive throughout the 1870s, boasting in 1878 four dry goods stores, one drugstore, one millinery store, one shoe shop, two cooper shops, two wagon shops, one grist mill, one combined sawmill and box factory, three blacksmith shops, three hotels, two churches, and one public school. The majority of landowning male residents of the Makanda area in 1878 listed their occupation as "farmer and fruit grower."[9]

Populations in small towns such as Makanda, Boskeydell, Pomona, and Cobden peaked around 1900, by which time houses had been built on nearly every forty acres of tillable or barely tillable land in Union and Jackson counties. In 1896, Makanda had grown to house a population of six hundred and was "the second heaviest fruit shipping point north of Cairo."[10] At about this same time, as coal had become profitable to mine and transport by rail in southern Illinois, the last of the huge oaks from the vast interior forests were cut for mine timbers as well as for building construction and railroad ties. Around Makanda, much of the cleared land was planted in orchards.

By 1900, as a result of the railroads, settlement had spread like a patchwork quilt of 40-, 80-, and 120-acre tracts over all of the land between the rivers. Even the most remote townships had several churches and schools with dirt roads leading to them from each log or frame house and barn and to the sawmills, fer-

ries, post offices, and stores. Self-sufficient for the most part, farmers sold wheat and produce from orchards and truck farms. They cut timber from the back acreage for the meager cash needed for shoes, cloth, coffee, and hardware.

The exploitation of the region's timber supply intensified between 1870 and 1920, until nearly all the land but that least accessible to horse and wagon had its trees cut and hauled to the mills. The hardwood timber industry in southern Illinois supported over 250 mills and cooperages between the Civil War and 1900 but then fell off dramatically, until by the 1920s it was meeting only the local needs for railroad ties, fence posts, fruit boxes, and baskets.[11] For the few decades between 1890 and 1920, the timber industry and agriculture meant chiefly for urban markets brought relative prosperity and stability to even the most inaccessible areas like those of Jackson county east of Makanda and to the west in Pomona township. But the economic situation rapidly deteriorated through the 1920s as crops failed, prices fell, and people lost their ability to earn cash, find jobs, and pay rent or mortgages. Even though most southern Illinois farmers were still self-sufficient in regard to their family's food supply, they felt the effects of the national economic depression before 1929. Tenant farmers and landless laborers suffered the worst through the 1920s and into the 1930s as the national economy gradually collapsed.[12]

Throughout all the years of the region's changing fortunes, from the 1850s through the 1920s, Giant City remained a place used as a commons. Beginning as early as the 1880s, the Illinois Central Railroad put on special cars to take pleasure-seekers on Sundays from Carbondale and Murphysboro to Makanda to picnic at Stone Fort and explore what was called by 1900 "Giant City." Under the ownership of a variety of families, among them the Rendlemans, Kennedys, Demings, Ashleys, and Robertses, the area continued to be used as a social gathering place. From its earliest years as

*Southern Illinois University Museum*

# Field Trip to Giant City
# By Geography Class, Circa 1900

ENDURING NATURE of the ancient Illinois Ozarks is best exhibited by this picture of a geography class field trip to Giant City around 1900. A gentleman named Mr. Ellis, in the lower right hand corner, was instructor of this class of young men and ladies at the Southern Illinois Normal, a teacher's college which has expanded into a large university in recent years.

Whether they took the train from Carbondale Makanda, or *North Pass* as it was known in its earlier day is not known. It was a distance of some eight miles fro Carbondale and an early start may have allowed them travel via horse-drawn surrey. Either way, it's a cinch th didn't use *Shank's Mare* or college students have chang more than we think.

Field trip to Fern Rocks at Giant City by SINU geography class, ca. 1900.
Southern Illinois University Museum, printed in *Outdoor Illinois* 1.4 (June 1962): 28.

a town, Makanda held an annual Fourth of July celebration at the "Old Stone Fort," to which as many as five thousand people a year are said to have attended to hear speakers, singers, and bands. From Makanda, the ride or walk to the stone fort was about a half-mile uphill. The streets of Giant City were a hearty walk to the south. Both sites continually attracted tourists, naturalists, and students, such as those from Southern Illinois Normal University (SINU, later known as SIU) who took the eight-mile train trip to study the area's geology and botany.[13]

## GIANT CITY STATE PARK IS ESTABLISHED

In the first decades of the twentieth century, a national movement to establish parks and recreation areas resulted in public lands being set aside in Illinois and throughout the country. Nevertheless, southern Illinoisans had to lobby actively to get a state park, just as they had to struggle for many years to see a national forest established in their state. No one lobbied harder to see the Giant City area become protected as a state park than John G. Mulcaster, who worked as the station manager at Makanda's Illinois Central Railroad station from 1902 to 1927. Mulcaster was the most active conservationist and tourism booster of Giant City and Stone Fort during the 1920s. According to his own words, he and two other colleagues conceived the idea and spent "four years of almost ceaseless work on it, writing story, song, and history, making twenty or more trips to Springfield and walking hundreds of miles [leading people] through it explaining its beauty spots and historic features." Mulcaster wrote many articles promoting southern Illinois's natural beauty for regional newspapers and for the *Journal of the Illinois State Historical Society* and was a regular columnist in Hal Trovillion's newspaper, the *Egyptian Republican*. Without his efforts over many years, it is doubtful that Giant City State Park would have been created.[14]

Fort Massac had been established as a state park in 1903 and Starved Rock State Park in 1911. An Illinois law passed in 1925 directed the development of a system of state parks to preserve historic sites and natural features. It conveyed supervision of state parks to the director of the Department of Public Works and Buildings, H. H. Cleaveland. Mulcaster knew of this statewide effort and pushed the Giant City area as a candidate. Herrin publisher Hal Trovillion and landowner Willis Rendleman also actively promoted the idea, along with Makanda druggist L. M. Brooks and nurserymen Arthur and Herbert Bradley. Another beautiful southern Illinois site, Fountain Bluff, had the support of Murphysboro's Chamber of Commerce, but many Jackson County citizens also pushed for Giant City's inclusion in the park system.

In 1927, after much study, three new parks were established in Illinois: for historic and scenic preservation, 200-acre Black Hawk State Park; for scenic preservation, 916-acre Giant City State Park; and for preservation of the virgin white pine, the 275-acre White Pines Forest. In the 1930s, New Salem State Park and Piasa Bluff State Park (later renamed Pere Marquette) were added to the Illinois system.[15]

The state legislature appropriated $200,000 to buy the initial central 800 acres at Giant City. The first tract purchased in September 1927 was 450 acres bought for $16,032.[16] The primary landowner, Willis Rendleman, who had bought out the farms of Jeff Bass, Edward Weiss, and Eugene Thomas in preparation for this sale to the state, received the governor's pen as a souvenir. Mulcaster and Rendleman were named as the two leading proponents in the *Carbondale Free Press*. Although it was Rendleman who gained monetarily from the sale, it was Mulcaster who wrote a thank-you to the public in the regional newspapers.[17]

Mulcaster consistently extolled the glories of the area after it became a park, and he continued to pass on his own theories about Stone Fort, maintaining that it was a fur trading post for a French company of old St. Louis, which he believed was active throughout the region between 1700 and 1763.[18] Mulcaster had fallen in love with southern Illinois and could be called upon as a guide to its beauty spots far and wide, but his imagination sometimes got the better of him.

## LOCAL CONTROVERSIES

When it became clear that a park custodian would be hired, Mulcaster was to many, and to himself as well, the obvious candidate. He approached Director Cleaveland directly in April 1929, offering to show him around the park and mentioning that he had "discussed things" recently with an Illinois state senator.[19] But in this tight economic time, a "bitter rivalry" ensued over the well-paying custodian's post. The other candidates were landowner and present township supervisor Willis Rendleman; Thomas Peak, ex-supervisor and old-time "Republican war-horse"; and Crawford Maddox, another prominent Republican. The local argument against Mulcaster was that he was "rich anyhow." Likewise, a newspaper article said that Rendleman was "paid a pretty penny for many acres of land that defied cultivation." Peak, the folks bickered, had already enjoyed certain party recognition.

According to a *Murphysboro Independent* article of July 3, 1929, the following logic prevailed, causing a furor in Makanda. Officials at the Department of Public Works and Buildings in Springfield decided "that to appoint either one of the 'native son' applicants would only make every other applicant angry," so finally, "through the influence of Union County Republicans, the appointment went to Ralph Lester (James) Corzine of Saratoga Spring, Union County."[20]

Ralph Lester Corzine, a forty-one-year-old resident of Anna, was a graduate of Anna's Union Academy. He had been a schoolteacher (1907–15), farmer (1915–18), and manager of a merchandise store (1918–28). Unemployed in the spring of 1929 when he applied for the custodian's position, Corzine was hired in June to be paid $100 per month. He would also be provided with housing. Rendleman offered to donate to the state of Illinois a shady site near his home for the custodian's house, where electricity was brought and a well dug.[21]

Jackson County men were angry that a Union County man got the job, but very quickly three other controversial issues arose that deepened the political divide: the cedar rust disease in the orchards, the location of the park's main entrance road, and the subsequent location of the custodian's house along the entrance road.

### Cedar Rust Disease

By 1929, much of the property surrounding the original strip of acquired state park land had been planted in orchards, mainly peach and apple trees. Edgar Roberts's orchards of ten thousand peach trees and ten thousand apple trees adjoined the park's land, as did Willis Rendleman's orchards and those of other landowners. Apple trees had been suffering for many years from cedar rust, an insect disease that requires nearby red cedar trees to spread. In May 1920, the Union County public was notified by the Illinois Department of Agriculture that red cedars were to be eradicated from properties near orchards by January 1, 1921. Evidence presented by H. H. Lamer, district manager of American Fruit Growers, Inc., stated that G. G. Patterson on the Union-Jackson line "had terrible cedar rust on Jonathan and Benoni apples. [The disease] defoliated the trees in September and the following spring [Patterson] did not have any fruit buds on these orchards." Lamer stated that after his employees cut every cedar tree, Patterson's orchards were not bothered again by cedar rust and enjoyed a fifty-dollar increase per acre.

When the state bought the Giant City property, the Illinois Department of Agriculture

THE LAND AND ITS PEOPLE

complained to Director Cleaveland that some orchard owners in that area had never cut down their cedars. Cleaveland received a petition by the following Union County orchard owners asking that all cedar trees in the new Giant City State Park be removed: from Anna, L. T. Hardin, T. P. Sifford, Mr. Hill, and Mr. Waterbury; from Cobden, A. Flamm, H. L. Lingle, Brimm, and Anderson; from Alto Pass, C. G. Keith; and from near Makanda, Alden and Leib.[22]

But not all of the farmers and orchard owners agreed. Some of the owners of the larger orchards sent their own petition to Director Cleaveland protesting "vigorously the ruthless destruction of the cedar trees" in the new park.

Orchard owners who lived closest to the park—Willis Rendleman, J. Wesley Neville, R. K. Loomis, Bailey H. West, and Edgar Roberts—argued that the cedars were one of the park's most scenic assets and that they could control the problem in their orchards with chemical sprays. As soon as Corzine was hired, Director Cleaveland sent the petitions and letters to him, asking for his opinion. Corzine responded that some of the orchard owners around the park were not concerned either way, while others, namely West, Loomis, Jerome Rendleman, and Ernest Allen, "vigorously protest" the cedar tree cutting. Finally, Corzine wrote that if the state of Illinois was going to require all the park's

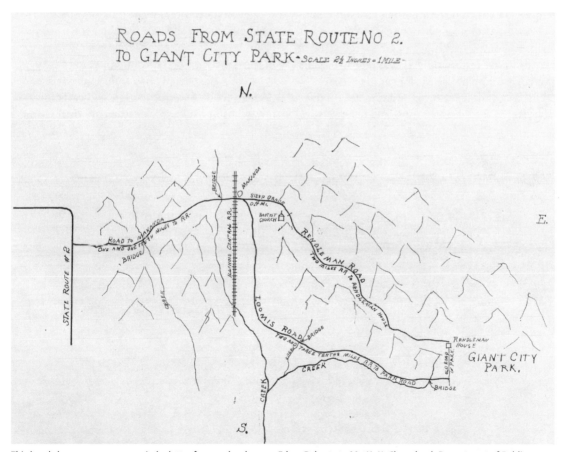

This hand-drawn map accompanied a letter from orchard owner Edgar Roberts to Mr. H. H. Cleaveland, Department of Public Works and Buildings, May 7, 1931. Roberts argued that the Rendleman route (northern) would be a better route into the park than the Loomis route (southern). Courtesy Giant City Visitor Center.

cedar trees to be cut down, then his "personal" view was that all cedar trees in the eradication area should be cut first, before money and labor were spent cutting the park's trees, but he would do whatever was required of him.[23] There is no evidence that cedar trees were ordered to be cut down in the park.

### Park Roads

Another major disagreement was over the building of roads. When the awarding of the custodian job was announced, a Murphysboro newspaper editor argued that "Giant City was conceived by Jackson county men, put through by Jackson county men, and the fruits of the victory, at least to the extent of the custodianship, was expected to remain in Jackson County."[24] Mulcaster argued that he wasn't born with a silver spoon in his mouth and charged that Henry Kohn, a state official, was trying to get the custodian's house built near his relatives' farms in Union County in order to get roads diverted to the southernmost and least historic

and attractive way into the park just to patronize Union County farmers.[25]

The heated fracas over the routes for road-building into the new park continued for years. Local landowners George and M. C. Lockard, R. K. Loomis, and E. W. Newman wrote Springfield advising the advantages of the Union County route. But in June 1929, a proposed course from Route 2 (which became Old Route 51) east through Makanda and on to the park was presented in a state bill. A simultaneous bill called for a road to be built from Route 13 east of Carbondale and southward ten miles to the park (today's Giant City Road). Eventually, both roads were built, as was the southern route through Union County, but not without some consternation on the part of Makanda's residents, who believed that their town would again be left stranded as it had been as a result of the construction of Route 2.

Roads—especially bad mud roads and flooded roads—were constant and consuming issues in Makanda, as was true throughout

An example of the sort of bridge needing replacement on the roads leading to Giant City, May 1934. National Archives, CCC records, SP-11.

Willis Rendleman house. Photograph by Hodde, Giant City Visitor Center, neg. print #33.

southern Illinois. Election outcomes often depended upon road repair promises. The roads through most of Union and lower Jackson counties were dirt roads, used mainly by farmers. In the 1920s, even the main route through Makanda Township, Star Route 2, was a terrible road. According to Charles Thomas, interviewed by Jane Adams, "It was really just a wagon track, full of ruts and mud holes."[26]

Then, in the summer of 1929, Makanda learned that an improved (graveled) road could be built coming into town from Route 2 but that the only appropriation the state would provide would be for the gravel, not for the manpower. Through the efforts of Mulcaster, landowners along the road, and other Makanda neighbors, $1,250 was raised to pay the freight costs of trucking the gravel from Chester's rock quarry. But who would pay for the labor to spread it?[27]

First, Director Cleaveland suggested that Menard Penitentiary inmates be used to spread the gravel. After Warden White objected, Dr. Oscar J. Hagebush of the Anna State Hospital and Rodney H. Brandon, Director of the Department of Public Welfare State House, agreed that about twenty patients from the state hospital could be used to spread the gravel from the trucks along the new road. Two or three hospital employees supervised twenty patients, who were housed and fed by local residents during the work, which took place in the first weeks of January 1930. Judge F. B. Herbert of Murphysboro objected both to using patients this way and to not paying regular laborers who desperately needed the work. Mulcaster and Brandon answered by saying there were twice as many hospital patient volunteers than they could use and that the road workers were being well fed and treated kindly. Not long after, when Corzine sought guidance from Cleaveland about the pay rate for roadwork within the park, he was told that thirty cents per man hour and another thirty-five cents per team were reasonable rates. It appears that the Anna patients were not paid at all.[28]

### Custodian's House and the Park Entrance

Yet to be decided were the locations of the park's entrance road and the custodian's house. Makanda citizens of course wanted the tourist trade to come through their town, not through Cobden from the south. On June 25, 1929, Makanda postmaster Bailey H. West wrote to Governor Louis L. Emmerson, "Our county went strong for you. South of our county is Union county which never went Republican in its history."[29] Three days later, orchardist and landowner Willis Rendleman, supervisor for Makanda Township, wrote to Cleaveland that "for the good of the park and the public," he would agree to donate a shaded house site near his home, east of Makanda and along the proposed route to the park directly from Makanda. Makanda's constable sent along to Springfield a notarized statement that the southern route, "the lower road," was covered completely with water several times a year when Drury Creek flooded.[30]

Representative Elbert Waller wrote to Director Cleaveland that the custodian's house should be built so that the road from Route 2 through Makanda would become the park's entryway because "the public spirit of the people of Makanda prompted the park's location" and the community had been "very hard hit due to the fact that the hard road [Route 51] just missed [the town] and deflected all the trade from its best trading community."[31]

The first official park entrance was an improved existing road from Makanda, past Willis Rendleman's property at the north edge of the park. A description of this road and the dwellings that existed along it before the improvement appear in a feature newspaper article of 1927. Along the two-mile "stretch of rocky ravine" were a number of old log huts that housed "free negroes." According to this source, the Makanda area was a refuge for runaway slaves during and after the Civil War. Steered toward the orchard owners and farmers by the Illinois Central Railroad conductors, former slaves and freed blacks sought work in the Makanda area. The huts along this road outside Makanda were reportedly the homes to a few of these blacks and their descendants. One such two-roomed hut with a leaky roof and no plumbing housed the family of John Reed and their three-legged cat.[32] Presumably, these log dwellings were among the first buildings dismantled when the park custodian began his job, displacing citizens like the Reed family, who were probably tenant farmers.

On the newly graveled road, many Sunday visitors traveled to the park in the summer of 1930. So popular was the park that 1,100 visitors in a three-month period stopped to ask for water at the Agnew home at the north entrance.[33] Corzine asked for funds to build picnic tables, and he wrote that he needed Rendleman's land immediately for a comfort station (bathrooms). He also asked permission for a couple of local boys to operate a "soda pop joint" at the campground.[34] Orchardist Edgar Roberts, who sold property to the state for the park, wrote Cleaveland to complain that Corzine was absent on a busy Sunday, gone in fact to a baseball game in Hallidayboro. Cleaveland reprimanded Corzine for his dereliction of duty.[35]

Corzine had a very difficult job. The land inside the new park's boundaries had been previously owned by over a dozen farmers and orchard owners and had been home to many tenants. The park had no use for most of these vacated houses, barns, and outbuildings, nor for the roads and fences that crisscrossed the land. Corzine was instructed on September 9, 1930, to inform the following former land-

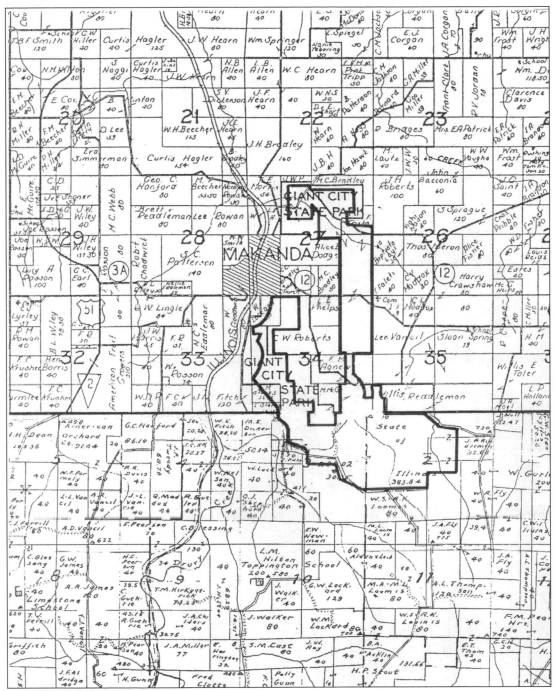

These are merged plat maps from Jackson County (1930s) and Union County (1930) with the 1943 outline of Giant City State Park overlaid. Because plat maps are inexact representations, some discrepancies are naturally exhibited. Map work by Kay Rippelmeye and Herb Meyer. Sources: Plat Book of Jackson County (Rockford, Ill.: W. W. Hixson and Co., n.d.); 1930 map of Union county (Map Library, Morris Library, Southern Illinois University Carbondale); U.S. Geological Survey, 15 Minute Carbondale Quadrangle (Edition 1922–43).

owners that they had sixty days to move their buildings from park property: Hattie E. Agnew, John B. Alden, Jeff Bass, Frank Benandi, Elsie C. Bennett, Earl Blessing, the Bradley estate, Pete Brilla, Felice Festa, James Gurley, Rufus K. Loomis, Lawrence E. McGregor, Jerome F. Rendleman, Willis Rendleman, Edgar Roberts, Eugene Thomas, Edward Weiss, and John J. Woods. After the sixty days, Corzine was to begin dismantling the remaining houses and other structures.[36]

Although there is no evidence that the state used eminent domain to take properties during the original land purchase of the 1930s, some of the local people have memories of forced removals from farms and homes to make way for the public use of their lands. It is understandable that many resented the public "takeover" of land, even if it was sold by their relatives to the park. Some of the acreage had been passed down through families for over a hundred years. Corzine was in an awkward position: he lived in the custodian's house next door to Willis Rendleman but was probably resented by many in Makanda, including Rendleman's friend Mulcaster.[37]

In August 1930, public consternation arose when locals read a story based on Mulcaster's comments in the *Carbondale Free Press* that eight hundred acres of Giant City State Park were allowed to burn under Corzine's watch. According to Corzine, Mulcaster circulated the falsehood in an attempt to get Corzine ousted from his position and replaced by Mulcaster's man, a Democrat. Mulcaster called the fire article a misunderstanding. He said he was talking to a reporter about a small fire that burned some of the park the year before and was misquoted.[38]

It would take some settling of the dust before the public's praise for the park would overcome the private disgruntlements of local individuals about its first establishment controversies. After the Democratic landslide election in November 1932, Ralph Corzine was asked to resign in April 1933. Franklin Delano Roosevelt's public works programs would quickly initiate great changes throughout the country. Southern Illinois's Giant City State Park was soon caught up in the tidal wave of change that made the previous few years of controversy seem like a manageable summer shower.

# 2

# The CCC Comes to Southern Illinois

During the late 1920s and early 1930s, regional newspapers and state publications described Giant City State Park as "the Playground of Southern Illinois" and even "the Switzerland of Southern Illinois."[1] Free entertainment and a place of undisturbed natural beauty had never been so sorely needed. Times were hard. Southern Illinois traditionally relied on agriculture, coal mining, and timber; all failed miserably in the economic depression beginning in the 1920s.

By 1930, the counties that had depended on the mining industry, such as Franklin, Williamson, and Saline, already had four times the national average of unemployed men. Unemployment was as high as 60 percent in some towns of the mining counties, farm produce prices dropped 63 percent, and the forest wood supply was depleted. These are merely statistics, though, that say little of the pain and deprivation, the hunger and fear, of the Depression years in southern Illinois.[2]

The national statistics were staggering. One-quarter of the workforce was unemployed; 10 million were without pensions or savings. Nine thousand banks failed, and the savings of 27 million families were wiped out. One-third of the nation was "ill-housed, ill-clad, and ill-nourished." Many people were camped, living near dumps, picking through garbage to survive, a number of them veterans of World War I.[3] The gap between the rich and poor was greater than it had ever been or would be until the 1990s. Five percent of Americans were taking in about one-third of all personal income. But the majority of people had run out of buying power. Teachers were paid as little as $280 for an eight-month school year. Often, they would get only promises to be paid or garden produce in lieu of money. Children

came to school with no shoes and nothing to eat for lunch. Throughout the country, crime and gangsters thrived, primarily because of the money that could be made bypassing Prohibition and later regulated liquor sales.

The years 1930 and 1931 were terrible for orchard owners in southern Illinois. The precious peach crop froze on the trees in the spring of 1930. Then a severe drought, the worst in the nation's history, nearly dried up the Mississippi River. Peaches that had sold for $3.50 per bushel in 1917 sold in 1931 for 65 cents. The bottom fell out of everything. Farm crops failed, farm animals died for lack of fodder, banks foreclosed, and then the banks failed. Local factories, such as the garment factory in Anna, closed.[4]

In 1930, the average-size farm in Illinois was about 143 acres, most of it planted in corn or in pasture.[5] Too much of southern Illinois's hill ground was cleared and planted in row crops out of desperation for quick cash, resulting in severe erosion of the topsoil, flooding, and muddied creeks and streams. Many farms, dotted with deep gullies, were abandoned as unfit for any production. The average southern Illinois land price in 1933 was sixteen dollars an acre.[6] Landowners were having a hard time paying the taxes on their acreage. Tenant farmers, the greater majority, were struggling to keep food on their tables.

Most rural families of the lower eleven counties of southern Illinois were scraping together an existence just as their ancestors had done for several generations, but they felt now that they were scraping the bottom of the barrel. Folks who lived through the Great Depression years tell of working sunup to sundown for five or seven cents an hour, or fifty cents a day. Around the towns of Makanda, Pomona, and Alto Pass, many were tenant farmers. The women could do the lighter farmwork: cut asparagus, hoe around the trees in the orchards, plant sweet-potato slips. The men cut timber, either for a sawmill or for cordwood. The most able could cut in a day a cord of wood, which sold for a dollar, the same price it had brought during the Civil War.[7]

The lives of most rural people in southern Illinois had changed minimally since the Civil War. Many still used horses for work and for travel. But their agrarian and sawmill-town ways of life were fading fast into America's past. Industrialism expanded its influence in the mines and on the farms, where fewer laborers were needed, and lands were being consolidated into larger farms. In each county, populations gathered into a few growing towns, until the villages and small towns located off the main highways and railways became isolated hamlets by 1930. And soon the highways would leave some of the railway towns stranded, as Makanda's townspeople were beginning to feel.

Although there are many reasons in hindsight to idealize the close and caring rural life in communities such as Makanda at the turn of the century, the facts cannot be denied that by 1930, many rural towns were populated by overworked people living on overused land and desperately needing a cash income. They watched their young people leave to search for work in the cities or to ramble the rails: "The Children's Bureau estimated that by late 1932, a quarter of a million [people] under the age of twenty-one were roaming the country. They hopped freights, bummed their food, and lived along the tracks with the hardened hoboes in squatter's camps called jungles."[8]

The country's two most important resources were being wasted—its people and the land. As had been done in small communities for generations, neighbors tried at first to care for each other. Township record books from these years show recurrent payments out of the township funds for village paupers' debts: for groceries, doctor bills, coffins.[9] By 1930, however, communities throughout Illinois, as well as throughout the entire country, needed outside help.

Illinois government did as much as lawmakers and the governor believed it could and should do to relieve the plight of the unemployed. In October 1930, Governor Louis L. Emmerson appointed a Governor's Commission on Unemployment Relief, but he did not request any funds for appropriation. Not until February 1932 was $20 million appropriated by the Fifty-seventh Illinois General Assembly, which also created the Illinois Emergency Relief Commission to administer the funds. But within six months, Illinois, as well as many other states, began looking to the federal government for practically all relief funds.[10]

Through the Emergency Relief Act of 1932, Illinois did receive some funding for direct and work-relief purposes. With the advent of President Franklin Delano Roosevelt's New Deal, federal projects began to relieve many Illinois families of unemployment, hunger, and need. Under the Civil Works Administration, people were paid a wage for labor, constructing parks, airports, stadiums, and other public buildings. Late in 1934, the Public Works Administration increased employment, and in 1935, Works Progress Administration projects began. The WPA was responsible for much of the improvement of roads in southern Illinois. The Agricultural Adjustment Administration regulated farm production. The Home Owners Loan Corporation granted long-term mortgage loans at low interest. The Farm Credit Administration provided long-term and short-term credit to farmers. The National Youth Administration provided job training for unemployed youth. New Deal programs affected nearly every family in the United States and did much to ease the poverty and unemployment of southern Illinois. Between May 1 and May 12 of 1934, the heads of 10,088 downstate Illinois families who were previously on relief rolls were transferred to work-relief projects.[11] The gratitude felt by southern Illinoisans for these programs and the subsequent adoration for Franklin Roosevelt lasted for generations in many families.

Although in 1930, Union County voted more than two-to-one against funding a state-wide system of conservation, forest preserves, and recreation ground, most Americans believed by 1932 that extensive land management throughout the country was necessary.[12] Many argued that it was a huge job that only the federal government could successfully manage. Individuals as well as public and governmental agencies began advocating a national forest in southern Illinois to achieve the goals of erosion control, timber production, and establishment of agricultural demonstration areas. The National Forest Reservation Commission approved land purchases in southern Illinois in the summer of 1933.[13] Thus began the Illini and Shawnee purchase units, which became the Shawnee National Forest. This nationalization and conservation of much of southern Illinois's most rugged and remote land was happening at the same time as the improvements at Giant City State Park—all through the efforts of a conservation army.

## FDR'S SOIL SOLDIERS

In the early 1930s, many young men from relief families across the country were given their best chance for success in the Civilian Conservation Corps. In southern Illinois, it was this program that simultaneously brought thousands of jobs to the area and began the crucial work of conserving soil, forest, and wildlife.

The idea of using young people as "soil soldiers" for a certain number of years was not originally Franklin Roosevelt's, but the U.S. Civilian Conservation Corps was his personal creation. Before his presidential election, the forest service in both California and Washington State had already organized cadres of unemployed people to work under relief concepts like those the CCC was proposing. It was

this kind of state-run system that conservative Union County voters did not support. Such programs for the unemployed had also been developed in Denmark, Norway, Bulgaria, Austria, and the Netherlands. The most controversial international model was the German Labor Service, originally created by the Weimar Republic to check unemployment in the cities. Like the CCC, the German Labor Service was voluntary and open to six-month enlistment periods, but under Adolf Hitler, it became an essential wing of the Nazi propaganda machine. The men in Hitler's camps drilled with weapons, and some of his work camps eventually became death camps.[14]

Roosevelt was aware of various state and international work programs. As governor of New York in 1932, he had developed an unemployment program that took ten thousand people off relief rolls by putting them to work planting trees. In his acceptance speech at the 1932 Democratic convention, Roosevelt had alluded to a million-man national conservation workforce necessary in the immediate future.[15] In January 1933, of the one-quarter of the national unemployed workforce, an estimated 1,500,000 were in Illinois.[16]

Two days after taking office in the spring of 1933, Roosevelt began organizing the camps for the Emergency Conservation Work (not officially called the Civilian Conservation Corps until 1937) by summoning a meeting of the director of the Bureau of the Budget, the judge advocate general of the army, the solicitor of the Department of the Interior, and the secretaries of war, agriculture, and the interior.[17] They designed a bill for the purposes of reforestation and humanitarianism. They would put a quarter of a million young men and World War I veterans to work by early summer building dams, draining marshlands, fighting forest fires, and planting trees. U.S. Representative Kent Keller of southern Illinois was a forceful, vocal proponent of public work projects to help the unemployed. He advo-

Jefferson Barracks, St. Louis, Missouri, July 1934, when CCC Company #692 was organizing there. Earl Dickey remembered that the company was there for about six weeks. He said, "That was right in July, the hottest wetter. They had the water pipe line just strung out over the ground. My job was to wash the dishes for the officers' mess, and we'd just draw water right out of those pipes. It was hot enough to burn your hands almost. We very seldom had to make a fire to heat the water." Photo courtesy of Earl Dickey.

cated in the U.S. House of Representatives for guaranteed work for all who wanted jobs.[18]

Congress pushed the measure through in ten days by voice vote.[19] The plan for the CCC quickly became a reality. The U.S. Army would organize the living arrangements of the men. The Department of Agriculture and the Department of the Interior would select work projects and provide personnel to manage them. The budget director would provide financial assistance and the judge advocate legal advice. The Department of Labor would coordinate the selection of enrollees.

Roosevelt knew that work with dignity was the key to a new spirit and hope for the nation. He gave a radio address as the CCC program was getting underway, on July 17, 1933. FDR's voice was undoubtedly heard by many southern Illinoisans as well as by the CCC men of Giant City's tent camp gathered around the radio, as citizens were likely to do in that era to hear one of their president's fireside chats. This one was directed specifically to the CCC enrollees:

Men of the Civilian Conservation Corps, I think of you as a visible token of encouragement to the whole country. You—nearly 300,000 strong—are evidence that the nation is still strong enough and broad enough to look after its citizens.

You are evidence that we are seeking to get away as fast as we possibly can from soup kitchens and free rations, because the government is paying you wages and maintaining you for actual work—work which is needed now and for the future and will bring a definite financial return to the people of the nation.

Through you the nation will graduate a fine group of strong young men, clean-living, trained to self-discipline and, above all, willing and proud to work for the joy of working.

Too much in recent years large numbers of our population have sought out success as an opportunity to gain money with the least possible work.

It is time for each and every one of us to cast away self-destroying, nation-destroying efforts to get something for nothing, and to appreciate that satisfying reward and safe reward come only through honest work.

That must be the new spirit of the American future.

You are the vanguard of that new spirit.[20]

## MOBILIZING THE CCC

Robert Fechner, a Boston labor leader, agreed to be director of the CCC. Fechner had a long career in the American labor movement and was to prove a capable director. Only thirty-seven days elapsed between Roosevelt's inauguration and the signing of the first CCC enrollee on April 7, 1933. This mobilization of bureaucracy and manpower has been called "a miracle of cooperation."[21]

A few groups, however, had serious concerns about the CCC bill. Organized labor voiced strong opposition and particularly disliked the idea of the army having any part in it.[22] William Green, conservative president of the American Federation of Labor, generally condemned the project. The army, he feared, would corrupt the labor force with its philosophy, regimentation, and army wage rates.[23] The Socialist Party spokesman, Norman Thomas, argued that larger measures were necessary. He thought that work camps "fit into the psychology of a Fascist, not a Socialist state." Some simply rejected the relief idea on the basis that a dollar a day was too little to pay a hard-working American. Others were against granting such further authority to the president by placing another agency under his direct control. And many opposed the CCC measure because they thought it might lead the masses to believe it was the government's duty to put them on the payroll.[24]

Only three amendments to the bill were adopted, the most important being the one proposed by the sole African American congressman, Representative Oscar DePriest, Republican of Illinois, that "no discrimination shall be made on account of race, color, or creed."[25] Another pragmatic precaution was taken to give jobs to the local unemployed woodsmen in the areas where the camps were to be situated. Roosevelt had been warned that unless local laborers were also hired, communities would not accept the outsiders.[26] These LEM (Local Experienced Men) were hired to supervise work crews as leaders and assistant leaders. Usually, the men were skilled in the woods or with machinery, but experienced cooks were also hired as LEM if complaints about the food grew too loud in the camps.

With the promise that jobs would become available, southern Illinois landowners in the Forest Service purchase areas offered their land to be bought by the federal government for an as-yet-unnamed national forest. Camps were to be established throughout the region under work supervision of federal forestry personnel. The Illinois officials representing the National Park Service also contracted with the CCC to establish work camps at the new state parks, Pere Marquette and Giant City among them. Pere Marquette's camp housed a company of CCC men who were veterans of World War I. These men were older and among the most vulnerable to the hardships of unemployment. In despair, thousands of these veterans from across the country had marched to Washington, D.C., in the summer of 1932 seeking payment of their wartime-service compensation pension. They argued that while they were fighting in Europe, many who had stayed home had gotten wealthy. They had been promised pension funds and wanted them now. President Herbert Hoover dispersed the "Bonus Army" with guns, bayonets, and tear gas. But when Roosevelt took Hoover's job, he immediately offered every veteran a chance to enlist in the CCC.[27] Several forest service camps in southern Illinois were veterans' camps: Camp Union in Jonesboro, Camp Cadiz in Hardin County, Camp Hicks in Pope County, and Camp Pomona in

Jackson County were all manned first by veterans from across the country.[28]

The enlistment period for all CCC enrollees was six months with the option of reenlistment for another six months, up to a maximum of two years. These rules were widely stretched, at least in southern Illinois. Initially, junior enrollees were between eighteen and twenty-five years old, unemployed, and unmarried. They came from families on relief. The enrollee was paid thirty dollars a month, of which twenty-five was sent home to his family. Room, board, clothing, and tools were provided by the government. The enrollee was expected to work a forty-hour workweek under the direction of his particular camp's supervisors.

All thirty CCC camps in the lower twenty-three counties of southern Illinois came under the supervision of one of three agencies: the U.S. Forest Service, the Illinois Soil Conservation Service, or the National Park Service (see appendix 1). Initially, all enrollees were sent to conditioning camps at existing army bases where they spent a week or more exercising,

receiving physical examinations, and adjusting to army-type discipline and routine. From Jefferson Barracks, Missouri, or Fort Sheridan, Illinois, men traveled in trucks or trains to their designated camps throughout southern Illinois. The number of men in each camp ranged from 170 to 200.

The CCC was a radical experiment. It meant to some people pervasive federal intervention. It was big government. The idea of it frightened some, but the prospect of continuing to live without work and without hope scared the public even more. For the hungry, unemployed young men riding the freight cars and bumming infrequent meals in alleys and at back-door stoops, it was a chance to eat regularly, work outdoors, and perhaps even succeed. When the idea was still new in 1934, Sherwood Anderson presented the human perspective in an article widely read in *Today* magazine:

> Into these camps have come boys, the greater number of them from American cities. They are young boys, most of them about

This and opposite, original CCC Company #696. All photos courtesy of George Oliver.

THE CCC COMES TO SOUTHERN ILLINOIS

high school age. But for this depression, in the natural flow of an older American life— it seems suddenly old now— . . . [they] would have come out of school and would have become clerks or factory hands. Or—and this would go for a lot of them—they would have become tough city guys—the kind that make bright young gangsters—the kind you see leaning against walls near gang hangouts in cities. "How much to kill a man?" How much? But, you see, even the rackets have become a bit thin now, clerkships have fallen away, prohibition has gone, the factories are not exactly howling for men.

. . . So these CCC camps have gathered them in, all kinds of them. . . . They had to build the camps, keep themselves clean, keep their bedding and their quarters clean, learn to swing an axe . . . to make beds, to learn the necessary sanitary laws that govern men living in camps, the give and take of man to man, so essential to life where men live, sleep, talk, dream in one great room—rows of cots all in the open—the door at the end of the room open—the sight of the wooded hills when you go to sleep at night, when you awake in the morning.[29]

Anderson could have been describing life in one of Giant City's two CCC camps, one of which was located in Jackson County (Camp Giant City) with the other just across the county line in Union County (Camp Stone Fort).

By April 1934, 300,000 men were stationed at camps throughout the country.[30] An average of 8,500 were enrolled each day beginning in May 1933.[31] The program was already getting very favorable press reports. And enthusiasm for the CCC did not diminish. From 1934 through 1940, Democrats as well as most Republicans viewed the corps as a great success.[32] Even the violently anti–New Deal

*Chicago Tribune* reported, "The CCC is one of the best projects of the Administration, and the great majority of its recruits, we believe, appreciate its opportunities and are being benefited."[33]

People in southern Illinois learned about the "Reforestation Army" program from the newspapers and radio and perhaps from the offices of the Illinois Relief Commission Agency, where young men had to go to enroll in the program. Between March 31 and June 1, 1933, the word of a chance for work spread quickly through southern Illinois. Men signed forms enrolling them in an organization first called "Emergency Conservation Work," but the name "Civilian Conservation Corps," used by Roosevelt in his congressional speech of March 21, was the name that caught on.[34] The young southern Illinois men who first enrolled were gathered at Jefferson Barracks to be divided into companies.

These first CCC recruits of the summer of 1933 were the initial wave of a great change in southern Illinois. As Jane Adams describes it, before 1932 the state and federal governments had very little impact on people's daily lives, but "during the twelve years between the beginning of the New Deal and the end of W.W. II, a sea change occurred in the country. . . . For the first time, government became a full partner in the economy."[35] The effects of this revolution in southern Illinois were all profound and some permanent. Thousands of men's lives, and women's as well, were forever changed while the regional economic pump was primed. The Shawnee National Forest was organized, and Giant City State Park was planned to be made accessible to the public year-round and presentable as the most manicured showcase of the region's natural beauty.

# CCC Companies #696 and #1657 and Their Camps, Giant City and Stone Fort

George Oliver was born in 1912 in Blyth, England, and grew up in southern Illinois mining towns—Tilden, Pocahontas, and Marissa. His father and older brother worked in the coal mines along with other English immigrants who had settled in the Tilden area. George managed to finish high school in Marissa but in 1932 and early 1933 could not find any work, not even in nearby St. Louis. He believed he heard about the CCC on the radio or from the newspaper and remembered that he had to contact the county chairman to get enrolled.

The guy we had to go see was in Steeleville; he ran a grocery store. So five or six of us boys hitchhiked over there; none of us had cars. We talked to him, but he said he didn't have the applications yet, but we should come back in a week or two. So we had to hitch back and go again. Then we were sent to Jefferson Barracks, from Sparta to Jefferson Barracks, to get our shots. They put us in companies of 220 men. . . . When they got ready to ship them out, they just took 200 in each company. They had lined us up by height. I was short— five-foot-seven. I was one of the shortest, so I was in the last twenty men. They pulled twenty out from each company and made up a makeshift company. My original company went to Oregon, and I was just lucky enough to come this way. That night they put us on an IC [Illinois Central] train. Didn't take long [to get to Makanda]. We stayed in the coaches all night. The next morning, they loaded our baggage on a Liberty truck, and we crawled up on top and rode out to the park, dodging limbs along the way. . . . We felt happy. I had

been out of high school for a year. . . . We were tickled to death to come down here.[1]

## COMPANY #696 ARRIVES

Oliver was headed to Giant City State Park's first CCC camp, one of the first to be built in southern Illinois. It was filled in June 1933 by Company #696, the country's 696th company to be organized, and was named Camp Giant City. Throughout the nation, between April 1 and June 1 of 1933, an average of eleven companies per day were created and sent out to camps in the woods and fields from coast to coast.[2]

An advance group of state park supervisory personnel had arrived at Giant City State Park earlier in the month. Superintendent Albin F. Olson and a technical foreman arrived first on June 2. By June 12, all of the supervisory staff members were there studying the park and planning the scope of work for the entire

George Oliver at his favorite resting spot, an old cedar leg near Devil's Stand Table. Photo courtesy of George Oliver.

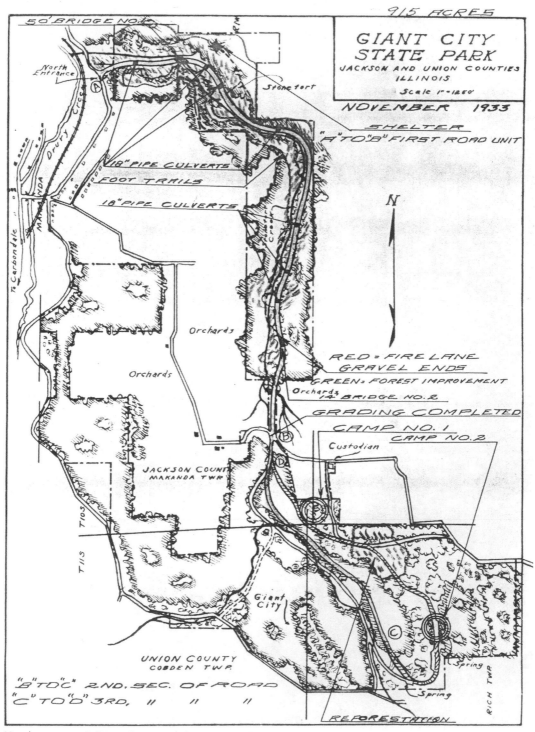

Map that accompanied November 1933 work report. Note the placement of two camps, Camp No. 1 (Camp Giant City), just north of the Jackson County line, and the proposed camp site (Camp No. 2) in Union County. National Archives, CCC records, RG 79.

View of some of the temporary quarters that were later made into winter quarters by the CCC.
National Archives, CCC records, SP-11.

Giant City State Park project. An early report by Olson states that the chief problem of the CCC upon their coming in 1933 to Giant City State Park was that of "making this natural beauty completely accessible to a varied public without in any way detracting from it by over-development." The "first and most necessary step" toward that goal was "the construction of an eighteen foot gravel road through difficult hillside terrain that would provide the visitor a safe, delightful drive from which he can derive a maximum of pleasure from the everchanging natural vista about him."[3]

The 2.1-mile access road to the park was deemed the first priority. This bumpy, curving road leading into the park turned east from north Makanda. It was referred to by the park supervisors as the north entrance. Other work projects envisioned within the proposed three-year agenda included surveying and marking boundaries, building five vehicle bridges, creating two miles of foot trails, clearing five miles along the side of trails, removing fifty acres of fire hazards, clearing ten miles of fire breaks,

improving fifty acres of forest and forty acres of erosion control, improving two miles of stream and twenty-five square yards of flood control, planting fifty acres, and collecting seventy bushels of seeds. The supervisors also planned four miles of telephone lines, three miles of fencing, a deep well and two thousand feet of water lines, twenty buildings and a tool house, four public campground buildings, and three picnic areas within fifty cleared acres. These projects would be directed by the state park supervisors. The building of the permanent camp barracks and camp buildings were under the work details of the army commanders.[4]

It was first estimated that all this work could be done with a CCC company of two hundred men in approximately three years. This proved to be a serious underestimation, mainly because the scope of work grew but also because the number of men available for project work crews from each company was less than the expected two hundred. The average number of men available for work details in September and October 1933 was only 119

Mess hall for Company #696, Camp Giant City, in summer–fall 1933 before barracks were built.
National Archives, CCC records, SP-11, photo #50A.

Army personnel of Company #696. *Back row, left to right*: First Lieutenant Roy Risk, medical officer and district surgeon; First Lieutenant Arnel B. Adams, Quartermaster Reserves, executive officer and post exchange officer; First Lieutenant Walter Urbach, Infantry Reserves, commanding officer, finance officer, quartermaster, construction quartermaster, and mess officer; First Lieutenant Barry, District Two adjutant; Second Lieutenant Harry F. Matheu, junior officer. *Front row*: Don D. Dewey, CCC superintendent, well drilling, Fort Sheridan, IL; Captain Mark G. Dawson, District Two commander; unknown person; First Lieutenant Thomas Bermingham, District Two chaplain. Photo courtesy of George Oliver; persons identified by Mary Schueller.

Department of the Interior staff, Company #696. *Back row, left to right*: Andrew Jackson Newlin, landscape foreman in charge of hewing of timbers; Carl F. Meyer, cultural foreman and engineer; Chester S. Harrell, erosion control foreman; Albin F. Olson, park superintendent; A. G. Ruediger, "Olson's right-hand man"; Daniel Brewer, landscape and road construction foreman. *Front row*: Carrol C. Collier, engineer; Charles Sanders, tool keeper; Floyd R. Boals, cleanup foreman and truck mechanic; Stanley O. Brooks, blacksmith and skilled workman; Everett F. Butler, landscape foreman. Not pictured: Red Thompson, "squirrel crew" supervisor; William Unger, road foreman; and William Stuemke, building foreman. Photo courtesy of George Oliver.

and 97, respectively. Of those 97 in October, 25 were needed for jobs around the camp: "chopping and carrying firewood, laying cinder paths, building septic tanks and putting different buildings in shape for winter weather." Furthermore, there was considerable turnover of enrollees.[5]

Most of Company #696, the first men to work at Giant City, were from southern Illinois towns. Eventually, all their names had to come from relief rolls, even the skilled persons such as typists and clerks. Many of their families had never been on relief rolls before the work projects required it, but according to George Oliver, all of the men's families were facing very difficult, if not desperate, financial situations. At Jefferson Barracks or Fort Sheridan, the

CCC enrollees spent a little over a week in an indoctrination program where they were issued clothes, received immunizations, and attended lectures on such topics as sex morality. They also did physical exercises, and some were instructed in the basic skills of grounds maintenance and kitchen duties.

When Oliver and his company jumped off the trucks after riding to the site from Makanda, the men saw a little camp of canvas tents. In southern Illinois's severe summer heat, the men settled into staked tents with dirt floors furnished with small cots, six or eight men to each tent. Some of the personnel, from both the army and the Department of the Interior, stayed in tents that had wooden sides and wooden floors. These had been erected by local carpenters. Others of the personnel who had accompanying families had already made arrangements to live in houses in the surrounding area. The original mess hall was an open-air tent filled with picnic tables. Cooking utensils and pots and pans hung on nails.

First Sergeant Jack Hellen called roll and asked the men to volunteer for various duties. Because Oliver admitted his typing skills, he was made clerk for the Department of the Interior at the camp, a job that proved to be a good deal, Oliver said. His high school degree in commercial studies, which had included bookkeeping, typing, and accounting, proved to be perfect preparation for the Interior Department's needs. This office supervised the men during their work hours under Illinois state park and U.S. Department of the Interior personnel and sent reports to state and federal officials. U.S. Army personnel, on the other hand, managed the men's transport to the camp and work sites as well as their living, medical, and eating arrangements. They were also in charge of granting the men permission to leave camp on weekends, disciplining them if necessary, withholding camp privileges, and administering their pay. Captain Walter S. Wood and Lieutenant Walter Urbach were the original officers in charge of the army personnel.[6]

## WORK BEGINS

In the summer of 1933, the first order for the outdoor work crews at the camp was to build

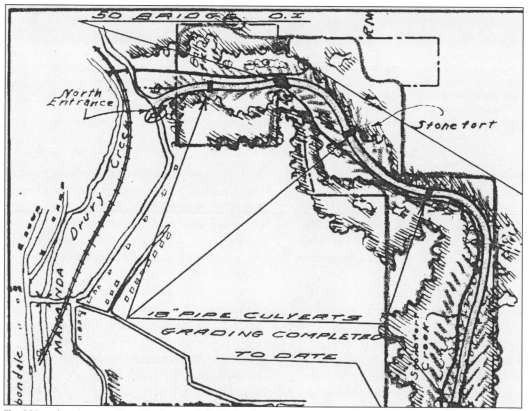

The CCC road engineers at Giant City State Park decided to develop the north entrance as the best route into the park. Note the ball field at the first clearing after the north entrance, where the CCC camps' baseball teams played their games.
From work report map, June–December 1933, National Archives, CCC records.

Drilling holes for dynamiting rock out of road right-of-way, October 1933. National Archives, CCC records, SP-11, photo #53.

William Unger and Daniel Brewer, road construction foremen. Photo courtesy of George Oliver.

the two-mile road and bridges that would establish winter access to the camp from the county road leading to Makanda—the north entrance. In just the initial phase, seventy dynamite blasts were set off to clear rock from the proposed roadway, and 270 yards of fill dirt

were dumped to reach an acceptable grade. Oliver reported that when the park was planned, the engineers wanted to make a loop through the entire area. It was foreman William Unger's suggestion that they create a road on top of the bluff by the Devil's Stand Table. The engineers surveyed the bluff top and decided that it could be done. Many Company #696 men thereafter referred to that road as Unger Highway.[7]

Company #696 was divided into various work crews. Although the men's wishes were often honored and foremen could request certain individuals, the officers in charge could also assign the men to a certain crew. Nearly one-third were put to work on road improvement, while two smaller crews worked in forestry improvements, clearing and pruning the deadwood in the park and constructing fire lanes. There was also a construction crew that built and maintained structures in the camp.

The park's boundaries between farms and orchards were not always delineated or made

Giant City Park hill at north entrance before CCC work began. National Archives, CCC records, SP-11, photo #2.

Giant City Park hill at north entrance after CCC work. National Archives, CCC records, SP-11, photo #2A.

During the summer of 1933, at least one-third of Company #696 enrollees were put to work on road improvement. National Archives, CCC records, SP-11.

clear to the enrollees. Or perhaps some of the enrollees had not yet learned to respect the property of others, particularly when that property was luscious, ripe peaches hanging from the trees. A Murphysboro newspaper story of July 1, 1933, titled "Giant City Woods Army Like Peaches" reported that landowner Edward Roberts shot at some of the new recruits as they were helping themselves to his peaches. This article referred to the "Reforestation Camp"; the name "Civilian Conservation Corps" would begin to take hold by the year's end.[8]

Later in the summer, Camp Giant City's men, along with other CCC men and many in the general public throughout the region, suffered from the mosquito-borne illness en-cephalitis. Although a few of the area's elderly persons and children died, the men at Giant City suffered only severe aches, pains, and headaches. Mosquito netting was issued for every cot, and Dr. Roy Risk also issued daily quinine tablets.[9] Work projects were substantially slowed for weeks because fewer men were able to work.

By September 1933, rock retaining walls had been laid at the first section of road. In addition, twelve truckloads of wood and twenty-six loads of brush were cleared from the roadside and hauled to camp to be cut into firewood. During the first year, wood fueled the kitchen stoves and during the cold months heated the tents. Later, coal, which was found

Building rock wall to hold fill on road at "big bend." National Archives, CCC records, SP-11.

to be more efficient, replaced wood for cooking and heating. The dirt work was done with picks, shovels, and wheelbarrows, while the trees were cut down with crosscut saws and axes. Railroad cars brought gravel to Makanda, where it was loaded onto trucks to be hauled and spread on the roads with shovels. By November, the enrollees were handling three railroad cars of gravel per day. The camp borrowed a concrete mixer from Carbondale's state highway garage to construct the footings for bridge abutments and piers on the fifty-foot bridge at the north entrance.[10]

The smallest work crew, a log-hewing department under the supervision of foreman A. J. Newlin, hewed logs for shelters, bridge posts and stringers, and guardrails. Only the

foreman had prior experience with such woodwork, but the efficiency of the "boys" increased monthly until they were receiving the most favorable comments from visitors to the park. The hewing crew also garnered much praise for their work from the camp supervisors in the inspection reports submitted to federal officials. This crew supplied almost all of the material for the original shelters and small structures built in the park.[11]

Two state agents visited the camp in July to inspect the work personally and to approve further projects. Harry B. Curtis, a regional CCC inspector, and Robert Kingery, the new Illinois director of the Department of Public Works and Buildings, approved the sites for new service buildings and the removal of the

Hewing logs for bridge stringers, guardrails, and parking barriers in the summer of 1933. The posts that were to go into the ground were creosoted in a vat heated over a dug-out fire pit. National Archives, CCC records, SP-11.

Bridge under construction, stringers in place, December 1933. National Archives, CCC records, SP-11, photo #86.

Assembling and placing new running rail, Project 132. National Archives, CCC records, SP-11.

Scenic view on first unit of road construction, autumn 1933. Notice how the tree in the middle of the photo fits into the guardrail. National Archives, CCC records, SP-11.

Sign at north entrance of Camp Giant City, home of Company #696.
Courtesy of George Oliver.

Original tents and building material for barracks at Camp Giant City.
Courtesy of George Oliver.

Camp Giant City buildings covered with tar paper and lathing strips. Courtesy of George Oliver.

custodian's house from its current location to one more convenient in the park. They also approved the plans for the building of a stone lodge. Joseph F. Booten, Illinois's state architect, would draw the plans or at least supervise the plan drawings. At the end of November 1933, a goal was set for having the lodge completed in six months. The lodge would actually not be completed for another twenty months.[12]

A mechanic and a helper maintained the camp's motor trucks: five Liberty trucks, two old Model A Ford dump trucks, and three new one-and-a-half-ton Chevrolet dump trucks. Less work was accomplished on the road in September than anticipated because the cost of renting a tractor and road grader proved prohibitive. Until a better price could be found, the roadwork was briefly suspended. During October, the enrollees were given leave to seek employment before the new six-month reenlisting period began in November. To assure steady work crews, only twenty men at a time were allowed to leave the camp for a few days.[13]

## CAMP GIANT CITY (SP-11)

As autumn approached, camp structures were built or improved to make them suitable for winter living, beginning with the tent-offices of the superintendent and commanding officer. A washroom and latrine were also built for them. Plans were drawn and the area surveyed for permanent barracks for the enrollees of Company #696 at their campsite near Standing Rock and for a new camp to be situated at the lodge site a half-mile to the southeast. In accordance with the federal regulation obtained by the burgeoning trade unions that CCC men were not to be used in the building of winter quarters, Easterly Lumber Company of Carbondale was granted the contract to build the barracks; they were completed just in time for the first November freezes. Around the same time, Bauer Bros. Construction Company of Belleville began the second campsite buildings.[14]

In November, a crew of enrollees was organized under foremen G. W. Thompson, Daniel Brewer, and Adolph Ruediger to plant 17,800 trees, shrubs, and vines, many of which the men dug out at the State Forest Preserve near Wolf Lake. (CCC Camp Union had been established there by Company #1621 about the same time Company #696 settled in at Giant City.) The Giant City men heeled in another 52,725 plants. As winter approached, the CCC camp construction crew stayed busy laying cinder paths, building septic tanks, winterizing buildings, and sawing and chopping the winter wood supply. A trail shelter made entirely of material from the hewing department and cedar shingles was completed in November on the cliff at the north entrance.[15]

Also in November 1933, the CCC boys were called in to extinguish six forest fires on the properties adjoining the park. Southern Illinoisans were accustomed to seeing fire in the woods. Most often set by local landowners and hunters of roots, the small yearly conflagrations usually just checked the understory's growth, but sometimes large trees and structures were damaged if a fire got out of control. One of the main missions of the CCC in southern Illinois would be to stop this practice by convincing local citizens that fire harmed the public resource.

Two of the main objectives of the Forest Service CCC camps stationed in the new Shawnee National Forest were fire fighting and the construction of a lookout tower. Camp Giant City also had a newly built observation or lookout tower for that purpose and had its fair share of fire excitement as well. Like most of the forest fires throughout southern Illinois, all of the Makanda-area fires occurred at night or on weekends and were thought to have been purposely set. Although farmers customarily burned the scrub from their woods and also some of their fields in the late autumn, there was substantial speculation that local young men may have wanted to keep the CCC boys busy in the camp and away from their girls at such times. This was known to be done around other camps as well. The men of Company #696 did work a lot of time beyond their eight-hour day controlling fires before any serious damage was done to the park property.[16]

Forest fires were less of a problem as the CCC and Forest Service officials gradually convinced the farmers of fire's harm and as the federal government acquired much of the cutover land for the Shawnee National Forest. While Camp Giant City was getting started, CCC officials and Conservation Service technicians identified sites for eight camps in southern Illinois where erosion was serious and a water supply available. Riverside Park was considered a likely location in Murphysboro.[17] These erosion camps along with the Forest Service camps and the fire watchtowers built by CCC enrollees succeeded in halting the fires that periodically burned much of the woods in southern Illinois.

None of the CCC men interviewed for this book who were sent to the camps in 1937 and 1938 recall ever fighting fires around Giant City, and the official reports note their sharp decline in number.[18]

## THE FIRST WINTER IN CAMP

There were a lot of comings and goings at the CCC camps, particularly at the end of the six-month enlistment periods. Men quit or were discharged for misbehavior. Some got better employment. During these first six months of the CCC at Giant City, the average number of men working at the camp vacillated between 127 and 192. The work crews continued through the winter with the construction of two bridges, three culverts, and the north entrance roadway, while the engineering department surveyed the creeks, road plan, and lodge site. The original

Erosion control, April 1934, near fire lookout tower, Camp Giant City. National Archives, CCC records, SP-11, photo #49.

When CCC Company #1657 reached Camp Stone Fort at Giant City State Park in December 1933, the men were housed and fed in newly erected, drafty buildings near the site of the lodge to be constructed in 1934–36. Courtesy of Floyd Finley.

Entire Company #1657 at Camp Stone Fort, March 31, 1934. Most of these men were from central Illinois, but some were from other states. Courtesy of Floyd Finley.

plans included a parking area, tennis courts, an area for lawn sports, a hotel, and a nine-hole golf course. In December 1933, the county relief office received word that there was room for eleven more local men at Giant City's camp and for twenty more at Murphysboro's Riverside Camp. Many men who enrolled after the initial organization were not required to go through the indoctrination at Jefferson Barracks, instead proceeding directly to their assigned camps.[19]

By December 1933, Forest Service camps were being built throughout southern Illinois: Camp Delta near McClure, Camp Glenn near Ava, Camp Pomona, Camp Eddyville, Camp Herod, Camp Kedron, Camp Hicks, and Camp Union. Camps run by the Soil Erosion Service (the predecessor of the Soil Conservation Service) were constructed at Metropolis and Murphysboro's Riverside Park. Later SCS camps were built at Dixon Springs, Grayville, Shawneetown, Anna, Benton, Waterloo, Norris City, Marion, Mounds, Sparta, Waltonville, Du Quoin, Red Bud, and Eldorado (see appendix 1). Camp Pomona, which began as a Forest Service veterans camp, would soon become the only African American CCC camp in southern Il-linois. This network of camps shared some resources, such as an ambulance, and some personnel, such as doctors and clergymen. Their sports teams played one another and their boxers competed against each other in games and matches to which the public was often invited. Men compared their situations and accomplishments with companies in other camps in friendly rivalries and competitions.

In the six-month summary of work accomplished by December 1933 submitted to the National Park Service, the following report was made on the CCC enrollees at Giant City: "The attitude of the CCC has shown that they certainly intended to work. With but few exceptions, they do as much work or more than could be expected on an outside construction job. Their morale is much higher than when they arrived and every man in the Company seems to be contented." As early as July 1933, CCC officials realized that rural recruits, such as the majority of Giant City's men, had "greater aptitude and enthusiasm" for their work. They were more familiar with outdoor work, and in the CCC they were making more money than they had as farmhands.[20]

CCC pennant and patches.
Author's collection.

## COMPANY #1657 ARRIVES

Shortly after southern Illinois's CCC Company #696 was organized at Jefferson Barracks, Company #1657 also organized there under Captain John F. Roehm. The men of this company were mainly from towns in central Illinois (see appendix 2 for a roster of names). In June 1933, they were sent to work just eight miles south of Springfield, near Chatham, at a place called Cotton Hill. Their tented campsite was a wooded area carpeted in poison ivy and weeds. The latrines and showers were out-of-doors, and the mosquitoes were terrible. Under the supervision of Frank N. Dalbey, these men began the construction of Lake Springfield. Their chief work was the blasting of limestone out of a stone quarry to be used as riprap on the shoreline of the proposed lake, created from the damming of Sugar Creek. Company #1657 included several older enrollees, men in their thirties and forties, who were hired as Local Experienced Men. After six months, the company was moved from its drafty tents to Giant City's new camp. This company was selected because of the experience its men had gained at dynamiting rocks from quarries.[21]

Twenty-year-old Floyd Finley of Mattoon was typical of the enrollees of Company #1657. He remembered clearly the company's summer in 1933 at Camp Springfield and the preceding indoctrination at Jefferson Barracks. "The worst thing about it was the hot weather. They gave us World War I heavy wool uniforms and shoes. But they didn't have any socks. We all had bare feet. We got blisters on our heels. That was awful. You would go to the first aid tent for help and they would put iodine on your raw skin." Along with the shoes, made by the prisoners at Ft. Leavenworth, the standard clothing issue included wool shirts, pants, and underwear, all surplus from World War I. Also issued were a toothbrush kit and a Bible.

Because of his prior work as an office boy and for a newspaper, Finley was hired as a company clerk for Company #1657 when it first began at Jefferson Barracks. He worked in that capacity through its months at Camp Springfield and for its five-month stint at Giant City. Finley said, "When I joined the CCC, like every boy, I was issued an identification bracelet, a 'dog tag' with my name on it. We wore these on our wrists. Never took it off for a bath or anything; it was clamped on. Everybody had a serial number. Later, you could buy a patch to sew onto your jacket shoulder. Each patch had an insignia to show rank and duty. Mine was crossed pens to show clerkship."[22]

Finley recalled that upon first arriving at Camp Springfield from the indoctrination period at Jefferson Barracks, there were two company clerks on Captain Roehm's staff, one too many. Roehm flipped a coin, which Finley lost, so he was sent to work in the first aid station. But after a few days, Roehm was dissatisfied enough with the other man to call Finley back to be his clerk. In that position, Finley accompanied Roehm to the state capital to appeal directly to Governor Henry Horner for office furniture, typewriters, wastebaskets, and other office items. The governor gave the camp several desks and equipment for the camp's offices.

Captain Roehm was of the field artillery, a "regular army" officer, as opposed to a more relaxed "reserve officer." According to Finley, Roehm "didn't have enough patience to sit to dictate letters, so he would walk up and down the tent office and dictate to me. I would sit there and type as he talked, no translation at all." In addition to his company command, Roehm was appointed to be the recruiting officer for central Illinois. He took Finley and a military doctor to the central Illinois towns where they had arranged recruiting days. The candidates would formally apply, get physically examined, and then be assigned to a camp. After the first great wave of recruits in the spring of 1933, when men were sent from Illinois to national forests out west and up north to Michigan, the leadership in the CCC learned that in

Captain C. G. (Guy) Whitney, commanding officer of Company #1657, in his office and living quarters at Camp Stone Fort in 1934. Captain Whitney had a Grundig German radio and a pet dog that followed him everywhere. Floyd Finley was among many alumni of Company #1657 who reported that Whitney was very well liked by his men. Courtesy of Floyd Finley

most cases, they should try to keep people close to their homes. Some enrollees, particularly the teenagers, had families whom they wished to visit on weekends.[23]

Although the men suffered in their uniforms all summer, the wool proved welcome in the late autumn on the central Illinois flatlands, as the men were living in wooden-floored tents when the night temperatures plunged to twenty degrees. Each tent had a Sibley woodstove in the middle, but it never warmed the whole interior. The CCC did not intend for the men to stay in the tents for the winter. The organization was moving many companies from northern areas in the state and from Wisconsin and Michigan farther south to spend the winter. As fast as new camp barracks could be erected, companies were moved in. Such was the case at Pomona's newly built CCC camp first occupied

by World War I veterans who had moved from a tent camp in Wisconsin to escape the harsh winter.[24] At Camp Springfield, Captain C. G. Whitney, a reserve officer and certified public accountant from Chicago, took over the army's command of Company #1657 in November 1933. A World War I veteran, Whitney was generally considered "an admirable gentleman and an ideal C.O." Upon assuming his new command, he informed his men that they were moving southward near Makanda where new barracks had just been built for them.[25]

## CAMP STONE FORT (SP-24)

On the night of December 10, 1933, the 162 enrollees, their army officers, and Superintendent Frank Dalbey boarded a southbound train. Most of the men had never been in the

Camp Stone Fort was built on "Gobbler's Knob," now the area of the lodge parking lot and new cabins. Courtesy of Floyd Finley.

Shawnee Hills of Illinois, so they "feasted their eyes" on the park's rock formations. Their barracks, situated on a hill known as Gobbler's Knob, just next to the proposed lodge site, were also a very welcome sight, even though these buildings too proved to be cold and drafty. Also newly built were a mess hall and a headquarters building. Some men, immediately upon arriving, climbed the observation tower on the hill to the south of camp to view the whole park, including Camp Giant City, just a half-mile to the north. In this camp, called Camp Stone Fort, barracks lined the east side of the road, and on the west side were the mess hall and other buildings. A central area had been arranged for the flag and company reveille.[26] Company #1657 stayed at Makanda's second camp throughout the winter, enjoying the results of a heavy snowstorm by building bobsleds to race down the steep snow-packed roadways and hillsides.

The infusion of these men to the Giant City CCC workforce doubled the average number of men reporting on work details outside of camp duties (such as kitchen and office work). Now, the supervisors had an average of 196 men to organize on special project details. The two companies established separate work crews, depending mainly on project priorities. When assigning men to crews, supervisors took into account the talents and interests of the men. Roadwork occupied more of the man-hours than any other detail. Reliable all-weather roads into the camp were essential to all the other projects.

In preparation for cold weather, the log-hewing department built solid roofs for the twelve tent buildings. At both campsites and along the newly surfaced road at the north entrance, trees were planted. Some crews blasted rock for a garage and a road subway and cleared the woods of underbrush. Coal was proving to

Interior of barracks at Camp Stone Fort. Courtesy of Floyd Finley.

be a sufficient fuel for the stoves, but the water problem was a major source of complaint for Company #1657. A well was eventually dug during the 1933–34 winter, and it finally provided a sufficient water supply for Camp Stone Fort. Until it was finished, the men hauled water from nearby Camp Giant City.[27]

During the week ending March 12, 1934, regional CCC inspector William P. Hannon made another routine inspection of both camps at Giant City State Park. It was the first inspection for Commander Whitney's men of Company #1657 at Giant City. The company had lost some of its original 173 men who had come from Springfield: eleven were dishonorably discharged (nine of those eleven had eloped), and of the nineteen honorable discharges, three took a medical discharge, two returned

to school, four transferred to other camps, and nine found employment. One, Jesse Baker, had died. On February 26, 1934, Baker had suffered a heart attack while walking up the Makanda hill from his home in Cobden. Baker, fifty-seven, had joined Company #1657 as a Local Experienced Man; he was buried in Cobden.

Hannon described Company #1657's Stone Fort camp on the high knob as standard, with six barracks buildings, one mess hall and kitchen, one bathhouse with seventeen showerheads and one twenty-foot-long urinal, and two pit latrines equipped with twenty-eight seats. There were also barracks for the army headquarters and for Superintendent Olson's office and staff headquarters. The health of the men was considered excellent, with only one man in quarters recuperating from a successful appendicitis

Camp Stone Fort's mess hall, ready for a meal, 1934. Courtesy of Floyd Finley.

operation. Mass was held every Sunday morning in the camp, and trucks transported Protestants to Makanda and Carbondale churches.

Hannon inspected Camp Giant City at the same time he was visiting Camp Stone Fort (see appendix 3 for a list of both camps' forestry personnel). Since Camp Giant City's inception in June 1933, there had been considerable fluctuation in the company. Sixty-two losses were due to honorable discharges; these were mainly men who declined to reenroll or accepted employment elsewhere. Other losses were due to dishonorable discharges: thirteen men had deserted, eight were discharged for serious misconduct and six for willful disobedience of orders, nine refused to work, two refused to obey rules, and two did not respond to urgent calls.

Although the army proposed to follow a strict regime, which was dutifully followed at some camps with reveille at 5:45 A.M., roll call at 6:45, transport to work sites at 7:15, and so on, the actual routine at Giant City was much more casual. Joseph Zimmerman, who was there in the winter of 1933–34 and later visited many CCC camps as an army recruiter, said what several other Giant City alumni expressed: "A boy scout camp was more organized and drilled than [this] CCC company."[28] This was not the case at most other southern Illinois camps, however, where a more disciplined regime was habitual.

The spirit of both companies was reported to have been very good as the new year of 1934 began. The morale of the newer Company #1657—which moved into unknown territory—remained high, due in great part to Captain Whitney's ability to get along with his men and to the weekly rallies he organized for

Camp Stone Fort's kitchen and staff, 1934. In front of the table are cooks William Jenkins *(left)* and Carl Lempe *(legs crossed)*.
Courtesy of Floyd Finley.

them. These gatherings, held in the mess hall, provided amateur theatricals, mass singing, musical programs, elocution, and exhibition boxing and wrestling. Finley remembered them as being for general purposes, including providing an opportunity for the men to talk to the captain about anything they wanted. At the weekly rally of February 28, 1934, the Overhead Quartet, made up of Finley, Howard O. Leonhard, Woodrow W. Brandon, and Ivan E. Rice, composed with the aid of Captain Whitney the following "Ode to Lieutenant Paul W. Nieman" to the tune of "It Ain't Gonna Rain No More." Lieutenant C. Jerry Boyd of Carterville took Lieutenant Nieman's place as second in command of Company #1657.[29]

Our Looic has a girl
    Her name is Gladys dear,
He sits around all day long.
    Hoping from her to hear.
[Chorus:]

Oh, the Looie's blue and we are too,
    Cause he got no letter today,
But don't you fret, you'll get one yet,
    And chase our troubles away.

He finally gets a letter,
    All pink and smelling swell,
The contents of the letter,
    He says he'll never tell.

[Repeat chorus.]

If he doesn't get a letter
    He's blue as blue can be,
But when he get a missive,
    He's beautiful to see.
[Repeat chorus.]

So we hope he gets a letter,
    He's a right good sort of feller,
And we hate to see him married,
    Cause letters are much better.

Although the Springfield men might have missed their girlfriends, there were never complaints about the food at Giant City as there were at some of the other camps, particularly early on. The men of Company #1657 remember eating well there. At least 80 percent of the food was procured locally with the remainder being shipped in from Jefferson Barracks, the army supply headquarters. The leftovers from the camps' good food drew a lot of dogs that the men fed and befriended.[30]

Sixty new enrollees were locally recruited to bring the roster of Company #1657 to 203 in March 1934. During March and April of that year, Captain Whitney approved an educational program led by the educational advisor, Russell E. Rigg, with the following goals: "to develop in each man his powers of self-expression, self-entertainment, and self culture; to preserve and strengthen good habits of health and of mental development; to assist each man better to meet his employment problems when he leaves camp; to develop an appreciation of nature and country life."[31] As novel and healthy as the camp was to these men, by March 1934 many of the original company missed being closer to home. They were nostalgic enough to compose lyrics to the tune of "Show Me the Way to Go

A number of dogs were adopted by CCC enrollees at Giant City's camps. Courtesy of Floyd Finley.

Home," a tune sung by the Overhead Quartet at the March 21, 1934, company rally.[32]

> Show us the way to Cotton Hill,
>     We're tired of old Giant City,
> We wanta go back to our old camp,
>     Where we were sitting pretty.
> Spring is in the air
>     And we're longing to be there,
> With all the girls at Iles' Park,
>     Up in the Springfield City.

After over five months of hard work at Giant City, the men of Company #1657 moved out of Makanda on May 3, 1934, but not back to Camp Springfield. The company occupied a newly built camp at the old fairgrounds of LeRoy, Illinois, where the men were put to work on soil erosion projects. Captain Whitney gave them a beer party before their departure.[33]

A great deal of effort was made by the army to make Giant City's CCC enrollees happy and enthusiastic. The officers of Company #696 arranged for the building of a boxing arena at the park. Over the next few years, boxing competitions became very popular with crowds made up of local residents and CCC boys brought from nearby camps. Jim Watkins, an enrollee at Camp Union, near Jonesboro, remembered that on competition nights at the Giant City camp, "The woods would be full, tied with horses, saddle horses and buggies, neighbors. [It was] the only entertainment they had, come see the CCC boys mix it up a little."[34]

Although most of the men in southern Illinois's CCC camps were contented, Giant City's men had it exceptionally pleasant. They were working in a park that was accessible to the public, which meant to many of the men "accessible to girls." The larger towns of Carbondale, Anna, Murphysboro, and Marion already were familiar to many enrollees and were within easy driving distance. They could attend classes at SINU as well as in the camp. On the weekends, most of the young men left,

hitchhiking to Cobden, Carbondale, or their homes. George Oliver remembered walking down the big Baptist Hill rather than using the north entrance because it was closer to Makanda. "By the time we got into Makanda, someone had already picked us up [to take us to Carbondale]. . . . With only five dollars a month, we couldn't have afforded that train ride." And around Makanda and Cobden, the locals were friendly. The men enjoyed romances with local girls from the first weekend of the camp's existence.[35]

One local girl, Fannie Lirely, lived about a half-mile from the camp with her parents. Her mother and father, Jacob Lirely, owned a farm and orchard. She had gone to grade school at Makanda but then went to Cobden to attend high school, as there was none in Makanda. The youngest of nine children, Fannie was eighteen years old in 1933. She had just returned from a trip to Florida with her aunt when she heard from girlfriends of all the goings-on at the park. They persuaded a neighbor to drive them in his Model A to see a boxing match there. She remembered: "I was standing back on the hillside and someone said, 'You don't look like you been to Florida.' And I looked around. I said, 'I don't have to look like a palm leaf just because I've been to Florida.' George was standing there beside a friend of mine, and he said, 'I'd like to meet that girl.' This friend said that could be arranged."[36]

Fannie and George began dating, often attending the weekend boxing matches where the champs from Giant City camp competed against the best of the other camps. George led her around where he worked in the new barracks of the Department of the Interior office and showed her a little model of the proposed lodge.

Some nights, Oliver's superior offered him the use of his truck. George had become familiar with the truck and the roads because his duties included cashing his supervisors' paychecks at the Carbondale National Bank and bringing their money to them. They trusted him. George and Fannie both remembered driving to Carbondale and hiding the borrowed truck on backstreets, not wanting camp officials to have to answer for its whereabouts.

Because of the CCC, hundreds of romances and subsequent marriages resulted in a more thorough stirring of the gene pool in southern Illinois than had ever occurred before. Men traveled to camps in states as far away as Massachusetts or Oregon. Forestry personnel came to southern Illinois from Washington State or Michigan and married local girls. The new opportunities for the enrollees made available by the CCC were not just economic or work related. Enrollees met women and men they would have not encountered in their hometowns—people with different ideas from their own. But at the same time, New Deal programs like the CCC were instilling common beliefs in their enrollees, beliefs in individual moral and social responsibility. FDR very much approved of the resulting democratization of the young "common people" fostered by the CCC.[37]

Boxing matches drew large crowds at Giant City State Park. Most of the matches featured serious competition, but some weekend matches were staged just for the crowd's enjoyment. CCC enrollee Kenneth Hawk said that in order to get out of some unpleasant punishment such as kitchen duty, he was recruited to box Mearle Hickam in a fake match. Hawk pretended to knock Hickam out, then they shook bolts and washers out of Hawk's gloves as everyone booed and laughed. "All for entertainment," Hawk said. Photo from *Official Annual: Civilian Conservation Corps, Jefferson Barracks CCC District, Sixth Corps Area, 1937* (U.S. Government), 52.

# Work Projects

On January 6, 1934, a meeting of CCC camp superintendents of state park projects was held in Springfield. Called by Robert Kingery, Illinois director of the Department of Public Works and Buildings, and attended by Dr. Service, procurement officer, and Harry Curtis and R. C. Van Drew, inspectors for the National Park Service, the meeting was arranged to verify approval of work projects for the coming months.[1]

One complicated proposed project at Giant City was accepted at this meeting. Through the park's center crossed two roads, one known as the Park Road, which ran north and south, and the county gravel road that ran more or less east to west in the park. A bridge and subway road, referred to as Project 47C, were approved for construction at this juncture. The first order of business to prepare for this long-term project was to build detour roads so the local farm-to-market travel would not be disrupted.[2]

## THE SUBWAY PROJECT

Throughout January, February, and March of 1934, the subway or underpass project demanded most of the energy from both Companies #696 and #1657. The average strength of the two companies combined in January was 393 men, allowing 298 men entirely for work details. Company #696 put a detail on the subway, and Company #1657 put men on the second unit of the road leading from the north entrance. For the subway construction, approximately

View of intersection before underpass project, looking east from county road meeting park road, June 1934.
National Archives, CCC records, Project 47C, photo #1.

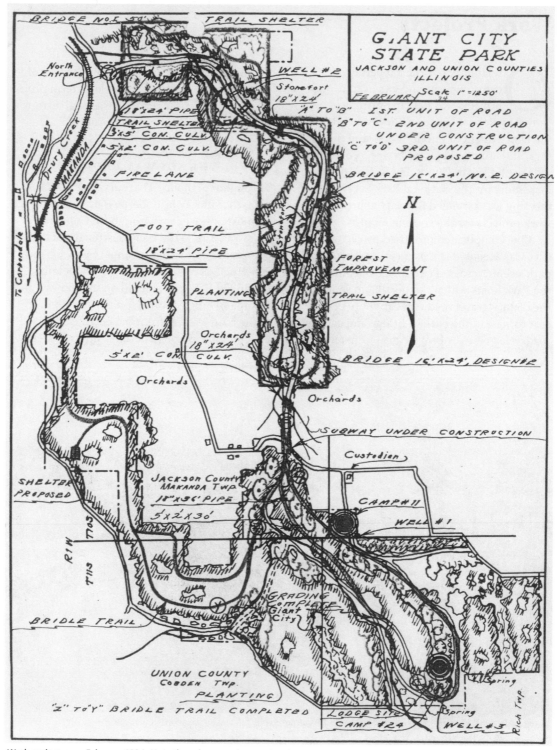

Work project map, February 1934. Note the subway under construction. National Archives, CCC records.

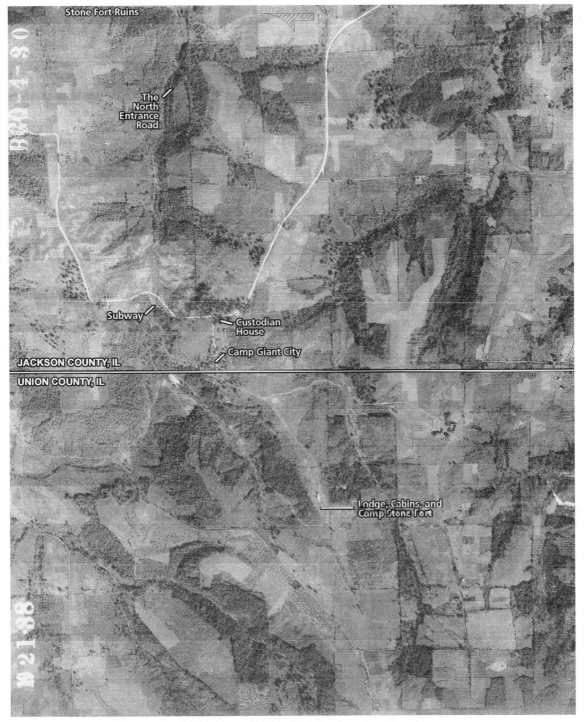

Stone Fort Ruins

The
North
Entrance
Road

Subway

Custodian
House

Camp Giant City

JACKSON COUNTY, IL

UNION COUNTY, IL

Lodge, Cabins, and
Camp Stone Fort

Aerial view of Giant City State Park showing the north entrance road and the subway location. Published by U.S. Department of Agriculture, 1938, Map Library, Morris Library, SIUC.

Excavating 50 percent complete on underpass project. National Archives, CCC records, Project 47C, photo #4.

Work on stone wall of underpass project, June 1934. National Archives, CCC records, SP-11.

**WORK PROJECTS**

fifty men per day were used to dynamite and shovel dirt and rock at the excavation area. Each month, as many as 192 sticks of dynamite were set into holes drilled five to six feet deep. Thousands of yards of dirt were then used as fill on the areas of road being prepared by Company #1657. Retaining walls were built to hold fill that was spread by the single shovelful. Foreman William Unger supervised this work. Stones for bridge abutments were carefully stacked, and two concrete culverts were poured for the northernmost sections of road. Superintendent Albin F. Olson highly praised the men of both camps, saying their work was beyond expectation and had been performed as fast and as satisfactorily as could be expected by a contractor "on the outside." Particularly the stonemasonry on the bridge abutments was compared by Olson to the fine work of professional stonemasons.[3]

George Oliver laid some of the rocks along the bridges and roads, explaining that the rocks were picked right out of the creek. The trick to laying the rocks, he said, was to slope each rock back a little bit. It was slow work, requiring the patience to try to fit a rock onto the wall, and if it didn't fit just right, the men would try another rock. "We'd just keep moving those rocks around until they fit right."[4]

## STONE FORT IS REBUILT

Everyone who was well acquainted with the Giant City Park area by 1933 had walked among the piled stones on the 125-foot bluff outside Makanda called Stone Fort. Many wondered about the ancient history of the wall's builders. Archaeologists have now determined that Makanda's Stone Fort is actually one of ten such enigmatic prehistoric walls located on bluff tops in southern Illinois. Although referred to most often by the public as forts, experts today consider it unlikely that they were built either for defense or as animal

Excavation at Bridge #1 for abutments and center pier, May 1934. National Archives, CCC records, SP-11.

Bridge #3, showing hewn stringers in place and stone abutments completed, March 1934. National Archives, CCC records, SP-11.

Bridge #3 completed with hewn superstructure in place, March 1934. National Archives, CCC records, SP-11.

WORK PROJECTS

enclosures or traps. Archaeologists now agree that the walls were constructed in the Late Woodland period, around 900 A.D., but they do not agree on why. Some wonder if they were created for ceremonial uses.[5]

John G. Mulcaster, who undoubtedly had explored the area extensively as an amateur historian, thought he had some answers about Giant City's Stone Fort and wrote about its supposed significance in several publications. Mulcaster was a reliable local authority on many aspects of Makanda-area history, but he was not a trained archaeologist, and he wrongly pronounced the fort either "a substation of a fur company, the Lingueste Mercantile Co. of St. Louis founded in 1750," or a defense built up by George Rogers Clark's men.[6] Most likely, Mulcaster was among the locals, or "natives," who told the CCC army and park officials about the site. But the officials "gave little credence to the stories" and ignored the archaeological site for several months.[7]

Then, in March 1934, Superintendent Olson reported with obvious excitement to headquarters in Washington, D.C., the "discovery" of a stone wall, 180 feet long and 15 feet wide, at a location "that offers excellent views in all directions."[8] When George H. French examined Stone Fort between 1879 and 1880, he described it as a "ledge of rocks" 280 feet long and on average 33 feet wide and about 30 inches high. It's possible that some of the rocks were taken from the pile in the historic period for building and other purposes.[9] A man among the CCC crews "experienced in hunting for Indian relics" was able to somehow "prove" to Olson's staff that the site was indeed prehistoric and authentic and a worthwhile addition to the park "if it was rebuilt."[10]

In the true military fashion of getting to work immediately on the job at hand, several CCC volunteers from Company #696, dubbed "the Stonefort [sic] Crew," were allowed to move all the stone into a new wall approximately eight feet high and three feet wide.

Olson wrote that as they tried to locate the original foundation by moving all the stone, "we found two good pestle and mortar sets, several dishes, loophole rocks, hoes, spades and bits of pottery. In an effort to locate the magazine or storehouse, we have been carefully turning over the soil in the vicinity of the wall. In the course of our digging we have found quite a few arrowheads, skinning knives and a half bushel pieces of pottery, but no whole pieces have been secured as yet."[11]

Superintendent Olson wrote in his monthly camp report with great enthusiasm of plans to start a park museum, as was eventually done at Black Hawk State Park, with the hope that the local people would donate the many valuable pieces they had found in the vicinity and that histories of the site would be available at SINU's library. The CCC completed a foot trail up the bluff, which gave easy access to the fort from the main park road. The plan of the CCC supervisors, who were understandably ignorant of archaeological methods, was to reconstruct the fort as they imagined it had originally stood "with the Chieftains post of command and flank observation and protection posts." Fortunately, this misguided phase of the ruinous project was not completed. Mulcaster, who was involved with some of the CCC efforts, reported in December 1934 that the wall was half re-reconstructed.[12]

There is no mention in any of the official reports that anyone with archaeological expertise was asked to advise on any aspect of the wall's deconstruction and reconstruction. One can safely guess that not all of the artifacts were handed over to the park officials by the men who found them, and one can also assume that some professional archaeologists and amateurs who knew of the site's significance were duly disappointed at the audacity displayed in so forcefully digging around this ancient construction. Of course, such plundering by private citizens into archaeological sites, even burial mounds, was common in the 1930s as well as in years before. Grave bones were typically thrown to the side in the search for artifacts. Looters were known to even use dynamite to blast open large mounds in the search for gold and other treasures. In fact, many people had reportedly dug around Makanda's stone fort in the previous hundred years looking for gold.[13]

In Mulcaster's often-reprinted "Old Stone Fort," he noted that some time shortly after 1870, a local Doctor Gallon tore down part of the wall hunting for relics. According to Mulcaster, none were found, so that therefore was proof that the fort was not of Indian origin. To further his argument that the fort was built by white men, Mulcaster quoted a man named George Owens who came to Makanda in 1862. Owens told Mulcaster of a small "one-pounder" brass cannon that was found in the wall of the fort. This was removed from the wall to use in Fourth of July celebrations around Makanda until it was sold to a junk dealer. Willis Rendleman told southern Illinois historian George W. Smith that the cannon was fired at Fourth of July celebrations from inside the enclosing "Stonefort" walls.[14] No one could argue that Makanda's Stone Fort was a pristine site when the CCC "discovered" it, but neither can the fact be argued that the site lost extensive valuable information as the stones were restacked and the artifacts removed. In 2002, the Center for Archaeological Investigations at Southern Illinois University completed a detailed technical report on Giant City Stone Fort that establishes many facts about this Late Woodland site and offers an intriguing hypothesis about the possible function of the "fort" as a ceremonial or sacred space.[15]

"Stonefort [*sic*] before starting work of removing stone to find old Indian relics for park museum" is the caption of this photo sent along with the Company #696 monthly work report for March 1934. National Archives, CCC records, photo #22.

Piling up stones removed from Stone Fort. National Archives, CCC records, photo #23.

"View showing a portion of the stone removed from Stonefort [*sic*] in an effort to find the foundation of the old fort with the idea in mind of building the fort as it stood originally." This caption accompanied the photo sent by Company #696 in its March 1934 work report. National Archives, CCC records, photo #24.

Dressing up the road by hand after the grading is finished, ca. March–June 1934.
National Archives, CCC records, SP-11, photo #72.

## OTHER WORK PROJECTS
## THROUGH 1934

By March 1934, the men were hand-grading the second unit of road. Head wells and catch basins of stone on steel were also fashioned. Both camps had crews that collected and transplanted tree stock from areas of the woods that needed thinning. In January alone, 632 black locust, 901 cedar, 165 maple, and 240 elm were transplanted. Nursery plants that had been heeled in during the fall were also set out in January, making a total of over 15,000 plants handled during the month. This crew, supervised by foreman Walter Dahl, also pruned and cleaned up approximately thirty-four acres, cutting up the fallen wood to be used as firewood by future campers.[16]

Each camp put a detail on the construction of a garage and service building. Foremen William Stuemke, W. H. Allen, and R. E. Kilgore were in charge of the construction and maintenance crews in 1934. The service building, which was completed in March, accommodated the mechanic, the tool sharpener, and all the tools for both camps. Quarry work was begun in January in order to furnish stone for all the masonry work in the buildings. The men from this construction crew quarried, cut stone, and unloaded supplies of cement, sand, and steel, which they then trucked to the appropriate job sites in the camp. The foot trail crew from Company #696 worked on a trail in the Stone Fort section of the park, while Company #1657 started on a bridle trail through the Giant City portion.

The log-hewing crew of #696, under the supervision of foreman A. J. Newlin, prepared and erected parking barrier posts and rails as well as footlockers for use in the barracks. The crewmen were called on to lay a 10-by-24-foot floor on Bridge #3. They also built a tight fence around the woodpile of Camp Giant City.[17]

A crew of engineers had planned the designs for the subway bridge as well as for the garage, service building, road bridges, culverts,

Men of Company #1657 working on the road. Courtesy of Floyd Finley.

Second unit of road, on the loop around the lodge site, nearing completion in January 1934. National Archives, CCC records, photo #102.

Start of work on garage and service building, March 1934. National Archives, CCC records.

Completed garage and service building. To the left is the temporary garage that was torn down and salvaged for materials.
Courtesy of Matthew Skertich.

**WORK PROJECTS**

Detail working on foot trail, March 1934. National Archives, CCC records, photo #14.

Finished portion of foot trail, February 1934. National Archives, CCC records, photo #114.

Breaking rock that had been placed for fill along bridle trails, April 1934. National Archives, CCC records, photo #41.

The log-hewing department, which hewed material for trail shelters, bridge superstructures, parking barriers, and guardrails, March 1934. National Archives, CCC records, photo #7.

Carrying a heavy log to be used as a ford on the bridle trail. National Archives, CCC records, photo #17.

Flood control work, clearing channel of Stonefort Creek, Project 52E. National Archives, CCC records.

and retaining walls. Topographical mapping of the entire park was underway, and the state architect was completing designs for the park's proposed lodge. February 1934 was an exceptionally dry and mild month, allowing for uninterrupted work progress by all the crews. On February 19, an inspection of Camp Giant City kept the men of Company #696 busy the entire day. They had won the honor of being the best company of the CCC in their district and would be judged next in a wider competition in the region. A holiday was allowed all the men on February 22, George Washington's birthday, and on the last three days of the month, a five-inch snow fell.[18]

March 1934 was a reenlistment month for the CCC. A large number of men chose not to reenlist in Company #696. As a result, work progressed slowly until mid-April, when seventy-seven replacements arrived, bringing the company strength up to two hundred and briefly allowing full crews to report to the work projects. When Company #1657 left Camp Stone Fort on May 3, 1934, all the work became the responsibility of the crews from Company

#696. The men of the bridge construction crew were completing their fourth and fifth bridges. A truck trail construction crew graded road by the shovelful and laid steel culverts. The log-hewing department was held up in its work, waiting approval of a bid submitted for materials, but it still managed to supply the timbers for five trail shelters completed in April. Completion of the subway was delayed pending certain construction approvals by the state highway department. Black walnut and oak trees, viburnums and roses were planted over thirteen of the park's acres. On steep banks, the men seeded lespedeza and planted vines.[19]

In June, the road construction crew used a tractor to grade roads. The planting and plant maintenance crew kept busy weeding and cutting sprouts off of old tree trunks. During June and July, the log-hewing department took the bark off 125 guard posts and 202 guardrails. The men also hewed some large trees, fourteen to sixteen feet long, into 10-by-10-inch and 8-by-8-inch timbers.[20]

The men got a long break beginning with a half-day on Saturday, July 1, and extending through midnight on Tuesday, July 4. From July 2 to July 4, CCC officials reported to headquarters that "the camp was over run by picnic parties encroaching within a few feet of the officer's quarters." Those men left in camp who did not or could not choose to take leave were "occupied patrolling the park for possible fires."[21]

In the heat and the drought that is typical for July in southern Illinois, Company #696 continued with familiar projects: clearing fire lanes, constructing picnic tables for campsites, sloping the banks of the subway for future planting, making fills and raking shoulders of road, placing guardrails and posts, cutting weeds and clearing brush from camping grounds and picnic areas. Some plants set out in the spring were lost to the drought, even though many were watered in hopes of saving them. Two teams of horses were hired from local farmers to plow ground, but only one team arrived on July 6. It was agreed that the ground

was too hard to work, so the horses were used to mow at five dollars per ten-hour day.[22]

New projects during this summer included a bathhouse, which required a plumbing detail, and excavation for water supply tanks. A fence was built around the camp, perhaps in anticipation of the next year's Fourth of July crowds. Managing park crowds each holiday and many weekends was an added burden to the supervisors of Giant City's camps, a burden with which other camps did not have to contend.

In early July, Superintendent Olson made a trip to Cook County Forest Preserves near Chicago in order to learn its method of constructing parking barriers, road barriers, bridges, and shelters out of hewn timbers. He was able to get blueprint copies of the work for his crews to use for future projects. Foreman Adolph Ruediger was acting commander during Olson's absence.[23] Enrollee Kenneth Hawk of Du Quoin helped build the stone floors of some of

Constructing picnic tables, November 1934. National Archives, CCC records, photo #18.

Trail shelter in course of construction at trail near the north entrance, June 1934. National Archives, CCC records, photo #65.

Trail shelter showing interior view of roof detail when shakes are used. The crew used cypress shakes rather than cedar.
National Archives, CCC records, photo #10.

the shelters and remembered that they followed blueprints "just exactly. . . . Most of them had sand laid, then leveled, then concrete on that, then these flagstones on top of that. Then you had to level that. . . . I liked laying rock. One guy ran around with a portable transit. He carried it in his pocket and could set [it] down and tell you when the rock was perfect. He was a state man. . . . These one-, two-, and three-stripers [indicating levels of rank] were over every gang. The three-striper was at the head of every barracks."[24]

Throughout May and June, the largest project of the camp—the subway, or underpass—was practically completed. Project 47C cost just under $2,000 and used over 1,400 man days.[25]

## CONGRESSMAN KENT KELLER

Camp Giant City provided weekly entertainment each Wednesday night for CCC boys throughout the region. Truckloads came to enjoy musical programs and boxing and wrestling bouts, and occasionally someone gave a presentation or talk. On July 25, a special visitor, Democratic representative Kent Keller, made an "almost unannounced" guest appearance before a "great concourse" of visitors.[26]

Keller, a great champion of public works projects during the Depression era, was born in 1867 and raised near Campbell Hill in Jackson County. He first entered into politics as a Democrat in 1912, winning an Illinois Senate seat. Keller didn't run again until 1930, when he defeated Edward Denison, an aged representative from Marion. Keller's platform included "guaranteed jobs for every man and woman who wished to work, infrastructure improvements, an interstate highway system, old age pensions, higher income taxes, unemployment compensation and liberal government spending to increase employment and consumption."[27]

Keller argued that labor was capital and that "jobs must be created to make the most of that capital and create wealth through labor."

He said that "people with jobs as capital should be favored over corporations and paper capital." Keller backed FDR's presidential nomination and won his own congressional seat again in 1932, so he was present during some of the most exciting days in the history of the U.S. Congress. FDR had Democratic majorities in both houses. His first piece of legislation, the Emergency Banking Act, passed after less than an hour of debate.[28]

In July 1934 at the Giant City CCC camp, Keller was campaigning for his seat in the House of Representatives. He entertained the crowd by playing a few fiddle tunes and then spoke. A newspaper reported, "He explained to the boys that it was he who assisted greatly in securing the first ninety-five million dollars for this great project."[29] Indeed, Keller was known then and still is today in many circles as the "Father of the New Deal." He introduced to Congress the first major bill on public works of FDR's term (HR 13,994), which was intended to put 2 million men to work. The day before FDR's inauguration, Keller spoke on the House floor, saying that labor was "the basic capital" and that "the first duty of government was to provide opportunity for all men to live by their labor." He said that because this right had not been recognized, the country was suffering an economic depression. He projected that "producing wealth through labor would lead to balancing the budget and end the depression." Keller was reelected in the fall of 1934.[30]

Keller believed that the Social Security Act was "the most forward-looking piece of legislation in America's history." He used his political clout to get authorization for Marion's veterans' hospital. In 1937, he would also initiate the construction of Crab Orchard Lake, Little Grassy Lake, and Devil's Kitchen Lake. The controversial Crab Orchard project, which was supposed to be the centerpiece of southern Illinois's revitalization through two coal-fired electric generation plants (the lakes used as cooling bodies), involved the purchase

Underpass project completed, ca. November–December 1934. National Archives, CCC records, photo #12.

of 44,000 acres and the forced displacement of many landowners. Four hundred Works Progress Administration men were working on the Crab Orchard project in 1937. For decades, however, angry southern Illinoisans, mostly displaced landowners, and other opponents to the project referred to Crab Orchard Lake as "Kent Keller's Frog Pond."[31]

The CCC program was not without detractors as well. Spending borrowed billions would surely have serious consequences for our economy, many argued. Public work-fare might allow too many men to feel that the world "owed them a living," a dangerous socialist attitude, according to some. Nevertheless, it was becoming more and more obvious that men and their families were benefiting from the work and life experiences in the camps. And the economy in southern Illinois was simultaneously improving.

# Lodge Construction and Arrival of CCC Company #692

Joseph F. Booten, chief of design for the Division of Architecture and Engineering of the Illinois Department of Public Works and Buildings, was the chief architect of Giant City's lodge as well as of the lodges designed at the same time for the other Illinois state parks: White Pines, Starved Rock, Pere Marquette, and Black Hawk. Booten has written of the great hurried pressure his staff was under in the planning of the lodges, for they were expected to design lodges and cabins for five state parks at the same time.[1] Records indicate that Joseph T. Gołabowski was the assistant architect who may have actually drawn the plans for Giant City's lodge. Ross Caldwell was the architect engineer for the National Park Service in 1938 who also worked on the lodge at Giant City.[2]

All of the lodges were built for the needs of the overnight camper and the daytime visitor. All of them except the lodge at White Pines enclose grand two-story spaces and massive stone fireplaces. The purpose of Booten's designs was to create the mood for woodland retreats and relaxation. He wanted the stone exteriors and big, hewn timbers to create a protected fortress effect. It has been noted that the obvious material strength conveys "a feeling of enduring security, perhaps necessary as an architectural narcotic for urban tourists." The lodges were all built of indigenous building materials: in the case of Giant City's lodge, native sandstone and hardwood trees.[3]

The lodge designs were to be exciting mixtures of the traditional and the new. The

The miniature model of the lodge that sat in the Department of the Interior office, where George Oliver showed it to Fannie Lirely just after they met in the summer of 1934. National Archives, CCC records, Project 28C, photo #8.

Truck being filled with surface dirt, which was removed down to rock bed, at stone quarry located off the park property, summer 1934. National Archives, CCC records, photo #10.

two folk building traditions of stonemasonry and horizontal log construction were used, but Booten and his assistants also employed "mixed horizontal and vertical wooden gables, roof purlins of round logs extended beyond the roof edge, wooden balconies, a variety of saddle-notching, and queen post roof trusses unknown together or individually in any building before the twentieth century." They also added decorative details to the ironwork in the hinges, lighting fixtures, and door bolts. Elaborate roof truss systems are exposed in all the lodges. Giant City's lodge originally comprised a central two-story building with two identical wings to the north and south, all made of stone. The north wing, which was built last, was designed as the dining and kitchen area. The south wing was to function as the comfort station, complete with restrooms and showers for campers. The identical east and west entrances would feature flagstone terraces and three double doors opening into the lounge. The lounge's impressive central interior would

rise up twenty-two feet from the floor to the exposed log ceiling trusses. At the south end of the lounge was to be a massive stone fireplace flanked by stairs on both sides that would lead up to a surrounding balcony overlooking the lounge. The effect was designed to be rustic but cathedral-like, something unseen before in a public building in southern Illinois.[4]

In June 1934, the construction of Giant City lodge began with the building of a miniature model. Also in June, a detail of about thirty men began digging the trenches for the foundation footings. All of the camp's dump trucks were constantly busy, hauling hundreds of cubic yards of dirt away from the lodge site or unloading materials for the lodge construction. The quarry crew was busy all during June and July, blasting, cutting, and hauling 233 yards of selected face stone to the lodge site from a quarry located near Makanda. Another crew unloaded from Makanda's train station two carloads of cement, two carloads of crushed stone, and four carloads of sand for the footings.[5]

Lodge foundation stonework, near the empty barracks of Camp Stone Fort, July 1934. National Archives, CCC records.

The concrete footings were poured the first week of July 1934, using 843 cubic feet of sand, 1,405 cubic feet of stone, and 698 bags of cement. The laying of the stone foundation began on July 10. By the end of July, the first floor level was attained after using 320 bags of mortar cement and 1,131 cubic feet of sand. In anticipation of the wood construction in the lodge, the hewing department began hewing the huge timbers for the center supports from oak logs cut from trees found in Union County.[6]

It became evident that Project 28C, the lodge, was going to require more manpower than the details allowable from the ongoing work crews of Company #696. The barracks of Company #1657, which had been empty since May, were situated very near the lodge site (where the present-day parking lot and new cabins are situated). The supervisors decided that the scope of approved projects at Giant City warranted bringing in another company that would supplement work details and fill the empty barracks.

## COMPANY #692 ARRIVES

Original CCC Company #692 had organized in May 1933 at Jefferson Barracks, but the outfit was sent to Missouri and transferred into the Seventh Corps District under a new number. The Sixth Corps District, headquartered at Jefferson Barracks, retained the number 692 and assigned it to a new company, numbered D-692. "D" signified it was established as a drainage (erosion control) camp. In southern Illinois, the work of the drainage camps was usually indistinguishable from the work of other camps, the "D" simply signifying a qualifying designation for a new company. The 244 men of this company, organized in July 1934 at Jefferson Barracks, were from central and southern Illinois (see appendix 4 for Company #692 officers, staff, and enrollee roster as of March 31, 1935).[7]

Among them was Earl Dickey of Newton, Illinois, the eldest son of a man who was both a farmer and a Methodist minister. Earl's father earned only five hundred dollars per year, so Earl and his siblings worked for farmers and at

Earl Dickey sitting above a 100-foot drop at Giant City State Park. Courtesy of Earl Dickey.

odd jobs as they could. In July 1934, Earl and another boy hopped a freight train to Fairfield to sign up with the "C's" and rode back in a coal car. The next week, they sat on seats in a train passenger car to Jefferson Barracks, where they stayed for six hot summer weeks.[8]

Lieutenant Walter Urbach assumed command of Company #692 at Jefferson Barracks in July and led an advance team of men to Giant City in August 1934. In order to maintain continuity and a knowledgeable staff, many of the men from Company #696 moved over to supervise the new company, #692, under the command of Lieutenant Urbach. Charlie Fiocchi stayed on as Urbach's company clerk, "Smokey Joe" Calbrecht was promoted to senior foreman, and Mike Kerkes of Virden became a senior leader. Others who came with the advance detail were George Bush, Dean Faeth, Junus Hobbs, Howard Hoyer, Charles McHenry, John Milan, Orrin Pauley, Mike Raws, and Homer Rawls. Six days later, Lieutenant Harold O. Highley and 208 men of the new company, including Earl Dickey, arrived at Giant City.[9]

Earl Dickey's family in 1929, Gibson City. *Left to right*: Phyllis, Helen, Erma, Mervil, Ray, Kenneth, Lora, Earl, Lilie, and Homer Dickey. (Yet to be born were Lilie, Ernest, Harlan, and Wesley.). Courtesy of Earl Dickey.

Planting trees around the water tower, newly painted to designate Company #692 at Camp Stone Fort. National Archives, CCC records.

The very next day, an enrollee named Peter L. Mobley from McNabb, Illinois, was bitten by a copperhead while he was playing with the snake as she was bearing young. He was rushed to Carbondale's Holden Hospital to receive an antivenom injection and recovered.[10]

Adolph G. Ruediger, who had been Superintendent Albin Olson's right-hand man for Company #696, now took responsibility for the National Park Service supervisory staff as the superintendent of new Company #692. William H. Murphy from Decatur, F. P. Brown from Elgin, and William Stuemke of Springfield were named senior foremen, earning $166.66 per month. The foremen answering to them and earning $155 per month were Charles R. Collom (Marissa), Elmer A. Klehm (Arlington Heights), Mark S. Greeley (Bristol), and Joseph A. Bangiolo (Murphysboro). Raymond Hamilton was named the machinist, and George Oliver, an original member of Company #696, was promoted from a regular CCC boy making $36 per month to an employee of the Department of the Interior making $125 per month, a salary that

"Smokey Joe" Calbrecht and his dog, Alibi. Courtesy of Earl Dickey.

Under Captain Edwin R. Morine in Company #692 were First Lieutenant Harlan D. Blackburn *(center)* and First Lieutenant George D. Markel *(left)*; all were reserve officers. Earl V. Bishop, M.D., a contract surgeon *(right)*, served both camps.

By 1935, Adolph G. Ruediger was making $191.66 per month as the project superintendent of Company #692. F. P. Britson was made superintendent of park projects for both camps. The following foremen made between $155 and $165 per month: F. P. Brown *(second from right)*, Charles R. Collom, John W. Newlon, Elmer A. Klehm, Mark S. Greeley, William H. Murphy, Herman J. Branca, Joseph A. Bangiolo *(first on left)*, and William Stuemke, the stonemason specialist. Raymond Hamilton *(second from left)* was the machinist and George Oliver *(far right)* the tool keeper and also company clerk.

enabled him to feel comfortable enough to ask Fannie Lirely to marry him. She said yes.

Fannie Lirely and George Oliver wed on December 22, 1934, and for the first year of

George and Fanny Oliver in the 1940s. Courtesy George Oliver.

their marriage paid twelve dollars from his monthly pay toward rent for a two-room house near the camp. The couple also bought a 1932 Model A Ford convertible from Vogler Ford for $325. They would remain living near Makanda throughout their lives. Like so many others, George credited the opportunities to learn professional skills in the CCC for his success in earning a good living in southern Illinois.[11] At Giant City, George was given the title of tool keeper, but in actuality, he continued his work as typist and bookkeeper for Ruediger. The newly populated Camp Stone Fort, now numbered SP-41, shared the services of the tool keeper from SP-11, Camp Giant City. Foreman Stuemke had been hired specifically because he was a master stonemason, and the lodge construction project was getting underway.[12]

Setting natural stone steps on a foot trail. National Archives, CCC records, photo #11.

Digging holes for guardrail posts, February–March 1935. National Archives, CCC records.

With two camps once again working at Giant City State Park, coordination was required between the supervisory staffs. Weekly meetings attended by the supervisors of both camps became essential. Matters such as the fair distribution of work trucks between the camps and their routing throughout the park required planning. As had been the procedure with Company #1657, both companies volunteered crews for whatever projects were deemed important at the time.

In September 1934, a proposed list of plants needed in the park for fall planting was put out for bids. Superintendent Olson planned to create an "arboretum trail." He proposed moving small plants and native trees along a designated trail where the plants would be labeled for the educational purposes of "botanical classes" for SINU. A topographical survey was done of a portion of the park that would lend itself to a five- or six-acre recreational lake. Based upon the results of a questionnaire answered by 459 recent visitors to the park, plans for such a lake were submitted for project approval. A sewage disposal

system was also being planned near the lodge site. Throughout October and November, crews continued their work on the trails, in the campgrounds, in the woods, and along the roads. They set over one thousand linear feet of guardrails, hewn by the log-hewing department, and built retaining walls where needed.[13] A carpentry crew, under senior leader Mike Kerkes, began the construction of cabins, 17-by-13 feet in dimension.

Of the many plants that suffered in the 1934 summer drought, 20 to 50 percent of some of the tree species, such as the maple and poplar, died. In the autumn, 5,760 pounds of walnuts were collected, as were 100 pounds of other seeds from thirty-five different kinds of trees, vines, and bushes. These were planted in the park's nursery.[14]

## THE STONEWORK

After the first year of road construction, the building of the lodge at Giant City required by far the largest number of workmen. Crews labored simultaneously at the quarry, at the

Looking north to lodge site and Camp Stone Fort from observation tower, before June 1934. Camp buildings are shown where current lodge parking lot and new cabins are situated today north of the lodge. National Archives, CCC records.

Stonework progress at lodge site, July 1934. National Archives, CCC records.

lodge site, at the hewing department's site, and eventually in the blacksmith shop. The stones for the lodge were first cut from the rock quarry just outside Makanda, across the railroad tracks from the park. The quarry crew kept busy throughout the building's exterior construction, from July 1934 to about May 1935.[15]

In midsummer 1934, a new quarry was opened up along a dry creek bed in the Stone Fort area of the park. Here, the quarry crew dynamited and quarried 760 cubic yards of stone in the month of August alone, using 212 sticks of dynamite. Care was taken to obtain enough large rock "to give the lodge wall a massive and sturdy appearance."[16]

Lynn Rayle was one of a group of young men from Michigan who enrolled into Company #696; he worked at the rock quarry. Rayle recalled one morning when he was hauled to work in the back of a truck and the truck driver didn't brake in time to stop at the railroad tracks. "We ended up on the tracks in front of a freight. Thank God it wasn't an express." At the quarry, Rayle explained, the first job was to get the shale off the top. "This was done with dynamite. We didn't get back far enough the first time[,] and a lot of rock went over our head. Someone started screaming[,] and we found out a woman living down by the tracks had a rock through her roof."[17]

Rock quarry near Makanda. "Isadore Costa, the leader or foreman[,] is standing on the bank at left. He was from Herron [*sic*]. . . . A Polish pal of mine and I went to Herron [*sic*] with him one night to a show. He dropped us off at an Italian tavern where they had the biggest schupers of beer I have ever seen. It was too much of a bargain for my friend. I had a hard time to keep him quiet to see the picture. We could still see the bullet marks from the shoot out they had in Herron [*sic*]." Photo and caption courtesy of Lynn Rayle.

Men of the quarry crew working at the rock quarry near Makanda. Photo courtesy of Lynn Rayle.

In the beginning and for the first months of lodge construction, there was no machinery at the quarry. The men drilled a line of holes into the rock with steel drills and sledgehammers. According to Scott Vancil, a member of Company #696, "When one guy got tired of swinging the sledgehammer, you swapped places, and he'd sit there and hold that drill. That was to drill down in that solid rock so you could blast it with dynamite. After you'd touch off a charge like that, big rocks would fly off there, and we'd use sledges and smaller hammers and smaller drills to make holes. Then you'd put a steel wedge in that hole. You'd hit on one side and the other to break that rock into a smaller piece."[18]

At least sixty-two men were detailed on the lodge construction during October and November 1934. The stonework progressed well during these two months with senior foreman William Stuemke in charge of laying the stone. His pay was at least six times the pay of the unskilled laborers he supervised. Some of the

Lynn Rayle, one of the few from Michigan at Giant City's camps.
Courtesy of Lynn Rayle.

Lodge construction with scaffolding completed as of August 1934. Note the newly erected water tower for Camp Stone Fort.
National Archives, CCC records.

Same view of lodge under construction in February 1935. National Archives, CCC records, photo #23.

young men, however, proved to have ability for the work and were consistently assigned to the lodge detail.[19]

By the end of November 1934, the south wall was laid up to an elevation about sixteen feet above the first floor level. The north wall was laid about ten feet above the first floor level, and two nine-foot-ten-inch stone arches were laid in place at the north end. The east and west walls were halted at about five feet above the first floor to allow for balcony corbel supports and knee braces. A large space was left in the middle of the west wall to allow for the hoisting of the four interior twenty-four-inch-diameter wood columns. The four huge oak columns and all the other columns and girders had already been hewn by the log-hewing department and were ready to set in place.[20]

December 1934 and the first three months of 1935 were cold and rainy, causing muddy roads and slower progress on all the projects

in camp other than the lodge construction. Supervisors made up for the lost time by requiring work details to labor on Saturdays. Considerable road maintenance was required, with hundreds of cubic yards of burned shale trucked in to be used as a subsurface on the roads. Twenty-one train carloads of crushed stone were hauled from the quarry at Chester's state prison and laid on the park roads during this period.[21]

At the lodge site, the four massive oak columns were raised in place along with two 12-by-12 oak posts. Hewn girders, floor joists, and stringers were also erected. The stonework was then able to progress more quickly, so that by the end of January, all of the stonework was completed to the second-floor line, including the first-floor stone arches.

Kenneth Hawk of Company #696 was happy to work a stint on the masonry crew at the lodge. He was just seventeen when he entered

One center column in place and one being hoisted with ropes, ca. December 1934–January 1935. National Archives, CCC records, photo #19.

Log hewers working on one of the four large twenty-four-inch columns for the lodge. According to CCC veteran Jim Watkins, who learned it from Bill Bartch, the oak logs for these center columns were cut on the Bartch land, southeast of Mountain Glen. They were hauled to Giant City State Park by Ray Coleman.
National Archives, CCC records.

One of the finished center columns, hand-hewn, showing an enrollee fitting a bracket to the column, ca. summer–fall 1934.
National Archives, CCC records.

Columns and girders in place, some arches completed, windows set, and wall continued as of January 1935.
National Archives, CCC records, photo #18.

Lodge fireplace, completed with arch and damper in place. National Archives, CCC records, photo #6.

Arch being set in place, ca. December 1934–January 1935. National Archives, CCC records, photo #17.

the CCC and admitted that he lied about his age in order to get in. He enrolled in Pinckneyville, where he was physically examined. "If you was alive, you passed," he said. CCC enrollees needed a family member's name as recipient of their salary, but since Hawk's mother was deceased and his father was absent, he used his brother's name. Each month, when he returned home to Du Quoin, his brother would turn over his money to him. Thus, he had more money to spend than many of the fellows whose money was needed by their parents and so "lived it up." He said he wanted to be sent to the state of Washington, but the way he remembered it, "I got in the truck and landed in Giant City Park, thirty-five miles from home." He recalled that there were a lot of boys in the truck from the Du Quoin and Dowell area, a few of them "colored." (There were five men listed as "colored" in the camp report of January 16, 1935, but none in the last years of the CCC at Giant City.)[22]

"Fact is," said Hawk, "the C's kept Dowell going for a long time. Dowell had a baker shop, Ogilini's that furnished bread for the camp. Frank Kosma, a three-striper, from Dowell had a lot to do with the local contracts." Kosma was Camp Giant City's mess steward, and his nickname, according to Hawk, was "Hands and Feet," because he was a great big guy with huge hands and feet. Through Kosma's arranging, Prairie Farms from Carbondale furnished the milk, and the meat came from the Du Quoin Packing Company. As a result, Hawk was able to ride the bread truck back and forth from Dowell if he'd catch it leaving for Giant City at four in the morning.

Hawk did a stint as a truck driver at Giant City after a driver parked an old 1914 or 1915 Liberty truck in his way in the garage. He and his friend Scotty Vancil wanted to move it. The state man said to them that if they were smart enough to start it, they could get it out of there. Hawk remembered that it had solid rubber tires, a four-cylinder motor, and "something like fourteen speeds forward and ten in reverse.

You had to crank it to get it started. So I backed it out and drove it for a while. Never did know what gear I had it in. Seventy mile an hour was as fast as it could go. An old clutch thing. So after that I decided I wanted to drive a truck." About his CCC assignments, Hawk summarized: "I don't regret any of it. I learned to do a lot while I was down there. I was young and full of vigor. I liked to do different things. We had 1933 Chevrolet dump trucks. They were new then and had racks on them. . . . You hauled sand or whatever. . . . You washed your own truck, kept your own truck clean, see that it had oil and everything in it. Turn it back in at night. If there was something really wrong with it, you took it back to the garage and the mechanics worked on it."[23]

Kenneth Hawk was determined to get a little practice at a lot of jobs at Giant City. He worked on the crew that cleaned around the

Kenneth Hawk. Courtesy Kenneth Hawk.

barracks. He gathered flagstone from the creeks in the park and on the neighborhood farms and laid it in the park shelters. Hawk recalled that while gathering creek rock one day, he was run off by a farmer on whose ground he was trespassing. Relations between the local landowners and the park personnel continued to be a little strained in the early years of the park.

Hawk also remembered that they unloaded "truckload after truckload" of the rocks from the quarry north of the lodge. Hawk joined the rock laying crew, spending time on the scaffolds laying the stones. He said that he'd have four boys on the ground cutting stone to his specified dimensions. If they got behind, those on the scaffold had to get down to help cut rather than stand around waiting. Hawk explained, "You had a hammer and a chisel. You had a small chisel you could hold in your hand and chip [with]. They furnished you goggles, and then they had some sledgehammers with big chisels you'd hold and chip [with]. That's what you worked with, and a trowel and a level."[24]

Hawk pointed out that there is a marked difference in the appearance of the stone on the lodge's south facing wall. The stone wall was about six feet up when they started trimming the face of the stone where it showed rather than leaving it rough as it was naturally cut at the quarry. Hawk asserted that this was the influence of Benny Baltimore, an enrollee from Carterville.

He was there and one day he started trimming his stones up. . . . The state liked it, so that's why they started trimming the stone. Otherwise, it would have been a rough rock stone building with no chisel marks in it, just how you picked it up. . . . Benny was the one to make them smooth on all sides and pretty flat in front, too, on the face. That was his idea.

. . . Baltimore and I laid the brick in the kitchen in the north wing of the lodge, a brick wall. I got mine crooked, off by a quarter-inch, and had to rebuild mine, tear it down, clean the bricks and start over. Baltimore was really good at it; he later made a living as a bricklayer. Everything had to be done right. If it wasn't done right, you had to tear it down and start over again.

As his memory was jogged about his toil on the lodge, Hawk laughed as he remembered that

North side of lodge before the dining room addition. Note the change in the color of stone at lower window level, which Kenneth Hawk attributed to the work of Benny Baltimore. Courtesy of Matthew Skertich.

Kenneth Hawk *(kneeling)*. Behind him are *(left to right)* Percell, "Nip" Griffin, Scott Vancil, and Bennie Baltimore. Names and photo courtesy of Kenneth Hawk.

from the front porch of the lodge, you could look over the hill to a farmhouse. With a transit, the boys would take turns watching a young woman in her yard.[25]

Scott Vancil also had vivid memories of his CCC years at Giant City. Vancil was living in Hallidayboro when he enlisted in Company #696 at Giant City in the summer of 1934. His father had been a coal miner, but since the mines had closed, he had been doing carpentry and brick mason work. Because there was no regular work and very little building going on, skilled men took any odd jobs they could get. Vancil knew some men from Hallidayboro who were at Giant City's camp: Porter Leslie, Cecil Griffin, and John (Jack) Barry. Since the camp needed workers immediately as some men left or were discharged, Vancil and many other recruits were not forced to go through the conditioning procedures at Jefferson Barracks. They enlisted and were enrolled directly at the camp. Vancil was skilled with his hands and so enjoyed, as did his buddy Kenneth Hawk, gaining experience at various jobs. "I worked on the camp detail, built things they needed as they came along. I built a couple

office desks. . . . We built some toilets there at Giant City that we took up to Kaskaskia State Park. Most of the men weren't confined to any one job down there. After a while, you'd get transferred around. Sometimes you just wanted to move. It gave us a lot of different experiences, and that was what it was all supposed to be about anyhow. . . . After camp detail, I was on the lodge [detail]. I wanted to [be] because I had friends up there. Then I went to the rock quarry."[26]

Vancil also stressed the patience and exactitude required to lay the stone: "You had to lay those rocks just so. . . . You had to put a thinner one [in] to break the mortar joint. You had to keep breaking the mortar joint in every direction. Each rock had to be cut a little different size, so that you didn't get any long seams in those mortar joints. They just measured the face of them; it didn't matter if you chipped the back side, because that would be out of sight. Each rock only had one face showing. You had a mortar joint down there between them." (The walls are two rocks wide throughout).[27]

The supervisors rented an air compressor, borrowed a jackhammer, and purchased a chip-

Stoneworkers using goggles. Courtesy of Kenneth Hawk.

Pneumatic drill in use at the rock quarry, January 1935. National Archives, CCC records, photo #12.

Using chipping hammer on stone for a shelter fireplace. National Archives, CCC records.

ping hammer in January 1935. The air compressor was rented for the large sum of $150 per month, but Superintendent F. P. Britson, who took Olson's place during the winter, reported that as a result of the new machinery, progress on the quarrying and cutting of stone increased 50 percent or more.[28] Lynn Rayle remembered breaking out stones at the quarry after an air compressor was acquired. The procedure was the same, but the drilling of holes went much quicker and easier. Rayle explained, "Black powder was put in these holes to break the rock into the large pieces. The next step was plug and feathers. Holes were drilled by hand with star drills. The feathers were put in the hole and the plug inserted. Then you gradually tapped them until the rock split." Rayle commented on the periodic disregard for safety at the quarry until the day his properly worn goggles were hit by a piece of steel bit, causing his eye socket to fill with fine glass. They were able to wash out his eye. "You can bet," Rayle said, that after that, "my buddies wore the glasses where they belonged." The unfinished blocks that had been chiseled out were then loaded onto trucks to take to the lodge site.[29]

Throughout February and March 1935, all the stonework for the main building was completed. Roof trusses, purloins, sheathing, and asphalt roofing paper were all put in place. On the first floor, all girder joists were positioned, and the subfloor was laid. Then the second-floor subfloor was secured. The lintels and lintel plates to the twenty-seven doors were bent, cut, welded, and riveted. The doors were hung and windows installed. Flagstone was laid on the lower observation platform and steps. The handrail of the exterior balcony with its hardware was installed. The main part of the lodge was reported to have been 98 percent complete.

Large expenditures were made to local businesses by the camps in the construction of the lodge and maintenance of equipment. Egyptian, Chas. Easterly, Union County, and Stotlar lumber companies profited from Giant City CCC camps in February and March 1935. The camp also bought from local businesses dynamite, cement, tires, plumbing and electrical supplies, oil and gas, hardware, and tools.[30]

Much of the decorative hardware used in the lodge was made on-site. One man was in

Gang cutting rock for lodge building in January 1935. Matt Skertich is surrounded by Moore, Condie, Hartline, Grant, and, in the back, Pop, a three-striper. Note the woodpile in the background. Names and photo courtesy of Matthew Skertich.

Moving dirt from in front of lodge and raising grade on road two feet, ca. October–November 1934.
National Archives, CCC records, Project 28C, photo #12.

Leveling grade with a mattock in front of lodge. Earl Dickey worked on this landscaping detail.
National Archives, CCC records, Project 53, photo #21.

ARRIVAL OF CCC COMPANY #692

charge of the blacksmith shop and the garage. Sheets of steel of the correct width—four to five inches wide—and the right length were brought in and were heated to flatten them. Holes were punched where the pins would go through the hinges. Kenneth Hawk allowed himself and Scott Vancil some credit for the designs on the hinges "to make them look rustic," but such an effect was in the architect's plans as well. The men decorated the hinges by hitting a rounded hammer with a sledgehammer. One would keep moving the rounded hammer on the metal, and the other would hit it with the sledge.[31]

By the end of March 1935, work remaining on the lodge included the circular stairway and the lower observation platform handrail coping. The oak shake roofing had not yet been delivered but had been purchased by the state. The building supervisors had to wait for the masonry to dry before laying the hardwood floor. Footings were dug for an attached comfort station to the lodge, which required removal of 115 cubic yards of clay. By March, the footings were poured, all the plumbing was roughed in, and all but the grout finish was completed on the concrete floor of the comfort station. In this addition, 75 percent of the stonemasonry was completed, and the window and door templates were in place. As the weather permitted, work crews of both camps continued with landscaping, the installation of guardrails, stream channel clearing, and erosion control. Sign construction and surveying also continued throughout the park.[32]

"Laying rocks just so." Stonework on the fireplace chimney, November 1934. National Archives, CCC records

Work on the lodge roof trusses began in February 1935. National Archives, CCC records, photo #10.

View of west elevation of lodge, March 1935. National Archives, CCC records, photo #24.

Lodge interior, southeast corner, showing stairwell partition, March 1935. National Archives, CCC records, photo #18.

Interior view of lodge, south end, taken from first floor, showing fireplace, March 1935. National Archives, CCC records, photo #21.

Hammered metal plates for decorative ironwork in lodge.
National Archives, CCC records.

South end of lodge showing the knee brace and preparation of columns for roof truss girders, ca. February–March 1935.
National Archives, CCC records, photo #12.

Roof framing on lodge. Note metal brackets on top of columns. National Archives, CCC records.

Drury Creek flood of March 10–11, 1935. National Archives, CCC records, photo #11.

### DRURY CREEK FLOODS

During March 10 and 11, 1935, one of the heaviest rains of the year fell on the park. Giant City and Stonefort creeks were swollen due to the backed-up water from Drury Creek, which inundated the entire north entrance area of the park. An estimated twenty-acre lake was formed due to this flooding. Drury Creek was notorious for flooding, or, as a local historian, Lesley Wiley Rossen, put it in typical accepting country fashion, "Drury Creek asserts its rights occasionally." James W. Thomas, a local poet who was born in England, traveled the world, and then settled in Makanda during the Civil War, wrote a poem, "Makanda Floods":

> Was you ever in Makanda
> When the water's on the rise?
> When 'tis pourin' down with rain,
> An' murky are the skies?
> When the dam across the Drury

Has thrown all the waters back?
When the houses are all flooded,
An' the stream's across the track?
When the youngsters are a'wadin'
In the water an' the mud,
An' the sidewalks are a floatin'
Like a reg'lar Johnstown flood?
When the people are a shoutin'
An' a laughin' when they see
Some tipsy cuss a tumblin'
Off the sidewalk in the sea?
Why then of course it's very nice
To be hung up in the dry,
A taking notes and laughin'
At your neighbors on the sly. . . .[33]

As the locals were well aware, these washouts required a lot of cleanup and repair work on the roads, drainage structures, and trails. George Oliver remembered that a conservation agent from Washington, D.C., advised the CCC landscape crew to build check dams in the creek that runs along the road through the park

Nearly completed riprap wall demolished in June 20, 1935, flood. National Archives, CCC records, photo #11.

from the north entrance. This advisor wanted the dams to be built out of rock and concrete to hold water and establish wildlife water holes. Oliver remembered, "We kept telling him you can't do it. When you get rain here, it will take them out. He didn't believe it, but while he was here a storm came up, a bad one. The next day after he saw the damage, he said, 'Well, just forget the check dams.'" It was decided, however, to build up the culvert headwalls in the Giant City area three feet above the crown of the road with leftover native sandstone from other projects. Another serious flood and windstorm on June 20 uprooted trees and demolished much of the riprap placed along the creeks.[34]

## WORK DETAILS

Earl Dickey remembered working that summer, mostly as a laborer, pushing a wheelbarrow, clearing and leveling the newly built roadbed at the north entrance of the park. Dickey also got

a chance to drive a dump truck, a one-ton Reo, hauling dirt loaded by hand from a pile and unloading at a needed place in the park. Fertile topsoil was trucked from the Stone Fort bottoms to spread at the park road underpass for future seeding and planting. Quitting time on work details was 4:00 P.M., in order to give the men time to get back to camp and take tools to the storage shed. One day, at five minutes till 4:00, as Dickey pulled up to the site where boys were to load the one-ton truck, he discovered he had a flat tire on his front wheel. Within five minutes, the tire was changed and the truck was fully loaded with dirt. Earl said, "They wanted to get out of there by 4:00."[35]

Now that new roads had been established throughout the park, crews began obliterating the old ones, salvaging with shovels and wheelbarrows as much old gravel as possible. During the spring months, crews were also sent out to the rock quarries to cover them over with dirt. The greater part of their need for stone was fulfilled, so three of the four quarries were covered over and regraded to a natural-looking slope and prepared for planting.[36]

All the stonework on the comfort station was completed by May, as were two flagstone entrance terraces. All the carpentry work on the toilet and shower stalls was completed except the hanging of the doors. The men were waiting to finish the sheathing inside until the plumbing work was completed.[37]

The CCC men and their superiors were taking great pride in doing jobs themselves, learning from someone more experienced and acquiring as they went along a great variety of skills. Learning to work was the purpose of the CCC, at the core of its philosophy. Of course, this approach was bound to be at odds with the burgeoning trade unions that had been watching the CCC work camps cautiously since their inception.

Dodge truck that Earl Dickey drove. On the right is shirtless John Allen. Courtesy Earl Dickey.

Comfort station under construction with roughed-in plumbing and completed foundation walls.
National Archives, CCC records, photo #28.

Comfort station at south end of lodge under construction, March 1935. National Archives, CCC records, photo #32.

Completed comfort station at south end of lodge. Courtesy of Matthew Skertich.

## UNION TROUBLE

During the construction of the lodge and its adjoining comfort station, which included bathrooms and showers, the CCC camp officials at Giant City State Park received complaints from the local trade unions, specifically from the plumbers' union.

President Roosevelt had promised that no skills would be taught that would compete with established unions, but the CCC often trod a very fine line. On November 20, 1934, C. C. Lindsey, the business agent for the Plumbers' Local #160, representing Union and Jackson counties, wrote a letter to Robert Fechner, director of the "Citizens Conservation Corps" in Washington, D.C. Most likely, it was one of scores of such complaints each year shuffled back down to the state, district, and finally camp commanders to explain and pacify. Lindsey's letter stated: "There is a man in the camp

at giant city Makanda, Illinois that is doing plumbing work and has charge of several camps in southern Illinois. He is not a plumber and has no license. We learn from him that there is a plan to put a plumber and other craftsmen on a repair truck in this territory steady. We feel like that we should furnish a plumber for this job as it is in our territory. Please give this your attention. I would like to make application for this job."[38]

This letter arrived at Fechner's office with an accompanying letter from Illinois representative Kent Keller verifying that this labor question had caused "a great deal of trouble in and around the camps of Southern Illinois." Keller asserted that it was not his business to interfere. Assistant CCC director James J. McEntee sent a letter to the chiefs of the three agencies that could possibly be involved: the army, the Forest Service, and the National Park Service. He also ordered William P. Hannon to investigate the matter. McEntee's advice and warning to all was a respectful direction to "employ competent mechanics who are licensed plumbers, in order that we will not run into any conflict with the sanitary laws of the state[,] and the health of the men will be properly protected."[39]

Special Investigator Hannon reported that the man in question was only a maintenance man and that there was no plan to set up a plumber to service the district CCC camps. Hannon continued espousing his own feelings on the matter, believing that money could be saved on car repairs if "real" mechanics were to be hired by the CCC. In his experience, the CCC enrollees were not adequately trained to run the garages and keep the cars in good condition. He mentioned to McEntee that he was also busy investigating other complaints from the masonry and stonecutting trade union representatives.[40]

The State Park Division of the National Park Service also sent an inspector to Giant City to find out what he could. Senior Inspector Carter Jenkins said that he was informed that the man in question "occasionally made small incidental repairs to camp utilities and buildings and general work as a jack-of-all-trades." Since the upkeep of the camp buildings, if that was where the work was performed, was within the duties of the army, Jenkins believed that the incident did not affect the National Park Service. Jenkins's opinion was that "there is no plumbing work being performed on the work project [probably referring the lodge's comfort station and kitchen] by the enrollee, as a check of our park plans will clearly show. . . . The work which this utilities man has performed is of such trivial nature that it would not be practical to retain the services of a licensed plumber[,] as this plumbing phase probably represents the smallest part of the man's duties."[41]

The army, under whose jurisdiction the man's work in the camp did fall, responded with a letter that stated that within each district, one enrollee was selected and given the title as leader for his special qualifications and aptitude for this work. This person did travel among the camps where "he is called upon to make only such immediate first aid repairs as may be necessary to the equipment mentioned above and plumbing at these camps. All major items of repairs or new installations are performed by 'job service' and employment of outside labor."[42]

The Forest Service responded by saying that enrollees were not used in their fieldwork but "have been used in the past on the laying and connecting of water pipes, under the direction of the camp commanders."[43] The immediate complaint seemed to be dropped, but the trade union tension remained throughout the existence of the CCC.

At Giant City State Park in April and May 1935, the landscaping crews took advantage of good weather to landscape the area around the lodge and comfort station after first excavating extensively to reduce the ground to grade. Many truckloads of scrap rock, wooden chips, and other construction debris were hauled away. Earl Dickey remembered working first with a heavy mattock leveling the lawn around the lodge and then on the installation of the lodge's septic tanks. A landscape crew planted trees around the lodge. The leader of that crew carried a pet chicken snake, four feet long, in his shirt pocket.[44]

Throughout the summer of 1935, the main part of the lodge was completed. The roof was covered with oak shakes, and wood flooring was laid on the main and balcony floors of the building. By October, the comfort station addition was nearly finished, lacking only plumbing fixtures. The lodge was open to the general public for viewing by day visitors, but the overnight cabins were only in the planning stages. Its official dedication would not be celebrated for another year. Robert Kingery, now state park director, visited the park on August 14 with Inspector Ralph N. Johnson and State Park Superintendent George H. Luker to approve the proposed sites for the cabins.[45] Work continued despite some labor objections. The press could always be relied upon to give favorable reviews of the progress at Giant City State Park.

In an article of May 6, 1935, a *St. Louis Post-Dispatch* reporter described the park's beauty, accessible on a road that wound through hills, "with the rock retaining walls, wooden bridges spanning clear, swift, small creeks." The lodge's large oak French doors impressed the reporter, who wrote that "they swing outward, surprising in the ease and soundlessness of their action." The reporter credited John Mulcaster for "getting Giant City made into a park." Surely, Mulcaster, the driving force behind the park's creation, was taking great pride in the changes taking place there. He would live just two more years, dying in February 1937.[46]

"We knew we were building something that would last," said CCC enrollee William Bodeker of Company #696.
Photo courtesy of Matthew Skertich.

Construction to be proud of: a bridge at Giant City State Park. National Archives, CCC records.

# 6 Camp Life

In 1935, after two years of operation, the Civilian Conservation Corps was proving to be an overwhelming success with the public and with Congress. In April, President Roosevelt endorsed the extension of the CCC and expressed complete satisfaction with the program: "The results achieved in the rehabilitation of youth, the conservation of our natural resources, the development of new recreational opportunities for our citizens and the quickening of business recovery have proved so worthwhile that I have not hesitated to recommend continuance for Civilian Conservation Corps camps for another two years." Roosevelt expanded the program to include men up to the age of twenty-eight and as young as seventeen. Congress provided funds through the Emergency Relief Appropriation Act of 1935 on April 8, 1935, for continuation of the program for another fifteen months. By August 31, 1935, the CCC enrollment throughout the country reached its maximum of 505,782, an increase of 115 percent since before the 1935 appropriation act, when 235,732 CCC men were enrolled in camps throughout the country. In September 1937, there were reportedly fifty-nine camps in Illinois. Between 1933 and 1942, Illinois had over 125 different CCC camps in operation.[1]

Approximately 20,000 of the total CCC men were put to work in the national park system, which included the state parks; 655 of the CCC camps were established among the 777 state parks, and 160 were established in 69 national parks. As Giant City State Park was undergoing its transformation and expansion for recreational use through CCC labor, so were Mesa Verde National Park and hundreds of others throughout the west, east, south, and Great Lakes region.

The public was duly impressed with the work done on public lands but praised still more the effects on the workers themselves.

Even the *Chicago Tribune* reported that the "CCC is one of the best projects of the Administration, and the great majority of its recruits, we believe, appreciate its opportunities and are being benefited." On November 29, 1935, six years after the great economic crash, FDR spoke in Atlanta in answer to those critical of the taxpayers' expense for his New Deal work programs: "I realize that gentlemen in well-warmed and well-stocked clubs will discourse on the expenses of Government and the suffering that they are going through because their Government is spending money on work relief. Some of those same gentlemen tell me that a

Richard Seyler, a three-striper, 1935. Courtesy of Earl Dickey.

114

Reveille. Courtesy of Earl Schmidt family, original photo at Giant City Visitor Center.

dole would be more economical than work relief. That is true. But the men who tell me that
have, unfortunately, too little contact with the
true America to realize that . . . most Americans want to give something for what they get.
That something, which in this case is honest
work, is the saving barrier between them and
moral degradation. I propose to build that barrier high and keep it high."[2]

The normal daily routine at CCC camps was
established by the U.S. Army and so was similar throughout the state and country; the main
difference in camp morale came from the atti-
tudes of the commanding officers. For the most
part, these men were reserve officers, captains
and first lieutenants. Most of them had held
civilian jobs before the Depression and fully
realized that the CCC camps were not military
installations. A more relaxed atmosphere was
usually understood as appropriate to the task
of getting the necessary work accomplished.
The men were enrolled for six-month periods,
not enlisted or drafted for a two- or three-year
tour of duty. They could choose to reenlist or be

honorably discharged after their time came to
a close. Improving the health and welfare of the
men in the ranks was the primary mission of
the CCC, but no man could be forced to stay in
the CCC or be punished for leaving. One could,
however, be dismissed through a dishonorable
discharge, as some at Giant City were. Joseph
Zimmerman, who served with Company #1657
at Giant City and who later visited Illinois
CCC camps as an army recruiter in the late
1930s, said he didn't recall any CCC men being
sentenced for committing a crime, but even if
an enrollee had been given a bad discharge for
being absent without leave, it did not bar him
from enlisting in the army.[3]

### DAILY ROUTINE

In military style, most camps began their day
with reveille as the flag was raised and with roll
call before breakfast. The flag was lowered at
the end of the day as the men stood in formation. The men slept and ate in military-type barracks. Saluting was not asked for in the CCC,
but enrollees were required to be courteous in

Camp Stone Fort, home of Company #692. Courtesy Matthew Skertich.

their answers with "yes sir" and "no sir" to officers and technical staff. Each man had to make his bed and straighten his area of the barracks before leaving for the workday.

On the job, the men wore issued clothing: two pairs of blue denim pants and shirts as well as shorts, undershirts, brown socks, and brown handkerchiefs. Along with their dress suit and long underwear, the men were also issued a pea jacket, a long army overcoat, towels and washcloths, a double-edged razor, and soap. At the canteen, the men could buy razor blades as well as cigarettes, candy bars, and beer for ten cents a bottle.

Immediately after breakfast, the men's energies were directed for eight hours by their project foremen. Among the enlisted men, a system of leaders and assistant leaders was developed. These men were paid ten or five dollars per month more than the beginning "dollar a day" enrollee was paid. This system encouraged and rewarded hard work and leadership abilities. In addition, a merit system was used at Camp Giant City, beginning around January 1935. Enrollees were rated A through D, with A designating an exceptional worker and D a very

unsatisfactory one who refused to work. An enrollee who merited a D could be punished with the loss of his entire weekend leave.[4]

The men were required by the barracks leader to complete camp duties and chores before or after their eight-hour workday was completed. In addition, they were expected to do their own laundry in the washhouse. Sheets and pillowcases were sent once a week to a commercial laundry in Carbondale or Murphysboro for washing, but denim work clothes, towels, and the like were washed in big buckets and ringers with GI soap. The shrinking of wool clothes was a common problem.

Until a bathroom was built at Giant City that had lights in it, urinal cans were posted outside the barracks for use during the night. One person's duty was to empty and rinse the cans each morning. Bedbugs were sometimes a problem in the barracks. Kerosene was sprayed, but another solution was to put each bed leg in a jar lid filled with kerosene. This at least was supposed to keep the critters from traveling bed to bed.[5]

Cold lunches were brought to the work site in the woods from many of the camp kitchens.

CAMP LIFE

"Smokey Joe" Calbrecht (senior foreman) and Cloice "Buck" Maples (leader).
Courtesy of Earl Dickey.

Earl Dickey remembered that the lunches brought to his wood-cutting crew in Wisconsin were always cold but still appreciated. The Giant City men were close enough to the mess hall to be trucked there for a hot noon meal, which was an advantage of working in a park rather than over a widespread forest area. At Giant City, one enrollee would stay behind to guard the tools at the work site. In exchange, he got the afternoon off. While on this detail, Dickey remembered practicing his hatchet tosses at a targeted tree and "getting pretty good at it."[6] Giant City's food was good and plenty, as the weekly camp menus attest. A typical lunch, such as that of January 15, 1935, consisted of fried chicken, giblet gravy, mashed potatoes, lettuce salad, bread and butter, and coffee with sugar and milk. For supper on that day, the men were served roast beef, boiled potatoes, canned peas and carrots, cabbage

Camp Stone Fort kitchen. Courtesy Matthew Skertich.

slaw, bread and butter, jam or jelly or apple butter, and coffee.[7] Early on in the program, it was noted that enrollees gained weight in the first three or four weeks of being in the camps due to the ample and well-balanced meals.[8]

The men in charge of the kitchen were notable figures at Giant City. Food was arguably the most important aspect of camp. Interviewees from other camps have reported serious problems, such as work strikes and riots, due to bad or insufficient meals. No one had such complaints at Giant City. Pop ("Cookies") Johnson was a good cook, as was Eddy Capps. The army personnel typically sat at a table separate from the Department of the Interior men; both of these head tables were served by waiters. George Oliver remembered that a friend of his, Russell Dunning from Herrin, waited on the table of the Interior Department. Dale Davison took care of the mess hall

and living quarters for the state men and the army. [9]

Camp life in general at Giant City compared favorably to other camps in southern Illinois. Although the army was responsible for discipline, all the men interviewed agreed that the officers were lenient "as long as you behaved yourself and did your work," as Kenneth Hawk explained it. An enrollee would get into some trouble for having a disarrayed bed or more trouble if he was gone when he wasn't permitted to be. KP duty was a common punishment. Hawk recalled that there was a period of only about six months when they had roll call and retreat, a regime followed by most camps every day for years. But after a while, the Giant City officers didn't require it. Every now and then the camp would have an inspection. Hawk remembered, "You'd have to put on your dress clothes, your army brown wool and

CAMP LIFE

Company #696 original kitchen personnel. Eddy Capps, a good cook, is in the second row with his arms around others. After the corps, he worked in cafés in Carbondale. Pop Johnson, another favorite cook, is in the third row, fourth from right. Courtesy of George Oliver.

tie, and you had to open up your footlocker and your bed had to be made and your other locker fixed up just like it's supposed to be. And you stood inspection. I stood inspection with four gallon of whiskey in my footlocker with clothes spread on top of it. They just seen it was real nice on top and went on."[10]

Hawk also admitted to short-sheeting his bed, which made it easier to make every morning. "I'd put one sheet on there and pull it down half way and fold it up above. The next morning all you have to do is tighten up your blankets. You put your other sheet in your locker and get it back out at night to use."[11]

Enrollees were typically not allowed to have cars, but many did. Willis Rendleman had a big barn and barnyard near the camp. The men paid Rendleman a dollar a month to park their cars in the barn, but he let them park in the barn lot free. Whenever officials were to come inspect the camps, Captain Arnel B. Adams would announce that everybody had better go hide their cars. Married men were allowed to live off base, as did a friend of Hawk's named Jones who lived near Ferne Clyffe. Jones's wife was pregnant, so he arranged with Hawk to take him home to her when the baby was coming. "Of course it happened about midnight, so we cut across country. We could leave anytime from [the camp], long as we were there when it was time to go to work."[12]

## RECREATION

The weekends and evenings belonged to the men. After supper, games, sports, a library, a canteen, educational classes, and movies were available in every camp. Alcohol, gambling, and firearms were strictly prohibited, but many camps were quite lenient regarding alcohol and

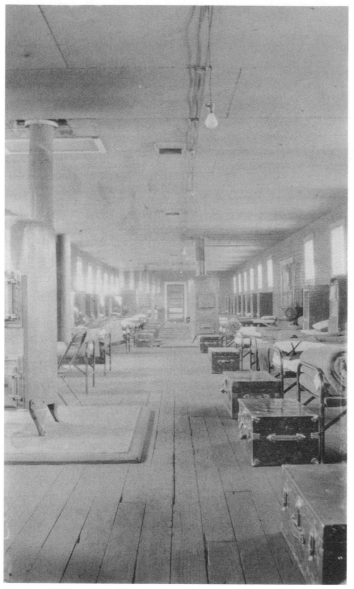

Barracks with Kenneth Hawk's bed marked with an *X*. Courtesy of Kenneth Hawk.

in itself. Most of the clothes did not fit the men. According to an article in the camp's newspaper, the *Stone-City Weekly*, there were only two optional sizes—large and larger. The smallest shirts were size 17, and the breeches were huge. Large shoes, "gargantuan" caps, and leaky raincoats were common. According to the article, the supply sergeant's answer to complaints was, "The CCC camps breed men!"[14]

The use of nicknames was more common than the use of given names. Many nicknames began for these men during their CCC years of living and working with a group of common buddies. Donald S. Blaase became "Newt," Woodrow W. Brandon was "Red," Floyd T. Finley was "Fin," and Howard O. Leonhard was "Howie." There was a "Big Horse" Hiller, "Hands and Feet" Kosma, and a German named Eschmann who was called "Nose."[15] Friendships were forged between men throughout southern Illinois and throughout the entire country that would last their lifetimes.

Poking fun, petty theft, and pulling tricks on one another were common antics in the barracks. Probably some boys were picked on, and some boys just had a hard time adjusting to being away from home. Earl Dickey said he could still clearly see some boys walking up and down Giant City's roads near the camp, tears streaming, "so homesick they could hardly stand it."[16]

Men were supposed to obtain permission to leave camp in the evenings or on weekends, but the rules at Giant City's camps were par-

gambling on the weekends. The boys were allowed a bottle of beer at weekend suppers for those who stayed in camp. Earl Dickey didn't approve of this and would sell his bottle.[13]

Hazing was also prohibited, but many companies did initiate the new enrollees in some unofficial way. Fitting into the army-issued uniforms was somewhat of an initiation experience

Willis Rendleman's barn and barnyard where enrollees could park their cars. Giant City Visitor Collection, neg. and print #32. Photograph by Hodde.

On weekends, the men of Company #1657 hiked the area around the camp, which included a cave they entered by crawling through a narrow opening and sloshed through water to explore. Courtesy of Floyd Finley.

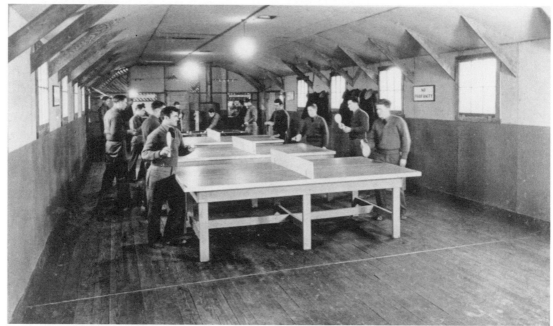

Playing Ping-Pong in the recreation barracks, Camp Stone Fort. Courtesy Matthew Skertich.

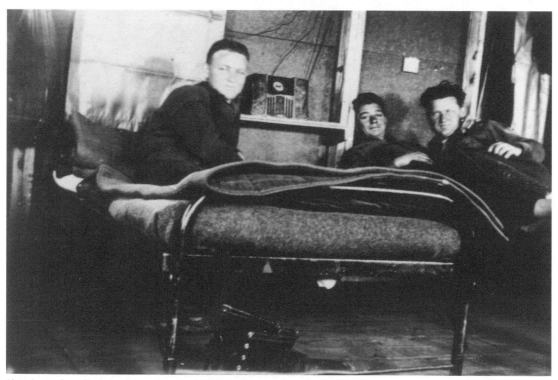

Listening to the radio during leisure time: Paul Wade, Joe Ainsworth, and Arnold Curtis. Names and photo courtesy of Earl Dickey.

Everett Ainsworth and "Whitey" Vick of Company #692, showing how well the overalls fit.
Names and photo courtesy of Earl Dickey.

ticularly lenient. An errant enrollee might have required reminding that any leave from camp was considered a privilege and not a right.

Men did go "AWOL," however. Some just left when they wanted and never came back. Others left early on Friday and came back to face the music on Monday. Although hitch-hiking was prohibited, the roads leading to the camps often had men on them walking or hitching rides. For many of the men, their CCC

Among those checking in the winter issue are Leon Kidd, Harry Stouse, Stike, Yuma (or Yuna), Ainsworth, and Goodwin in the spring of 1935. Names and photo courtesy of Earl Dickey.

Included in this photo of "the gang" are Serfs, Dudas, Boday, Penrod, Weeks, Ham, Dio, Adio, Porter, and Snoops (the dog). Names, nicknames, and photo courtesy of Kenneth Hawk.

job was the best time they had ever had and perhaps ever would have in their lives. They loved it. As Kenneth Hawk gleefully expressed it more than fifty years later, "I just had a ball in there. I tell you—a little old country boy from a hick town, never had a dime in his life getting five dollars a month and would come home and get my twenty-five—shoot, I was a king."[17] Hawk and Scott Vancil would often save

their weekends off until they could build up six or ten days. Then they'd go wherever they wanted to go. Vancil reminisced, "We'd take off and have a ball. When we'd get broke, we'd come back."[18]

Several interviewees mentioned that the harmony at Giant City was mainly due to the fact that the men were for the most part all from southern Illinois, which meant greater

Friends: Hickman, Kennie Hawk, Hiller, Garner, Haught. Names and photo courtesy Kenneth Hawk.

understanding between them as well as easy visitation to their families and girlfriends on weekends. Kenneth Hawk said all of Company #696 but a few were from towns south of Olney. "I don't remember any Chicago kids. Maybe that's the reason we all got along; we were all hillbillies down there."[19] It became obvious as early as 1933 that rural recruits, like most of those from southern Illinois, displayed greater aptitude and enthusiasm for CCC work because they were used to toiling outdoors and handling tools.[20] Many camps, however, such as Pomona's and those in outposts of the newly bought lands of the Shawnee National Forest, were placed too far away from all-weather roads or large towns to allow for easy weekend entertainment, which caused dissatisfaction among some enrollees.

Although the park filled on the weekends, the barracks of Camp Giant City pretty well emptied on Friday and Saturday nights. Most went home, but Oliver remembered that those boys who drank would go over to Murphysboro to a downtown dance hall called the Grey Stone. "Others managed to get some white mule [homemade corn whiskey] and pass that around; [they] probably all got drunk. Most of us stayed together in groups." Oliver did recall quite a bit of gambling, mostly with dice, especially on the nights after the monthly paydays. "Wouldn't take some long to lose their five dollars," Oliver chuckled.[21] Hawk maintained that on pay night, the gambling would last all night "in the washroom. . . . You had to go in the washroom. Lights out at ten o'clock, so [you] had to go to the washroom to play the dice. Just the camp boys. . . . Don't remember any fights. Guy by the name of Halstead won everybody's money one weekend of those of us left in camp that weekend. He was from Carbondale. There were a lot of good card games there—poker—in the bathroom too. We set on the floor."[22]

Vancil, who continued to moonlight as the camp barber, cutting hair for a quarter a head, remembered "a few friendly card games, mostly poker." But at one game he got mad at the company doctor: "I was playing cards and he wanted me to go cut his hair. I said that I was off duty on a Saturday. He kept talking and talking along about it and I was trying to play cards. Some of the guys knew that I was getting mad. He was standing right behind me. Finally he told me, 'Cutting my hair ain't like cutting an enrollee's hair.' 'Oh,' I said, 'it ain't?' 'No,' he said. 'Oh,' I said, 'maybe I better go find out.' So I threw my hand in, looked at my watch, and I knew those guys were watching me. In five minutes I was back in that card game. He had his hair cut. He never come back to the barbershop anymore. . . . I just give him a quick once over. . . . There was a place in the card game when I got back."[23]

Hawk also remembered cockfights right out in the company streets. "These guys in camp had little pens fixed out there in the woods." Lynn Rayle confirmed that there was prodigious gambling at the camp: "The boys would bet if it would rain the next day." Earl Dickey said it was common to know of boys who gambled against their next month's pay and then end up having to pay $1.50 for each dollar owed.[24]

Enrollees tried to make extra money in lots of ways. Rayle sold watches through a wholesale dealer in Chicago, and since he didn't have kin to visit close by, he'd do KP for another enrollee "for a buck." Those with cars gave rides to others for fifty cents or a quarter. Dickey ironed shirts and trousers, pressing the fashionable creases down the pant legs with a fifty-cent iron he had bought. Finley had a darkroom set up at one end of a barracks. One older man was a tattoo artist. Rayle said a lot of his buddies got tattoos there that embarrassed them later. Some of the men set tomato slips for nearby farmers to earn extra money. One enrollee's wife made candy out of sugar packs taken from the dining hall, which was then sold by the piece in the barracks. Although there were some reports of stealing in the camps, the problem was not severe. In August 1935, someone stole ten pairs of shoes from Barracks #5 of Camp Stone Fort. Rayle recalled that one boy stole the major's raincoat and traded it to a bootlegger. "We had a boy taking a mail-order course in finger printing, and he nailed the varmint." Some interviewees remembered something about "a bordello" along the Illinois Central tracks just north of Cobden, but all declined to go on record with a firsthand account.[25]

Bootlegging, however, was a more open problem throughout the years at all the CCC camps. Although the prohibition against the sale of alcohol had ended in December 1933, there were still a lot of bootleggers because their product could be gotten cheaper. Hawk remembered that he could get alcohol for one dollar a gallon when it cost five dollars a gallon at the store, "but it was pretty rotten. They called it rotgut, pretty rotten, but what the heck."[26] There were known bootleggers within two miles of Giant City, "so many of them," an official report from January 1935 reads, "it is difficult to eliminate them." In the same report, the men are described as very well behaved and the morale "splendid."[27] Rayle

Company #696 baseball team before acquiring uniforms. Courtesy George Oliver.

recalled that when the weather was cold out while they were working, somebody would pass the hat and someone would disappear for a while. "A shot or two out of the jug he brought back would warm you in a hurry."[28] Dickey believed he learned some useful lessons for his later ministerial work as he helped the drunks get into their beds after being brought home from weekend drinking bouts.[29]

Giant City camps were so lenient that at times, long-term guests stayed with the men in the barracks. Women in the barracks were strictly forbidden, but Hawk remembered that two Kosma brothers from around Dowell kept their twelve- or thirteen-year-old brother with them in the camp for three weeks. Hawk's father stayed with him there three days. "If there was an empty bunk to use, kitchen fed him and he went out on the job with us and set there and talked. . . . It was a loose arrangement."[30]

The men's morale, generally speaking, was excellent in both camps at Giant City. The CCC

army personnel and project staff cooperated to keep the men happy in their off hours, believing that "contented workmen do a better job." Trucks were made available by the park service staff to take the enrollees to Carbondale and Murphysboro each Wednesday and Saturday night when special movie rates of ten cents were offered for CCC men. Several groups from SINU entertained the men at the camps, and the camps' recreation rooms had Ping-Pong tables, checkerboards, jigsaw puzzles, playing cards, and a well-stocked library.

## SPORTS

The athletic program offered both camps equipment for basketball, football, soccer, track, pole vaulting, horizontal bar, gymnastics, boxing, wrestling, baseball, kittenball, and horseshoes. All sports were wildly popular at the camps, but the CCC budget did not include money for uniforms. Funds had to be secured through charity and other means, which some

Company #692's baseball team, 1935–36. *Back row:* Gisinawib, Davis, McKinney, Allan, McNear, Nunn, Fenwick, Johnston. *Front row:* Teets (manager), Kays, Rubell, Tracy, McKalister, and Wreck.
Names, nicknames, and photo courtesy of Earl Dickey.

might call "kickbacks." The baseball uniforms were obtained through the efforts of Dr. Andrew Esposito and Father Tom Bermingham, the chaplain at Giant City.

Giant City was the headquarters for all the medical staff of the region's CCC camps. The doctors and Father Bermingham traveled throughout the region, serving various camps. Esposito and Bermingham became good friends as they rode together to perform their duties. Esposito explained how he and Bermingham acquired the uniforms needed for the summer 1934 season: "We had nine camps in the area, so we had a league of nine teams. They played intramural, baseball primarily. Baseball

was the big thing, the summer thing. Bermingham and I went to St. Louis, and we caged all this stuff. We asked the big companies, 'Won't you help out the poor guys in the camps, now, how 'bout donating?' Or, 'We got just so much money,' and they'd give it to us at cost. . . . We'd get the money from the wholesale grocer who was making money on the camps, but he was making nominal. How much could he make in the Depression days? Well, we got enough money to buy nine sets of uniforms."[31]

Basketball continued to be the most popular winter sport, and Giant City's Stone Fort Company #692 had a terrific team. In the fall of 1934, a serious lover of basketball came to the

Company #692 champion basketball team, 1935–36. *Back row:* Chester Rabold, Raymond Cannady, James Winkleman, Mr. O'Brien (educational advisor), Cecil Brewer, "Chub" Kays, and Howard Nunn. *Front row:* Eugene Crawford, Raymond McNair, Charles "Christy" Davis, Claude [?], and Walton "Pug" Manuel. Names and photo courtesy of Earl Dickey.

park in the person of Captain Edwin R. Morine, the camp commander. Earl Dickey, five-foot-six, who played guard, said Morine was their man. When the captain came to camp, he weighed 285 pounds. If the team lost, he'd "jump up and down and click his heels; he didn't like it a bit. But he treated us nice when we won a game. And we won a lot."[32] The boys of the Stone Fort team had beaten Murphysboro's Company #1625 team for their nineteenth straight victory on March 5, 1935, and won the honor of being the champions of the Twenty-second District. The next week, however, they lost to Shawnee-town's Company #624 for the title of champions of southern Illinois.

The team's center was Charles Davis. On the 1934–35 team were Francis Wenger/Wag-ner, John Dunn, Kenneth Fenwick, Raymond McNair, Gene Williams, Eugene Crawford, James Fellin, Kenneth Bierbaum, Raymond Goodwin, Walton Manuel, Philip Genet, Philip Janesh, William Allen, and Walter Otten. The team rode to games and practices at the gyms at SINU or Carbondale's First Methodist Church in canvas-topped GI trucks. Dickey said they never took showers after games.

However, after a good practice or a winning game, Morine would lead them all to the camp's kitchen, where he had waiting for them juice and a freshly baked cake with icing "a half-inch thick." According to Dickey, when Captain Morine left camp in April 1935, he weighed 325 pounds.[33]

**CAMP LIFE**

## PUBLIC RELATIONS

The camps first appeared to the public very much like army base camps. And of course, in the same ways the public worried next to an army base, landowners and parents next to CCC camps worried about trespassing and their daughters' welfare. Some CCC boys continued to fill their shirts with peaches from the orchards on their way walking to camp from Makanda.[34] Kenneth Hawk's wife remembered that when the CCC boys moved into Camp Du Quoin, the girls were told to just stay away from them. One CCC alum told me, "At the time the C's started, we were rats. We were the underdogs, the poor class people. [The public] didn't think too much of us. You could tell, from the way people looked at you. You weren't too wel-

Captain Edwin Morine, the basketball booster for Company #692. Courtesy of Earl Dickey.

come in a lot of places. . . . Later on, it eased up and it didn't make too much difference. I think it finally got so that we were the few of the kids who had fifty cents on a Saturday night to spend at the businesses."[35]

Thelma Baker of Pomona left her home near Pomona's CCC camp because the country seemed overrun with unsupervised CCC boys. Kenneth Hawk admitted, "The saying back in those days if you saw a CCC boy coming down the street was, 'Mary, get in the house, cover up the rain barrel, anything with a hole in it; here, Queeny, get in here.' . . . That's the saying they had about us, even call the dog in. . . . But we weren't bad, just ordinary poor kids."[36]

Although the road through Makanda was established as the main route into the park, tensions arose between Makanda businessmen and the park's custodian, Charles Gore, who had taken over after Ralph Corzine. Very quickly there was trouble between Gore and the Rendlemans, both T. W. Rendleman, who owned the Makanda General Store, and Willis Rendleman, Gore's close neighbor. Evidently, Gore neglected to pay his bill at the store and then refused to do business there. In December 1934, Gore charged Willis Rendleman with letting his stock loose on Gore's property. Gore had the seventy-year-old Rendleman arrested—twice. Rendleman reportedly complained to state authorities that Gore "wasn't fit to live in their community" because he'd been a coal miner and did not attend church. One state official sent down to straighten out the mess in December reported that "unless the custodian was one of the Rendlemans or their following, they [the Rendlemans] couldn't get along with them [the custodian]."[37] The feud continued for years, with charges flying back and forth of both Rendlemans' and Mr. and Mrs. Gore's improper conduct. The CCC also had its problems with Gore. A report by Carter Jenkins, assistant regional officer of the National Park Service to Charles Casey, Department of Public Works, concluded that Gore "consistently tried to undermine the prestige of CCC superintendents and foreman."[38]

Even if Gore did not take his business to Makanda, the camps at Giant City did a great deal of trade with other local markets. Most of their nonperishable subsistence supplies came from the district quartermaster at Jefferson Barracks, as did the bulk meat, potatoes, butter, and cheese, but the camps maintained contracts with dozens of local businesses.[39] The other twenty-eight CCC camps in southern Illinois were having the same rejuvenating effect on the economy in their areas, putting a little bit of money into the pockets of CCC families to spend and even more money directly into the local markets.

The average number of men on work projects in May 1935 was 177, making up crews from both camps considerably smaller than expected when the work projects were planned. The organization of work using crews from both camps continued to require supervisory coordination. The administration for both camps was divided into four distinct divisions: engineering, landscaping, general projects, and office. Cooperation was also essential between the CCC administration at Giant City and various local and state highway departments, as well as the U.S. Forest Service and various units in the National Park Service.[40]

Early in the spring of 1935, the CCC administrators at Giant City State Park decided it was time to start showing off the program's two years of work. Acting Superintendent Albin Olson contacted various newspapers, luncheon clubs, businessmen's associations, and SINU to tell them of the opportunities for recreation facilities. The following groups arranged picnics and tours at the park: Carbondale Business Men's Association, Illinois Federation of Women's Club, Carbondale Rotary Club, southern Illinois 4-H clubs, Southern Illinois Teacher College faculty, Illinois Convention of the Women's

Christian Temperance Union, Southern Illinois Editorial Association, and L. O. Trigg's Ozark Tour group, which made Giant City the destination of its annual trip into the wilder country of southern Illinois.[41]

In truth, the CCC's effect on Giant City was a substantial taming of the wild, a change that most folks heartily approved.[42] Underbrush was cut back, fields and picnic areas were kept cleared and mowed, and wider foot and horse trails were maintained. The roads into the park and through it had been radically altered and improved for vehicle traffic. The *Herrin News* on May 9, 1935, read:

> If you want to see what can happen to a place when the national government takes hold and starts developing it into a national park, take a run down to Giant City.... It does not look like the wild woods that Governor Len Small took over during his administration and started a state park for the people of southern Illinois.
>
> A wide gravel road, winding through the hills of the beautiful orchard country and terminating in a loop in the heart of the park a mile and one-half east of Illinois State Highway No. 51, is the work of many pairs of youthful hands grown strong from the days spent in happy labor.[43]

The general public opinion was that the natural wonders that had been enjoyed for many decades at Giant City, such as the Hazard Stairs, the Devil's Stand Table, Balanced Rock, and the old stone fort, were now made easier to enjoy. Long picnic tables and stone fireplaces with piles of firewood nearby were being used by hundreds if not thousands of visitors each weekend. Steps and paths led to the favorite sites and overlooks. The men of the CCC at Giant City had substantial improvements to show for their years of labor, most notably a lodge that was quite a showpiece, even as it was, in late 1935, unadorned and partially landscaped. The work of other Forest Service and Soil Conservation CCC camps throughout

Scenic drive. Photo by Bill Hedrich, Hedrich-Blessing, Giant City Visitor Center, neg. #10680-2.

Illinois was just as difficult and important, but their goals were often for less-immediate picturesque results.

During the weekends, when visitors crowded into Giant City State Park, the enrollees often acted as "freewheel guides." During one month, between July and August 1935, 4,317 persons visited the park, of whom 436 were from out of state. For one weekend barbecue, an enrollee counted 1,125 cars coming into the park. Barbecue pits were dug and long picnic tables spread with food. CCC baseball games drew crowds to the summer gatherings and were played on the Stone Fort

---

CAMP STONEFORT 692

# STONE-CITY WEEKLY

CAMP GIANT CITY 696

VOL I.  WEDNESDAY, SEPTEMBER 4, 1935  NO. 2

# OVER 4000 TREK TO PARK IN MONTH

## GIANT CITY STATE PARK

Last week a general description of Giant City Park appeared in the Stone-City Weekly. The following will conclude the article:

Within the Park may be found a group of rocks whose sheer walls form a rock city known as Giant City. The spot is located about four hundred yards south of the Giant City picnic grounds. A foot-trail leads through the streets formed by the sandstone walls. The streets, five in number, are from two to eight feet wide. The upright walls average about forty feet in height. A perfectly carved heart appears on one of the walls. It was carved by the wind and rain. Too, there are names and dates carved in the walls which date back as far as 1862, during the Civil War.

Trees, moss, ferns, and flowering bushes abound on the building-like rocks. At the edge of the main street, known as Kingsway Street, are large trees which furnish nice shade and gives the street the appearance of a city residential street. In the spring of the year a large poplar tree blossoms into a thing of beauty. The blossoms overhang the walls of the Giraffe Dining Table. The latter is a

(Continued on Page Two)

### LABOR DAY VISITORS NUMBER 1600 HERE

On Sunday and Labor Day, September 1 and 2, there were one thousand six hundred and forty-six (1,646) visitors in Giant City State Park. This should be ample proof that this is fast becoming one of Illinois' most popular play grounds.

The greatest number of visitors were from Herrin, while Marion residents ranked second. In all, a total of about twenty-five cities were represented by the visitors.

Lieut.-Col. W. A. Smith, commander of the Jefferson Barracks District, visited Camps Giant City and Stonefort yesterday on a tour of inspection.

## Work Details in Park

The following work details have been completed recently in Giant City State Park:

The north entrance shelter house, with rock floor and stained wood work; the Fire-place shelter at Giant City; the foot bridge at the north entrance; East Fire-place shelter practically completed; the shelter near Cedar Hill; the foot-bridge at Giant City; the abutments of the east foot-bridge.

The following are in various stages of completion:

The open shelter at the Boy Scout cabin; the guard rails for roads which are constructed by the Hewing department; the raising of the road at Three Rocks; and the beautiful lodge, which lacks only lighting fixtures, door hardware, hardwood floor and plumbing.

Additional work being carried on by the Camp 696 detail includes the addition of a porch to the kitchen, the construction of a cabinet in the kitchen for pies, cakes and bread, installation of new lockers, removal of the District office into the old State office building which was rebuilt and remodeled both in and outside, the assembly of a ping-pong table and two pool tables in the Recreation Hall, and the construction of a recreation hall in the Mess Hall for the use of ping-pong and pool.

The above and many other projects have greatly increased the appearance and comfort of Camp 696. The Camp detail was completed with Curry as leader; Brinkman, assistant leader; and A. Smith, workman.

## State Health Officers Inspect the Camps

On Monday, August 26, Camps 692 and 696 were inspected for trachoma by State Health officers. The camp boys were found to be perfectly free of the infection and far above the average in their eye condition.

Trachoma is a very serious and communicable infection localized in the eyes.

## 692 REMOVES ITS TONSILS

Company 692 has gone tonsil out-ish. Several of the boys are having their tonsils removed under a special plan evolved by Dr. Bishop.

The operation is performed by a local specialist and the individual is usually able to report back in two or three days.

The cost is very low. Any one suffering from infected tonsils would be wise to take advantage of this special plan and have the diseased objects removed.

We are appreciative for the cooperation given to us by the business men who have purchased advertising space in the Stone-City Weekly. Without their aid it would have been impossible to edit our paper without cost to Camps 692 and 696. Please keep this in mind and patronize those who make this paper's existence possible.

## GUESTS OF GIANT CITY STATE PARK

Last Thursday a group of children, escorted by a St. Louis Post-Dispatch man, visited Giant City Park and had a weiner roast. After the weiner roast the children attended the wrestling and boxing matches.

There were about twenty car loads of people from Southern Illinois visiting in Giant City State Park last week. Among them were the following individuals: Mr. and Mrs. Hill and daughter, Betty, of Makanda visited at the Charles Gore home Sunday.

Mr. and Mrs. Bruhlman of Chicago visited Giant City Park Sunday. Mr. Bruhlman is a member of the Conservation Council of Illinois. He was interested in the work done here by the CCC boys. Mr. Bruhlman stated that our Park

(Continued on Page 3)

## Visitors From Nearly Every State Enter the Park

A compilation of the number of visitors to Giant City State Park during the period beginning July 21, 1935 and ending August 25, 1935, reaches a total of 4,317 persons, as revealed by the record maintained by the Park Headquarters at Camp 692. This number includes Sunday visitors only.

The record further shows that of this number 436 individuals were out-of-state residents, whose respective addresses practically present a roll call of every state in the Union. Truly, the old phase "from the blue water of the Pacific to the rock-bound coast of Maine" is not an inaccurate manner to describe the territory from which the Park's visitors amassed.

Every Sunday an almost unbroken line of cars stream into the Park. One sees every type and vintage of automobile represented, from a 1916 Model T Ford to a 1935 custom built model. The richest and the humblest intermingle as visitors and picnickers in Illinois' most beautiful park.

In summer Giant City State Park is not only one of the outstanding beauty spots of Southern Illinois, but of the entire nation. Acre upon acre of verd and timber, high towering rock bluffs, worn and weathered down through the ages, caves, streamlets, the famed Devil's Stand-Table, and innumerable other scenic objects, all combine to make this the most scenic park in the state.

For the comfort and conven-

(Continued on page 2)

## Camps 696, 692 Enjoy Vacation

Camps Giant City and Stone Fort 692 enjoyed a rather lengthy vacation this last week-end due to the Labor Day holiday.

The boys secured passes Friday afternoon which gave them permission to visit their friends and relatives until Tuesday.

Front page of the *Stone-City Weekly*, September 4, 1935, issue.

diamond near the north entrance. In August 1935, Giant City's team was in first place.[44]

## THE STONE-CITY WEEKLY

Companies #692 and #696 jointly published a weekly newspaper they called the *Stone-City Weekly*, edited by Carl [or Carol] Woody of #692 and Charles Triplett of #696. In each issue of the four-page mimeographed paper, articles appeared written by the officers and staff on items of general interest, notable guests to the park, sports reports and team standings, and news of promotions or outside employment for CCC enrollees. Some columns were devoted to gossip. First-page articles in the issues from August 28 through September 25, 1935, focused on such topics as the "Indian" relics found at Stone Fort, the variety of flora found at the park, and work progress on the subway project. Reporters noted individual visitors, families holding reunions, and groups such as CCC men en route from Indiana to Oklahoma. A 4-H club and the young ladies' classes of the Johnston City Christian Church were mentioned. The greatest number of visitors on August 18 were from Marion and Du Quoin. At least five hundred visitors came to Giant City on a typical Sunday. The September 4 issue read, "Every Sunday an almost unbroken line of cars stream into the park. One sees every type and vintage of automobile represented, from a 1916 Model T. Ford to a 1935 custom built model. The richest and the humblest intermingle as visitors and picnickers in Illinois' most beautiful park."[45]

Other news items included the titles of monthly motion pictures available for viewing: three reels of Daniel Boone, two reels of a cougar hunt, and a Mickey Mouse comedy entitled *The Haunted Ship*. The "Barracks Chit-Chat" sections of each issue contained humorous gibes at enrollees. One writer commented, "Love is a funny thing isn't it? It even got the 'Shylock' of 692 to spend sixteen dollars in one

night on one girl." A full page of advertisements featured various businesses in the area.[46]

The little publication used one full page of ads to sell the four-page paper, but the CCC companies found it increasingly difficult to sell the ads. So the editorial staff appealed to the men for the ten-cents-per-month subscription, which would buy four newspapers and would mean "just one less drink or just a few cigarettes less. . . . Won't you and your buddy 'spare a dime'?"[47]

In the last extant issue of the *Stone-City Weekly*, dated September 25, 1935, the writer, most likely one of the army commanders, praised the work and more pointedly the skill of many of the CCC "boys," twenty of whom had been learning from the stonemason William Stuemke "and are now able to go ahead with building construction without supervision using southern Illinois sandstone as building

Landscape foreman Everett Butler. National Archives, CCC records, photo #8.

material." The writer continued to brag, "Fifteen of the boys are accomplished carpenters on the rustic type of woodwork found in the park. Ten boys are experts on landscaping and planting, using native shrubs and plants, and five are capable of running survey, both lineal and topographic, on their own responsibility" (see appendix 5).[48]

### EDUCATIONAL ACTIVITIES

In the fall of 1933, just a few months after the arrival of Company #696 at Giant City State Park, Commanding Officer Lieutenant Walter Urbach met with SINU's president Henry W. Shryock to plan night courses that the CCC men could take to earn high school credit in English, biology, and American history. Many men did take advantage of this opportunity, catching rides together to the Carbondale campus one night a week. Camp Giant City enrollee Joseph Zimmerman remembered taking a rhetoric class at Southern Illinois State Teachers College.[49] Encouraged by his classroom

experience, he took an entrance exam and was awarded a scholarship to the University of Illinois, so he quit the CCC in April 1934.[50]

In the spring of 1934, thirty men began taking advantage of the education classes in English, biology, history, and botany at SINU in Carbondale, transportation being furnished each Tuesday night. Enrollee Floyd Finley recalled taking a class in English in the Old Main building on SINU's campus. Educational movies also were made available at the university. Within the camp, Commander C. G. Whitney instructed fifteen men once a week in accounting. All men in Company #1657's camp were listed as literate, and many worked on their high school degrees while with the CCC at Camp Stone Fort.[51]

Since drought relief camps were considered temporary, they were not allowed an educational advisor. However, Company #692, first established as a drought relief camp, had access to the educational classes offered by John M. Eddy, the educational advisor for Company #696. Enrollee Kenneth Hawk's

John M. Eddy, educational advisor to Company #696 and to the staff of the *Stone-City Weekly*. National Archives, CCC records, photo #18.

CAMP LIFE

assessment of both the army and the "state men" was that "you couldn't have found a better bunch than we had there. The state men were really cooperative in showing you and teaching you how to do things." Hawk remembered Captain Arnel Adams as a particularly good and gentle man.[52]

## AUTUMN 1935 AND THE DEPARTURE OF COMPANY #692

CCC enrollments were down in the fall of 1935 for the first time since its inception.[53] This seemed proof to many of some return of national and local prosperity. In September 1935, the Illinois CCC quota allowed was 38,300, but the reported strength was only 22,661. In the same way, the U.S. quota allowable was 600,000, but national enrollment had dropped to 430,000. Thousands of federally sponsored jobs had opened up for young men, and many CCC enrollees moved into these jobs.[54] George Oliver left Giant City at this time along with Superintendent Adolph Ruediger. They worked within the WPA system in southern Illinois on soil erosion projects.[55]

The trees lost their foliage early in the fall of 1935 due to cold weather and high winds in October and November. As any native knows, autumn and spring are the glory times for southern Illinois but are sometimes too short-lived. The two companies at Giant City made the most of the season, though, hosting a barbecue picnic on October 20 under the bluffs near the north entrance for all twelve camps of the southern Illinois CCC subdistrict. The families of all the enrollees of the twelve area camps were invited, so five thousand were expected. Eight thousand came. They enjoyed local bands and company orchestras. District baseball trophies were presented. Lieutenant Colonel William A. Smith, district commander, and Major Ernest J. Teberg, subdistrict commander, were guest speakers.[56]

This picnic proved to be a farewell to Company #692, which departed from Giant City

State Park the first week of November 1935, leaving the barracks near the lodge once again empty. CCC Honor Medals, awarded for character, loyalty, and excellence in performance of duty, were presented to the following men while they were at Giant City: Joe Calbrecht, Cloice Maples, Oliver F. Jones, Mike Kerkes, John W. Allen, Dean Faeth, Richard M. Seyler, Charles A Fiocchi, Frederick W. Kollman, Orrin Pauley, Harry R. Jeffries, and Anthony E. Hoffman. They had lost one member of their company, Paul E. Faulkner, who died at the Jefferson Barracks hospital from pneumonia. The men of Company #692 prepared for their move to Copper Falls State Park, Wisconsin.[57] In an area where clear-cut logging had left behind dangerous debris that could fuel wildfires, the expertise of Company #692 was needed in erosion control, fire suppression, and reforestation.

They left at 7:30 A.M. on a train in which (without official permission) they had four dogs traveling with them. They arrived in Wisconsin about thirty hours later in the middle of a winter blizzard. Earl Dickey, who had chosen to reenlist and move with his company to Wisconsin, wrote to his girlfriend, Juanita Ernest, of Newton, Illinois, that his new home at Copper Falls State Park had "beautiful scenes, waterfalls with pools as black as pitch and coppery colored spray." He mentioned that a CCC company from Granite City, Illinois, was also en route to Wisconsin, and a company from Anna, Illinois (Company #625), came up at the same time to Highland, Wisconsin. It was ten degrees below zero when they arrived.[58]

## WINTER AND SPRING 1936 AT CAMP GIANT CITY

There were periods of cold temperatures in December 1935 and January 1936 that were the coldest on record for southern Illinois and the entire Midwest. Superintendent Olson admit-

Company # 692, Makanda, Illinois, summer 1935. Photo and names courtesy of Mary Schueller.

*Lower row, left to right:* 1. Ralph D. McAlister 2. Melvin W. Moore 3. Dean Faeth, leader 4. Frank W. Hough 5. Matt J. Skertich 6. John Cankar 7. Roger Guthrie 8. Norman P. Lloyd 9. John W. Allen 10. Richard M. Seyler 11. John Burlison, assistant leader 12. Paul E. Chambers 13. Steve A. Durbin 14. Peter L. Mobley 15. Leslie Boyd 16. Everett Ainsworth 17. Raymond H. Smith 18. John F. Kays 19. Harold A. Pettit 20. Cloice M. Maples, leader 21. Byrl Strange, assistant leader 22. Harry R. Jeffries, assistant leader 23. Andrew Persich 24. Elden Mantle 25. Carl M. Woody 26. Kenneth R. Mason 27. John Selski, assistant leader* 28. George H. Bush, assistant leader 29. Carmine Stompanato 30. James R. Gregory 31. Grant W. Brissman 32. William E. Vedell 33. Mike Kerkes Jr., leader 34. Vincent Mastroianni 35. Charles M. Johnson 36. Kenneth W. Jeffrey 37. Charles A. Fiocchi, leader 38. Kenneth E. Kays 39. William E. Tieman

*Second row from bottom, left to right:* 40. Ernest Henderson 41. Frederick W. Kollman 42. Stanley Fesler 43. Joseph Gaffney 44. Bertrum Burke 45. Melvin A. Clark* 46. Raymond D. Morris 47. Harold Ohl 48. Kermit W. Dunnigan 49. Edward T. Morrison, assistant leader 50. Darrell M. Stroupe 51. Tom Turcol 52. Stanford B. Kessler 53. Kenneth S. Fenwick 54. Wilbur Towell 55. Raymond Goodwin 56. George R. Fox 57. Earl W. Dickey 58. Lyle J. Vick 59. Eugene B. Crawford 60. Glen D. Keen 61. Dillon S. Rudolph 62. Harvey H. Floyd 63. William H. Long 64. Ralph O. Rider 65. James H. Babbs 66. William G. Munden 67. Walton Manuel 68. Frederick W. Jenkins 69. Chester R. Rabold 70. Walter Carlton 71. Walter Oldham 72. Raymond C. Calvert 73. Clarence A. Sutter 74. Elmer Smith 75. Robert A. Curry 76. Joseph F. Kupryn 77. Ralph B. White 78. Robert E. Johnson 79. Walter D. McAdam, assistant leader 80. Frank H. Guennewig, assistant leader 81. Donald R. Glenn 82. Henry G. Zilm 83. Irvin A. Jones 84. Ernest G. Stauss

*Third row from bottom, left to right:* 85. Robert C. Pudney 86. James D. Bartram 87. William G. Wedlake 88. James E. Smith 89. Ralph O. Freeman 90. Frank T. Akers 91. John Johnson 92. Everett Canerdy 93. Delbert Garr 94. Raymond A. McNair 95. Densel R. Atteberry 96. Ben J. Wyss 97. James A. Christison 98. Williard W. Leonhard 99. John Yuna 100. Robert A. Wys 101. William H. Evans 102. Emil S. Nickel 103. Winnifred A. Erwin 104. Ebert A. Hileman 105. Junus L. Hobbs, leader 106. Glenn Smith 107. Hollie A. Roberts, leader 108. Veril Brewer, assistant leader 109. Charles F. McHenry 110. James H. Purdum 111. Glenn A. Glover 112. Adam H. DeSherlia 113. John Selski* 114. Glenn Cummins 115. George F. Fry 116. Harold Howe 117. William T. Allen 118. Roy J. Fansler 119. James M. McFarland 120. Kenneth E. Bierbaum 121. Joseph H. Lake 122. Edward King 123. Elmer H. Shoemaker 124. Robert L. Coan 125. Ira H. Sage 126. Anthony E. Hoffman 127. Orrin Pauley, assistant leader 128. Delbert Lewis 129. LaVern Van Houten, leader 130. Ralph Sheaks 131. Adolph Mikolased

*Fourth row from bottom, left to right:* 132. John Rupalites 133. Carl Miller 134. Joe J. Waitkus 135. Lowell Short 136. Robert Nethercott 137. Paul E. Brummett 138. Robert L. Fiedler 139. Arthur Hangsleben 140. Ray Shelton 141. Hower Hoyer, assistant leader 142. Howard C. Phillips 144. Harold E. Holt 145. Howard Nunn 146. Joseph Fetsko 147. Fred D. Gerzema 148. Ellis Grear 149. Robert McBeth 150. Wayne Phillips 151. Marvin Serby 152. Floyd H. Buress, leader 153. David E. Lambert 154. Harvey L. Nichols 155. Woodrow R. Kirk 156. Glen B. Young 157. Arthur E. Westemire 158. George A. Benedict 159. James H. Walters 160. Marian A. Manning 161. Francis L. Wenger 162. John Welty 163. Guy Shaffner 164. Daniel A. Binegar 165. Van C. Crawford 166. Gilbert K. Shaw 167. Charles L. Davis 168. Harold R. Robeen 169. Edward W. Anderson 170. Arthur L. Ulrey 171. Warren I. Kircher 172. Lawrence Mangum 173. John Doczy, Jr. 174. George A. Mathias 175. Milford Davis 176. Lawrence Ankovitz 177. Arnold O. Curtis 178. Lloyd W. Youngblood 179. Oliver F. Jones, leader 180. Theodore T. Dennis

*Top row, left to right:* 181. Frank W. Pozzi 182. Sylvester Olszanowski 183. Frank Tidaback 184. Gene Williams 185. Earl Schilling 186. Theodore J. Fowler 187. James A. Fellin 188. John E. Hamlet 189. Wilfred A. Kniepkamp 190. Jack Kuegler 191. Cletus Sprouse 192. John L. Dunn 193. John G. Frey 194. Thomas T. Ware 195. Melvin W. Lunn 196. Dennis T. Harris 197. Adam R. Condie 198. Don F. Shields 199. Melvin A. Clark* 200. Clayt R. Whisman 201. Chester J. Pacione 202. James H. Friel, assistant leader 203. William H. Murphy, senior foreman 204. Adolph G. Ruediger, project superintendent 205. Earl V. Bishop, M.D., contract surgeon 206. Captain Edwin R. Morine, commanding officer 207. 2nd Lieutenant Jesse A. Bartlett, exchange officer 208. Charles R. Collom, foreman 209. Joseph A Bangiolli, foreman 210. Elmer A. Klehm, foreman 211. Mark S. Greeley, foreman 212. George Oliver, tool keeper 213. Nildo V. Tozzi 214. Frank Orlandi 215. Albert Chiesi 216. Charles Wallock 217. Ted Masilonus 218. John Gugliemetti 219. Gilbert M. Clouse 220. Henry Raab 221. Fred Peck, Jr. 222. John A. Myers 223. Edward M. Forbes 224. Elwin W. De St.Jean 225. Carroll G. Moore 226. Robert Benson 227. Howard Boers 228. Ben Malmberg 229. Grant Marshall 230. H.A. Hunt 231. Walter Rogers 232. Ray Corzine 233. Anthony Gambo

\* These names are duplicates.

The north end of the lodge, preparations for dining hall addition, January 1936. National Archives, CCC records, Project 120, photo #A50.

Construction of overnight cabins, March 1935. National Archives, CCC records, Project 107.

ted in his February–March 1936 report that "two years of experiencing mild and pleasant winters left us unprepared for the length and severity of the winter just passed." The extreme cold required that the work on the dining hall/refectory addition to the lodge be entirely suspended for a time. Grading and planting were halted because the ground was frozen solid. Excavation for the sewage disposal plant for Camp Giant City and the lodge's comfort station continued because they were so badly needed.[59]

Basketball and educational activities were very popular during the winter, and an amateur radio station was outfitted from the camp. In 1936, classes were being held in a section of a barracks building and in various small buildings around camp under the direction of John M. Eddy, the educational advisor, in reading, spelling, penmanship, trigonometry, accounting, auto mechanics, mechanical drawing, blueprint reading, forestry, civil service, postal work, bookkeeping, radio code, radio principles, shorthand, typing, and public speaking. The basketball team was playing about two games per week at a gym in Carbondale with other teams from nearby towns.[60]

The facilities of Camp #11 and the men of Company #696 were again inspected by William Hannon at the end of February 1936; of the 202 men enrolled, 19 were from Michigan and the rest from Illinois. Hannon reported that the roads were considerably improved but could stand even more work. The food was excellent, far superior, Hannon wrote, than at other camps he had inspected of late. All effort was being made by the quartermaster to contract all perishable food locally, trucking only nonperishables from Jefferson Barracks. Both Hannon and Superintendent Olson reported during this February–March period that the morale of the men at Giant City was excellent. Each inspection report mentioned that no communistic activities had been reported at this camp, a concern of some of the conservative public.[61]

March 1936 proved to be a welcome warm change from the record-breaking cold of the preceding months, and the stonemasonry work on the dining room addition resumed "splendidly," according to Olson. The overnight cabins were completed in March, and two of the empty buildings of Camp Stone Fort near the lodge were razed, their materials salvaged for use in other projects.[62]

Overnight cabins about 90 percent completed by end of March 1935. National Archives, CCC records, Project 107.

April and May 1936 were very productive work months for the men of Company #696, even though their hoped-for work strength of 200 enrollees was reduced to 154, due to men leaving for other jobs and a lack of new recruits. Nevertheless, the "ideal construction weather" allowed for more "splendid progress" on the dining room addition to the lodge as well as on the sewage disposal system. Scott Vancil remembered working during that winter on five particular rocks for the dining room fireplace arch, which in his opinion was "the nicest arch in the lodge":

> The nicest one of those arches is the one in the big dining room [presently the bar], and that was cut with a chipping hammer. I cut those rocks for the fireplace myself. They built the arch to set them on, then I got me a helper and he and I set them. I was working in a building that had been a [#]692 barracks. . . . That was in the winter months, so I cut those rocks in there. They brought them in as big chunks. There were no two sides of any one of those rocks that had the same dimensions.
>
> You'd use a square and a chipping hammer. An engineer had figured these rocks for size the way they wanted. There were six sides to each rock and no two alike. He cut a pattern out of cardboard or something, the size of each one of those rocks. So I had to cut a rock according to that pattern. There were six patterns for each rock, because no two sides were the same. So I got all the rocks cut, then he told me to go up and lay those five rocks. I was three months cutting them five rocks. That archway of the fireplace was the most particular part of the whole building.[63]

Robert Kingery, director of the Department of Public Works and Buildings, visited the park in May, as did hundreds of citizens each weekend and numerous schoolchildren enjoying end-of-the-year picnics. A large crowd celebrated Decoration Day, May 30, at the park.

Superintendent Olson wrote in his report at the end of May, "The daily appearance of these picnics is very gratifying to us, in that it is evident that Giant City Park is taking its proper place as the recreational center of Southern Illinois." To further advertise the park's facilities, Olson was beginning the plans for a dedication ceremony for the lodge.[64]

The date for the lodge dedication was set for August 30, meaning that the work toward its completion also had a deadline. Throughout June and July, the dining hall was nearly finished, along with its requisite water supply, electric power, and kitchen equipment. The parking area was graded and the area surrounding the lodge further landscaped. Labor on Camp Giant City's bathhouse and sewage system continued.[65]

## LODGE DEDICATION CELEBRATION

A crowd of at least 20,000 was expected to attend the lodge dedication ceremony. Lieutenant Thomas P. Bermingham, subdistrict chaplain, aided considerably in the planning and promoting of the event through advertisements in four hundred newspapers. Committees were established of CCC officials from camps throughout southern Illinois for publicity, programs, decorations, transportation, first aid, construction, entertainment, parking, and information. As Giant City was often used as the central locale for all the CCC camps for southern Illinois and as it was, of course, a public park as well, all of the CCC companies in the near region of southern Illinois were invited to attend, along with their families.

An emergency job crew was created and approved by CCC authorities to build temporary toilets, concession stands, and a speakers' platform. A temporary public-address system was installed. The whole camp was kept "on edge" anticipating the event and until the great day was over. Hugh Roach, who took charge as acting superintendent for the camp in August,

Form for arch and stones ready to be cut for fireplace arch in dining room. National Archives, CCC records.

Detail of fireplace construction for dining room addition, ca. April–May 1936. National Archives, CCC records, Project 120, photo #6.

expressed "tremendous gratification" in his report following the event as all the efforts of the men were amply repaid. Coming to celebrate the CCC and the new lodge at Giant City State Park on that late August day were 22,000 people, "by far the largest crowd ever in Giant City Park, and one of the largest ever assembled in southern Illinois."[66]

Congressman Kent Keller of the Twenty-fifth Illinois District acted as chairman of the dedication committee. Other speakers were representatives of the National Park Service and the CCC. Then Governor Henry Horner spoke: " I feel that the project to recruit young men who otherwise would be out of work, give them useful and instructive employment, house them decently and comfortably, and direct their labors to constructions dedicated to public use and advantage, deserves our gratitude and applause." The governor concluded his address saying he hoped the park would "be a sanctified spot where our people will meet happiness and recreation and instructive interest. To that end it was created and to that purpose I dedicate it." The lodge was described by the speakers as a monument to all men of the Civilian Conservation Corps, and walnut plaques were presented to enrollees who represented all the camps in the district. Music was provided by the Carbondale American Legion Bugle and Drum Corps, the Carbondale Community High School band, and the Murphysboro American Legion band.[67]

### NOVEMBER 1936

William Hannon had represented CCC director Robert Fechner at the August lodge dedication, and he returned to Giant City again in November for a routine inspection. Several changes in personnel had occurred in the intervening months, and the strength of Company #696 was down to 160 men, mainly due to the fact that men were obtaining work. The previous camp superintendent, Albin Olson, had

been temporarily discharged for using government gasoline in his private car, so in November 1936, John J. Biggs was appointed acting project supervisor. First Lieutenant Sidney I. Wald was the new camp doctor, and Estel H. Winegarner became the new educational advisor. Captain Harold H. Capers was commander for the army officers, with Captain Arnel B. Adams as second in command. The food, according to Inspector Hannon, continued to be exceptionally good at Giant City, thanks to Lieutenant George F. Cooper, the mess officer, and Frank Kosma, the mess steward.[68]

The New Deal programs were having their desired effects both locally and nationally. On November 3, 1936, President Roosevelt was re-elected in a landslide over Republican Alfred M. "Alf" Landon. At the Democratic National Convention on June 27, 1936, FDR said:

> Liberty requires opportunity to make a living—a living which gives man not only enough to live by, but something to live for.
>
> For too many of us the political equality we once had won was meaningless in the face of economic inequality. A small group had concentrated into their own hands an almost complete control over other people's property, other people's money; other people's labor—other people's lives.
>
> These economic royalists complain that we seek to overthrow the institutions of America. What they really complain of is that we seek to take away their power. In vain they seek to hide behind the Flag and the Constitution.
>
> Governments can err. Presidents do make mistakes. But the immortal Dante tells us that divine justice weighs the sins of the cold-blooded and the sins of the warm-hearted in different scales.
>
> Better the occasional faults of a Government that lives in a spirit of charity than the consistent omissions of a Government frozen in the ice of its own indifference.
>
> . . . This generation has a rendezvous with destiny.[69]

Cars parked at Giant City for lodge dedication, August 30, 1936. National Archives, CCC records, photo #3.

Crowd gathered around speakers' platform at lodge dedication. Congressman Kent Keller and Governor Henry Horner spoke. National Archives, CCC records, photo #1.

# 7

# The Last Years of the CCC and Its Legacies

As Giant City State Park and the Shawnee National Forest were made publicly accessible by Civilian Conservation Corps labor, so were all the Depression-era forests and parks in Missouri, the Great Lakes region, the south, and the west. The evidence of CCC work is in nearly every state's parks and national forests. The goals of the corps were accomplished, and President Roosevelt and the Democratic Party reaped the benefits of the New Deal programs for many years. CCC alumni interviewed for this history expressed profound gratitude and praise for the chance they were given in the corps. Kenneth Hawk said in all seriousness that if the CCC hadn't come along, he "probably would have starved to death. . . . I don't know what would have happened to me, probably would have been in jail with the rest of them."[1]

The positive impacts of the CCC at the level of the low-income (or no-income) family were tremendous. Along with the money and the skill training also came pride and hope. Matthew Skertich of Gillespie was one of ten siblings whose father had lost his job. Skertich enrolled into Company #692 when it was taking in new recruits in 1935 and came to Camp Stone Fort. His job as a truck driver was to drive men to and from work sites in the mornings, at lunch, and at the end of the day. He helped the crews once at the sites in a variety of jobs: cutting dead trees, making bridle paths, planting trees, and cutting the stone for the lodge, of which he says he was "extremely

"Like a bunch of brothers," February 6, 1935.
Courtesy of Matthew Skertich.

Earl Dickey on back of Kermit Dunnigan in Wisconsin.
Courtesy of Earl Dickey.

Earl Dickey on swinging bridge over Bad River in Wisconsin.
Courtesy of Earl Dickey.

Skertich wrote that in "in all honesty our group was like a bunch of brothers who all got along so well" (see appendix 6 for Skertich's name among the roster of Company #696 in 1937). Since one of Skertich's real brothers, Rudy, enrolled into a CCC camp in Salem, Illinois, their parents received fifty dollars each month, "which at the time," Skertich wrote, "was like a million dollars." In 1937, the job market began to inch open. After leaving Giant City, Matthew Skertich worked with CCC Company #2659 in Elmhurst for a six-month stint. He left the CCC to work at Inland Steel Company in East Chicago, Indiana, where he remained for the next forty-two years.[3]

## CCC COMPANY #692 AT COPPER FALLS STATE PARK, WISCONSIN

The other members of Company #692 were spending their remaining enlistment periods at Copper Falls State Park, four miles from Mellen, Wisconsin. The area had been clearcut for lumber, and the CCC was expected to work on reforestation, fire suppression, erosion control, and park development. Company #692 was chosen because of its special skills in drainage and erosion control. Lieutenant George D. Markel was still the unit's commander. The winter of their arrival was one of the snowiest and coldest on record. In early February, temperatures reached forty degrees below zero. A severe cold spell lasted twenty-three days, during which time the boys were stranded in their barracks trying to keep the wood stoves filled. The roads to town were terrible, there was a lot of illness in camp, and the outfit had some trouble in keeping competent cooks. By the end of March, half the company left when their enlistment period ended.

But some stayed. Some of the Illinois boys had met girls in Wisconsin, courting them while attending basketball games, dances, and ice skating parties. Mike Kerkes met Irene Pray working in a store in Mellen. They

proud." Skertich did a lot of boxing and Ping-Pong playing. He remembered classes being offered in masonry, carpentry, forestry, and cooking.[2]

Fine cooks at Giant City in 1937 were Pete and Paul Kosma of Dowell, "Talky" Salwin of Herrin, Emmalline Swinigan of East St. Louis, and Pop Johnson of Murphysboro. Camp inspectors often combined "mess" and "morale" in one category of their typed reports, proving the effect on the camp mood of good, plentiful food. Good food proved so important to every CCC camp's success that the corps learned early on that experienced cooks had to be hired. In many camps, such as Giant City, promising cooks and bakers were sent away at CCC expense to short-term cooking schools to return ready to share much appreciated recipes and skills.

Company #692 veterans from Camp Stone Fort on swinging bridge at their new home at Copper Falls State Park, Wisconsin, March 8, 1936. Ralph Keets from Greenup, George Mathias, Earl Dickey, behind him is Walton Manuel, Charles Davis (with the *W* letter sweater) from Effingham, Arthur Hansleben (also not vet), Eugene Crawford from Palatine [or Palestine], and Elmer Shoemaker from Peoria. Photo and caption courtesy of Earl Dickey.

married in 1939. "Smokey Joe" Calbrecht met Marguerite Polencheck; they wed in December 1936. Frank Smith met Marion Kron, and he married her in August 1936.[4]

Even before the snow had melted, the men were put to work planting hardwood trees in cut-over areas of the park. Most of the seedlings died, however, in the unusually hot and dry summer of 1936. Because of the severely dry conditions, fire hazards became the main concern. The men of Company #692 fought many fires around their camp location, but on August 7 they were sent to Houghton, Michigan, to catch a nine-hour ferry ride to fight an out-of-control fire on Isle Royale. Other Illinois CCC companies from Hinsdale and Glenview were already on the island. This fire raged for eleven days until August 18, severely damaging over one-third of the island.

A simultaneous fire on Stockton Island (one of the Apostles Islands) kept the rest of the Company #692 firefighters stranded for ten days. When the fire season ended, Company #692 built roads bridges, foot trails, a garage, and a combination building to be used by the park. The company demobilized in the late summer of 1937.[5]

The year 1937 marked the midpoint of the life of the CCC, although at the time no one could say how long the country would be in need of the New Deal's workforce relief agencies. Created in response to an emergency and operated on a six-month and then a yearly basis, the CCC stabilized in 1937, as business conditions improved, at an enrollment strength of 350,000 men in 1,991 camps. This is a substantial reduction from the CCC enrollment peak in September 1935 of 505,782 men in 2,652

Group from Company #692 in Bayfield, Wisconsin, on their way to fight fires on Stockton Island, Lake Superior. They are Elwin De St. Jean, Moore, Veril Brewer, Raymond Cannady, Syler, Mikolased, Upton, Anklevitch, —noski, Grosteni, Spiller, Sweet, and James McFarland. Names, spelling, and photo courtesy of Earl Dickey.

camps. In the early years, as many as 1,000 applications for new camps had been on file.[6]

The CCC grew more popular with the public each year until 1941. Even though its broad sociological goals were never exactly clear, and even though many believed that the corps was not giving the youth enough work experience that had long term value, its continuation seemed inevitable through the late 1930s. Congressmen were hurt when camps closed in their districts because many camp jobs and outside contracts were available as political largesse,

Firefighters leaving camp for Stockton Island. Courtesy of Earl Dickey.

although the effect of politics in other ways on the corps has always been considered mild.[7]

Local businesses greatly benefited economically from the camps. It has been estimated that nearly $5,000 per month was spent by each camp in the local markets. Martin Bakery of Murphysboro, for example, came to depend heavily on getting the contract as the supplier of thousands of bread loaves that the bakery delivered daily to the four Jackson County camps.[8] Not only was business up but crime rates had dropped as a result of the CCC and other employment programs. A Chicago judge attributed the city's 50 percent reduction in crime to the work supplied by the corps. And many city employers indicated preferences for young men with CCC experience.[9]

On June 28, 1937, Congress approved the extension of the CCC for another three years, limiting the maximum enrolled strength to 300,000 and formally establishing the Civilian Conservation Corps as an independent agency, no longer under the agency of the Emergency Conservation Work. Unemployment was still a widespread problem in 1937, and the CCC was proving itself as one solution.[10]

Manning the kitchen on Stockton Island, August 1936, are Markel, Anklevitch, and Veril Brewer.

Names and photo courtesy of Earl Dickey.

The bosses of Company #692 at Copper Falls State Park, February 1935: Dick Seyler, three-striper; Jim Friel, two-striper; and Mr. Greeley, the state boss. Courtesy of Earl Dickey.

## TEACHING SKILLS IN THE CCC

Nevertheless, "make-work projects," as some derisively described the projects of the CCC, WPA, and others of the "alphabet soup" legislation, could be improved upon, as many of the CCC leaders admitted. The immediate crucial benefits of the corps to the desperate unemployed men were obvious. But there was just as obvious a need for training that the men could use on "the outside" for lifelong employment. This fact was evident to CCC officers and superintendents. John J. Biggs, project superintendent at Giant City from 1936 to 1939, wrote a request in January 1937 to his superiors addressing this issue and how to train the class of young men who were admitted into the corps, many of them

men who were without any specific interest in life. . . .

These men were in many cases underweight because of lack of proper food. Few of them had ever had a job which lasted over a few days. Their social conditions at home were depressing. With no chance to secure legitimate work, many of them were in danger of becoming potential criminals.

We in the Corps directed our efforts to building them up physically and mentally. Our jobs as a whole were merely common

Woodwork shop tools. *Official Annual: Civilian Conservation Corps, Jefferson Barracks CCC District, Sixth Corps Area, 1937* (U.S. Government).

**Woodwork shop.** *Official Annual: Civilian Conservation Corps, Jefferson Barracks CCC District, Sixth Corps Area, 1937* (U.S. Government).

Cabin interior with original red cedar furniture made by the CCC at Camp Giant City. Hedrich-Blessing photo, courtesy of Giant City Visitor Center.

labor. We tried to teach the men not only to work but to like to work. Because a large part of their pay went to help out needy members of their family, a sense of responsibility was developed. These men as a whole went back to civilian life physically fit, willing and wanting to work, but handicapped because their training was general and no definite profession or trade had been chosen.

Because of the foregoing facts it is my opinion that each of our projects should have at least one job set up which the more ambitious enrollee can strive to get on, and which will develop sufficient skill to be able to take over in civilian life.

Biggs proposed using the teaching skills of an experienced cabinetmaker and foreman at Company #696 to train a small crew of enrollees in the trade of furniture carpentry. He recommended equipping one of the abandoned camp's barracks with woodworking equipment and tools for this long-term commitment. The regular carpentry crew had recently completed the construction of twelve overnight cabins; Biggs suggested that the new crew make furniture from red cedar for these cabins: chairs, tables, benches, beds, dressers, washstands, and hat racks and coatracks. In the first days of February 1937, Biggs's request was approved.[11]

Giant City's CCC companies had already produced experts in other trades. Some would carry their trades directly to outside employment. In 1937, Howard Watson of Williamson County and Johnny Miller of Murphysboro were singled out for their abilities in cutting and placing stone in the continuing construction of the lodge additions and other stone structures in the park. There were many ways through work experience and classroom instruction that CCC men could broaden their opportunities for success in civilian life, which was, as Superintendent Biggs expressed, one of the central goals of the corps. In the summer of 1937, classes were offered at Giant City in carpentry, plumbing, electrical wiring, motor and gas engines, woodworking, photography, journalism, cooking, and table-waiting as well as in academics such as arithmetic, economic geography, U.S. history, eighth-grade proficiency, and basic literacy.[12] In 1938, thirty boys successfully completed a truck driver's course. Additional weekly classes were initiated in 1939 and 1940 in radio and code, landscaping, teacher and leadership training, public speaking, bookkeeping, commercial art, fruit production and marketing, poultry husbandry, salesmanship, tree surgery, and social dancing.[13]

## FLOOD RELIEF OF 1937 AND CCC CONTRIBUTION THROUGH 1941

The nation's other central goal of the CCC—conserving the country's forests and topsoil—was being met on many fronts by the corps throughout the United States. Some of the public argued the advantages of maintaining the CCC as a permanent and ready national workforce. The usefulness of such a "conservation army" proved apparent during the devastating midwest flood of January 1937. The CCC camps of southern Illinois were called out to assist the National Guard in the evacuation of such river communities as Shawneetown and Rosiclare. They assisted in the efforts to save Mound City and in sandbagging the levee at Cairo, Golconda, and other river towns. Floyd Boals, an original Company #696 enrollee, remembered working day and night carrying sandbags and doing "almost everything that we could to save the town [Cairo]."[14] The CCC helped construct refugee tent camps at Anna and Wolf Lake. Former CCC camps Hutchins and Hicks were also occupied as refugee camps.[15] A detachment from Giant City's Company #696 was sent to Cairo and participated in the Army Corps of Engineer's dynamiting of the Bird's Point–New Madrid waterway as a means to arrest the rise of the Ohio River at Cairo. The flood's destruction required the CCC workforce along the Mississippi and Ohio rivers for many months.[16]

First Half of Entire Company #696 in 1937.

*First row, left to right*: T. Heater, H. Cauble, M. Pledger, E. Crisler, M. Evans, L. Chapman, K. Stanley, V. Caterino, C. Hagler, A. Anderson, D. Leonard. *Second row, left to right*: D. Jones, R. Stecher, W. Callis, J. Godsil, J. Martin, D. Bittle, E. Costa, R. Coy, H. Simmons, E. Cook, J. Kendrick, H. Rix, A. Dunning, J. Campbell, W. Corbett. *Third row*: left to right A. Reames, V. Rowatt, H. Hazelwood, J. Koros, C. Rushing, E. Youngblood, J. Reynolds, W. Johnson, A. Salvo, L. Dunn, F. Sanders, S. Dudas, A. Slack, A. Dunlap, H. Scott. *Fourth row, left to right*: W. Sims, T. Myers, V. Mathias, A. Toler, C. Pearce, J. Foster, G. Pulcher, C. Guenther, S. Lezu, W. Stokes, L. Padgett, R. Mills, G. Lauder, H. Richmond, B. Edwards, S. Farthing. *Official Annual: Civilian Conservation Corps, Jefferson Barracks CCC District, Sixth Corps Area, 1937* (U.S. Government).

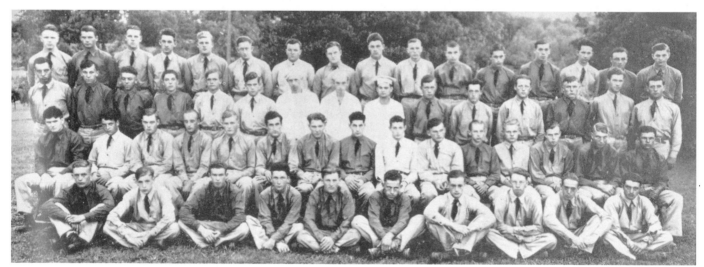

Second Half of Entire Company #696 in 1937.

*First row, left to right*: C. Beaver, W. Bradley, A. Bradshaw, R. Davidson, H. Sumner, C. Burns, E. Tinsley, Edward Mitchell, G. Allen, W. Barker. *Second row, left to right*: S. Krisfalusy, W. McGhee, K. Benefield, T. Carroll, J. Morefield, C. Cox, A. Lindsey, R. Eschmann, K. Stanley, A. Polonowski, L. Yancy, E. Peterson, C. Berry, J. Wilmoth, D. Rendleman. *Third row, left to right*: R. Sweazy, W. Miller, G. Alexander, L. Eubanks, W. Matlock, G. Gould, W. White, D. Whitecotton, E. Morgan, A. Westbrooks, F. Blessing, R. Nethercott, R. Myers, J. Blessing, W. Hobbs. *Fourth row, left to right*: M. Griggs, K. Davis, R. Fries, P. Simpson, S. Patterson, E. Gerl, H. Watson, T. Hindman, F. Sawin, D. Thomas, J. Fitz, C. Long, V. Campbell, C. Zimmerman, V. Berry, W. Lucas. *Official Annual: Civilian Conservation Corps, Jefferson Barracks CCC District, Sixth Corps Area, 1937* (U.S. Government).

*Members not in picture*: R. Robinson, B. Baltimore, W. Lence, W. Smith, C. Triplett, D. Newlon, Eugene Mitchell, H. Harmon, L. Dial, H. Hileman, T. Stanley, D. Bishop, R. Ossig, S. Ball, R. Penrod, M. Malone, E. Bradley, C. Cheek, C. Sanders, R. Griffin, D. Henderson, T. Hogan, R. Lindhurst, L. McDaniel, H. Miller, F. Rodgers, H. Ross, T. Smiley, R. Bradley.

Aerial photo of Camp Giant City, foreground, 1938. Lodge and cabins in distance can be seen at end of loop.
Division of Parks, courtesy of Giant City Visitor Center.

An article in *Life* magazine dated June 6, 1938, stated that the CCC was "the one New Deal measure that has won universal approval even from diehard Republicans."[17] Partially because of the great use made of the CCC workforce in local and national emergencies during the 1930s, there continued strong bipartisan support for the agency, even though the cost of FDR's "Santa Claus" agencies was a main cause for Republican criticism.[18] Still, the removal of a CCC camp from a constituency could spell political trouble for the incumbent in an election.[19]

In Washington, however, federal officials were constantly arguing over the CCC program and its general purpose. According to Francis Perkins, FDR's secretary of labor, the president was so pleased with the personal effects on CCC enrollees that "he wanted to find a way for well-to-do boys, as well as relief boys, to go to CCC camps (to get the advantages of the training and democratic living)." Nevertheless, army personnel and investigators were continually on the watch in the camps for "communist" activities. As trouble had brewed abroad in the 1930s, those such as General Douglas MacArthur became increasingly interested in the possibilities of the CCC as a reservoir of military strength, pushing to introduce compulsory military training at all the camps.[20] Others, fearing fascism, argued against the army's growing militarization of the camps.[21] It is a daunting fact that while the CCC camps were sprouting up throughout the United States, work camps were also being erected throughout Germany and Austria, also in out-of-the-way, obscure rural places such as Neun Gammen, Mauthausen, Buchenwald, Lublin, and Auschwitz-Birkenau. In the United States, without intending it at the beginning, the CCC did prepare men for a military lifestyle, but, more important, by keeping the men unarmed, the American camps reminded everyone of the ideals and values that made a war worth fighting.

Many men did leave the CCC to enlist in the regular military, where they made better soldiers because of their CCC lifestyle experiences, but the corps remained at the end as it had been formed at the beginning, committed to two principal objectives: the relief of unemployment and the accomplishment of useful conservation work.

At Giant City, the work crews of Company #696 continued through 1937 and 1938 their long-term projects of road-building and other park improvements. The cedar furniture construction proved to be a very successful endeavor, but camp morale fell until November 1938, when Captain William G. Lefferts

replaced Captain A. O. Fink as company commander. Lefferts and his subordinate officers were credited with the improved morale. In October 1938, a group of men from Company #696 transferred to Company #1625 and moved to Golconda, Nevada. A large group of newcomers was taken into the ranks at Camp Giant City at the end of 1938.[22]

John J. Biggs remained as Camp Giant City's superintendent until the latter part of 1939, when he was replaced by Stirling [Sterling] S. Jones, who continued through 1940 directing the work crews on the lodge additions and interior, cabin furniture, roads, picnic areas, and latrines as well as on the continuous timber stand improvement, planting, and the building or repair of foot trails.[23]

In 1938, the lodge's first concessionaire, Clarient Hopkins from Harrisburg, began offering hot lunches for fifty cents and dinners featuring steaks and lobster. Hopkins allowed dancing and served beer at ten cents a bottle. Local tourism advocate Wayman Presley wanted Giant City to remain a "pure clean recreational spot," so he complained to state authorities, warning them that he would not

Latrine, completed except for outside paint as of March 1937. Job #3-113, National Archives, CCC records.

Aerial photo of lodge and original cabins, May 1938. Some remaining barracks of Camp Stone Fort are at the end of the parking lot.
U.S. Department of Agriculture photo, Map Library, Morris Library, Southern Illinois University Carbondale.

include it on his tours if it did not remain dry.[24] Even though some locals grumbled about the drinking, dancing, and gaudy neon advertising signs, Camp Giant City was surely solidifying its place as the choice CCC camp in southern Illinois.[25] Camp inspectors reported that the morale and mess were both excellent in 1939 and satisfactory in 1940. The southern Illinois public was falling in love with Giant City State Park. Attendance in 1938 was 47,566; in 1939, 49,000 visited the park, making it the seventh most popular of all Illinois parks. Its popularity grew immensely so that by November 29, 1940, over 120,000 visitors had come that year to Giant City State Park.[26]

Dr. Andrew R. Esposito, who became a longtime Murphysboro resident, was south-ern Illinois's CCC contract surgeon in 1939. In March of that year, he diagnosed enough cases of mumps in the camp hospital to place all the men under a working quarantine, meaning they were not allowed to leave camp for a specified number of days. Thirty-five men went AWOL, breaking the quarantine order, and were there-fore called before hearings where punishment of some kind was declared.[27]

The average company strength in 1939–41 remained about 178, which allowed approxi-mately 100 men on work projects outside the camp details. At the end of each six-month enrollment period, men left for employment or simply did not renew their enrollment. New en-rollees were assigned to established work crews and filled up some of the empty cots.

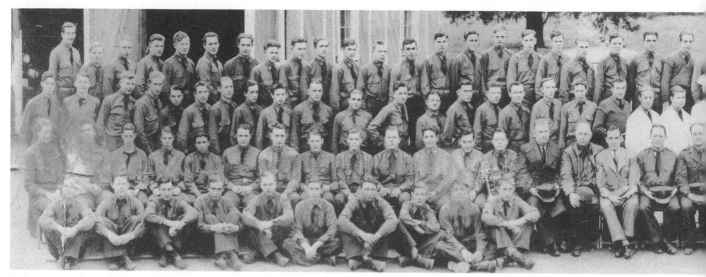

Entire company photo of Company #696, February 1940. Poster at Giant City Visitor Center and in Giant City State Park Civilian Conservation Corps Collection in Special Collections, Morris Library (MSS 280), Southern Illinois University Carbondale.

The CCC director, Robert Fechner, died on January 1, 1940. James J. McEntee, who had been the assistant director since 1933, became director.[28] McEntee was not as forceful, and the concept of the CCC was already experiencing problems regarding segregation, leadership weaknesses, and desertion. Much of the erosion in the ranks of the CCC must be attributed to international events. After Hitler invaded Poland in 1939 and overran western Europe, the U.S. economy gained strength through military spending, and unemployment declined dramatically.[29] The most enthusiastic of the unemployed were not entering the CCC any longer but instead joined the armed services. Many CCC reserve officers were also returning to regular life in the army.

On February 27, 1940, a photographer came to Camp Giant City to take official photographs of the camp and Company #696 (see appendix 7 for names from photo composite of entire company). William Lefferts had been company commander since late 1938. His subaltern was Arthur W. Fox. Dr. Ellis Crandle was the civilian physician, and Ernest Plambeck was the educational advisor, assisted by

Carrol L. Wilson. Thomas Bermingham continued as the area chaplain. Oscar L. Raines served the officers as their orderly, and J. H. Tindall was their official car driver. Ralph Hancock was the inspection clerk, and William Neber served as the night guard.

Fred H. Mills was the company clerk, and F. Paris served as his assistant. Henry J. Bayers ran the commissary, Milburn C. Taylor ran the canteen, and Walter H. McDonald was the supply leader. Carl I. Hagler was the company's cabinetmaker and Frederick D. Shoemaker the head carpenter. The chief mechanic was Harold Harmon.

William Burbes operated the camp's radio. The bathhouse overseer was Robert Payne. Allen L. Hood blew the bugle each morning and evening at reveille and when the company was called to retreat.

For the National Park Service, Stirling S. Jones supervised the work projects. Roy D. Shockley was the NPS assistant clerk. Almond V. Robertson was the senior leader; Clinton Cox and Joseph Fitz were leaders. Specialists for the Park Service were Sumner M. Anderson, geologist; Carl F. Meyer, engineer; Arnold

E. Roehl, landscape architect; Floyd Boals, mechanic; and Charles Sanders, tool keeper. Andrew J. Newlin and William L. Parker were foremen of the work crews.

In the kitchen, Boniface Humm and William W. Johnson were first cooks. Second cooks were William Dudas and Thomas F. Hodges. The mess steward was Bruno De Giacinto. Kenneth Burnett was the baker. Paul Turner was in charge of the first aid station and was assisted by Orderly E. G. Rodgers.

CCC officers, like those in the regular army, moved around quite a lot within the CCC system and out of the system as the country began gearing up its military strength. Company #696 was left short of administrative personnel in the last months of 1940. Arthur W. Fox became the acting company commander but had to double his duties as the educational advisor. Although a camp inspector stressed in his January 1941 report the immediate need for additional qualified administrators, he reported on the good general camp condition, the much-liked chaplain who is "very competent in dealing with morale problems," the wide range of athletic and recreational activities, and the "very fine reading room."[30]

Liberty parties under escort were trucked to Carbondale every Wednesday and Saturday nights to satisfy the men's social needs. "The work progress," according to the inspector, "was excellent." It appears that by 1941, the structured routine and the work ethic of the men were naturally running the camp, with minimum army direction. The menus continued to rate excellent with the inspectors.[31]

Company #696 greeted a new commander, Lieutenant Kubiak, in March 1941, but Burnell H. Mathis was in command by November 1941. The great majority of work projects planned at Giant City had seen completion, and national enrollment in the CCC was falling. W. Sam Bunker became the new project superintendent with Charles V. Pragaldin as a new foreman, but company strength had fallen to 150, allowing fewer men than ever to be available for park work details. The company was in fact ordered to disband on November 1, 1941, but those orders were rescinded in order to finish the water supply system for the park. In late November 1941, only seventy-five men were reported to be in the camp. A side camp of over sixty men had been split off out of Company #696 and sent on a construction detail to Decatur to build a five-hundred-man capacity army USO recreation center.[32]

Company #696 called to reveille, February 1940. Poster at Giant City Visitor Center.

The men remaining at Giant City were kept busy with the building of a concrete reservoir and pump house, a vehicle bridge, stone barriers at a parking area, and furniture for the Pere Marquette lodge. By November 1941, night classes were strictly vocational: welding, machine lathe operation, airplane sheet metal, woodworking, and motor vehicle driving. The country was gearing up for war. The Civilian Conservation Corps had run its course.[33]

Some historians of the CCC believe that a great opportunity for the United States was squandered in letting the corps dissolve completely. Early on, progressives in the New Deal wanted programs like the CCC to go on indefinitely. Harry Hopkins, who oversaw the Works Project Administration, argued that large-scale projects such as the development of national forests and the building of great recreational centers were not possible under "the profit system." He said that programs like the CCC would be self-liquidating and "represent a contribution of the unemployed themselves of enormous social value to the nation." But

the CCC was an emergency relief measure that never shook off that mantle. The combination of the conservation concept and the unemployment relief never fused to solidify into a cohesive plan to meet the country's future needs. It wasn't just the needs of the immediate raging war that blocked such a vision. A permanent workforce relief and conservation program would have been a sharp departure from the United States' conservative train of thought powered by its trust in individualism and its faith in unlimited natural resources. Furthermore, Americans tend to view the holding of private property as a sacred and necessary right. The CCC and the concurrent establishment of national forests were radical steps away from individualism and private property ideals. Even though a departure from these traditional ideals proved necessary to rescue this country in the 1930s, more liberal tenets could not hold a lasting grip. The leadership of the CCC had always been of a more conservative bent. "The CCC was not run at the highest level by liberal intellectuals such as Harry Hopkins or Aubrey

Camp Giant City library, February 1940. Poster at Giant City Visitor Center.

Williams, but by conservative trade union officials," which, according to one CCC historian, "was undoubtedly a factor in explaining the CCC's relative popularity with even right wing congressmen and commentators."[34]

### CONCLUSION OF WORK

Enrollment in the CCC dropped from 300,000 to 160,000 in the year 1941. Hundreds of camps closed as jobs became more plentiful and recruitment into the corps more difficult. After the bombing of Pearl Harbor on December 7, 1941, the CCC was asked to offer its camps to the army for military projects and to the American Red Cross for war emergencies.[35] Camp Giant City closed in late spring 1942; the camps at Pere Marquette and Kickapoo state parks closed at the same time, their buildings turned over to the state of Illinois. Some CCC campsites, such as those at Waterloo and Pomona in

Illinois, were soon to be retrofitted for use as German prisoner of war camps.[36] The Civilian Conservation Corps officially went out of existence on June 30, 1942.

For a brief time in the fall of 1942, there was a plan by the federal government to use Giant City's empty CCC barracks as a place for military conscientious objectors, but in January 1943, Illinois governor Dwight H. Green gave 4-H clubs permission to use the camps. Some of the remaining CCC barracks near the lodge were removed to the SINU campus, but those of Company #696 remained in the park for many years.[37]

By 1941, Bond Blackman had become the park's custodian with Howard McGinnis as his assistant. In February 1942, Blackman was reprimanded by A. R. Kugler, assistant superintendent of parks, about Blackman's responses to a work questionnaire that indicated that his work was directing the activities of his as-

Juanita Ernest (Earl Dickey's bride-to-be) among the bluebells near Newton in the spring of 1935. Courtesy of Earl Dickey.

ways prided itself as an agency of real workers, whereas the public's joke on the WPA workers, who were too often seen roadside, leaning on their shovels, was that their initials stood for "We Piddle Around."[38]

Most agree that in its nine-year history, the CCC did an impressive amount of work, advancing the cause of conservation. It saved millions of acres of forest and topsoil on cropland that were in danger of being lost forever. One-half of all the trees planted in the United States were planted by the CCC. It has been said that without the help of the corps, it would have taken fifty years to accomplish for the National Park Service what was done in nine.[39] This was assuredly the case at Giant City State Park.

Over its brief history, the CCC had employed almost three and a half million men, and 4,500 CCC camps had been established.[40] Illinois greatly benefited; only New York and Pennsylvania had more men enrolled from their states than the 165,300 whom Illinois sent to the more than 120 different camps in operation at various times between 1933 and 1942. According to one historian, fifty-four camps a year on average were operated within Illinois with a total cost of approximately $103,600,000.[41] The cost expended in 1939 for each enrollee for food, clothing, overhead, and twenty-five-dollar monthly allotments to dependents was approximately $1,000 per year.[42]

In southernmost Illinois, in addition to the two state park camps at Giant City, twenty-eight other CCC camps were established by either the U.S. Department of Agriculture (Forest Service) or the Soil Conservation Service. Nearly every one of southern Illinois's counties had at least one camp. Jackson and Union benefited from four camps established in each of their counties. (See appendix 1 for information on other camps in southern Illinois as well as a map showing locations of camps.)

The CCC was a bold experiment. According to Leslie Alexander Lacy, "It was the first genuine effort by an American government

sistant, implying that Blackman himself did no work. Kugler wrote, "I would be ashamed to give a general impression that we are going into competition with the W.P.A." The CCC al-

World War II veterans and their new families enjoyed the free recreation in public parks created for them during the Depression era.
Courtesy of Giant City Visitor Center.

to undertake, on a massive scale, a basically practical and anti-ideological program for its dispossessed youth."[43] Commenting in 1938 on the success of the CCC, the *St. Louis Post-Dispatch* wrote, "It has done more than any other program to lift the morale of the indigent and despairing. . . . It has taken the cold business of government and made it human." Dozens of CCC alumni interviewed in southern Illinois remembered it as the rescue they found for themselves and for their families during desperate years. Earl Dickey said, "It gave boys a chance who weren't having a chance." Most attribute their skills and employment in later years to their work in the CCC.[44]

Scott Vancil worked in the coal mines after his time in the corps. He said he had a bad time for a few years, "worked construction all over the country." He recalled fond memories of Giant City, of learning to work and live with all kinds of men and of jumping over to the Devil's Stand Table to have a few cold beers stashed in the rock hole with his buddy Kenneth Hawk.[45]

Hawk left the corps in November 1936, after nearly two years of work at Giant City. A friend of his left his CCC stint at the same time, and the two planned a trip to California in a Model T Ford. "I don't know what I was going to do there. . . . It was the land of milk and honey. But in those days you had to have somebody vouch for you if you went in [to California] without a job. . . . We never did get anybody to vouch for us, so we didn't go." Hawk worked in the Chicago steel mills, then in a tavern, then in a foundry. He finally settled on work at Du Quoin's Bluebell Packing House for thirty-five years.[46]

When Company #692 left Illinois for Wisconsin, Company Clerk George Oliver, by that time married to Fannie, did not go. He quit the corps to be a foreman for a WPA crew that was clearing the woods along the Cache River and the Post Creek cutoff. His crews helped sandbag the levees at Cairo, working sixteen to twenty hours a day. In the fall of 1937, Oliver entered SINU, studying accounting and bookkeeping. He worked at various office jobs until he was drafted into the navy in July 1943. After the war, he became supervisor of central receiving at the university, where he worked for sixteen years.[47]

Earl Dickey stayed with Company #692 at Copper Falls State Park, Wisconsin, cutting firewood and working outdoors, but he also learned to type well. He regularly sent typed letters to Juanita Ernest, who went to Illinois Eastern College for two years and then taught school. Earl had been sending his twenty-five dollars to his parents each month and indicated mixed feelings when he learned his dad had bought a new car with the money. "Guess they needed it," he said, smiling. His parents did give Earl his last twenty-five-dollar check, with which he was able to purchase two white shirts, a suitcase, and a railroad ticket to Adrian, Michigan, where he would attend college. He left the CCC in September 1936. While working as a janitor and winning a scholarship, Dickey continued on to seminary at Westminster, Maryland. He and Juanita married in 1941. Earl ministered for sixty-four years in Illinois Methodist churches in Enfield, Shipman, Murphysboro, Jerseyville, Carterville, East St. Louis, Benton, and Mt. Carmel. In the 1950s, the Dickeys volunteered in the development of the United Methodist Church camp at Little Grassy, just north of Giant City. After they retired, they moved to a house near Giant City State Park and up through 2008 volunteered as guides at the park's visitor center.[48]

The CCC taught men at an impressionable age not only to work but also to live with others and to become friends with strangers from distant regions. Those who traveled far with their CCC companies learned that people do things differently in other places. In one letter, Earl Dickey expressed to Juanita his surprise to learn that in Mellen, Wisconsin, adults

THE LAST YEARS OF THE CCC

Governor Jim Thompson at the fifty-year anniversary of the Civilian Conservation Corps with CCC veterans. Among them in the front on the right is George Oliver. Courtesy of George Oliver.

More recent aerial photo of new water tower and new cabins under construction at site of old Camp Stone Fort.
Courtesy of Giant City Visitor Center.

didn't go to Sunday school. He closed the letter, "There are two hundred men in camp, but no one to talk to."[49]

Years later, when sharing their experiences with this author, Giant City State Park CCC alumni spoke with great affection and obvious pride as they saw their work still being used and enjoyed, even though most acknowledged that few younger people realize that the Civilian Conservation Corps was responsible for the first roads, trails, bridges, shelters, and lodges in their national forests and parks. The federal government had seized a national conservation opportunity—to reclaim exploited natural resources and build recreational and educational natural areas. As a result, forever changed was the American public's understanding of what its federal government could, or should, do to invest in its citizens and protect its natural heritage. The New Deal's legacies are many: social security, unemployment compensation, stock market regulation, the federal guarantee of bank deposits, collective bargaining, and wages and hours legislation. Added to that, through the work of the CCC, the United States can claim an extensive national forest system and rejuvenated state park systems.

Even when the impressive material legacies of the CCC are understood, perhaps the immaterial ones are more arresting and profound. Historians have a difficult time quantifying or even describing in general the effect of the CCC on a generation of poor young men. Each man had his own profound story with some common similarities with his fellow enrollees. They were given a chance to work. They were allowed a way to be useful to their families and even enjoy personal success. While earning paychecks, they also learned skills, but more important, they earned self-worth. The character lessons they learned were apparent in the men's stories, in their demeanor, and in their eyes as they shared them even fifty years later.

After World War II, a new generation of southern Illinoisans gradually came to understand and fully appreciate that a natural treasure, Giant City State Park, had been made beautiful and accessible to them during the Depression era. Veterans and their families "swarmed" over the state parks, eager for recreation and open spaces.[50] Giant City's cabins typically opened in May. During the 1940s, George W. Williams was the park superintendent, and Anna Cook ran the lodge.

In 1959, U.S. senator Everett Dirksen, from Illinois, unsuccessfully tried to revive the Youth Corps idea, proposing conservation corps camps for boys sixteen to twenty-one in the nation's public lands. In 1961, U.S. senator Hubert Humphrey, from Minnesota, sponsored the Youth Conservation Corps bill again. In 1970, the Youth Conservation Corps Act was made public law, modeled on aspects of the CCC experience.

Through the 1960s, the park property expanded and the popularity of the lodge and grounds grew. The empty barracks of Giant City's first CCC camp, Company #696, remained across the road from the Devil's Stand Table, a reminder of the corps. The CCC was fondly remembered by a generation as a bright, green spot in the dark Depression years—when a favorite playground was created for Illinoisans at Giant City State Park by boys who came to work there, on their way to becoming men.

**Appendixes**
**Notes**
**Bibliography**
**Index**

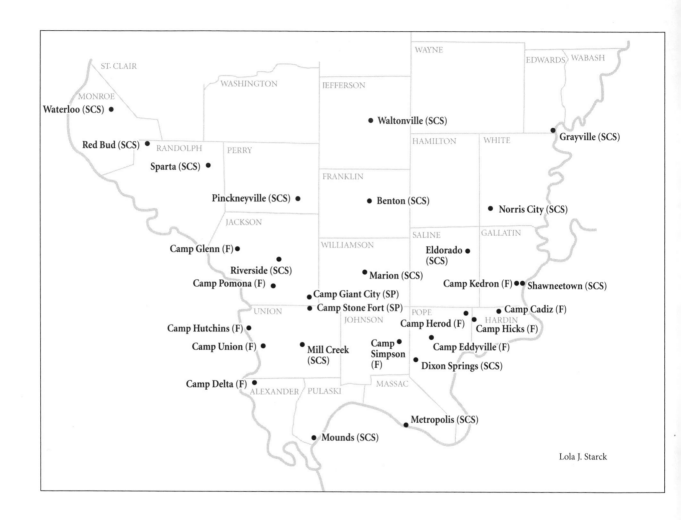

Waterloo (SCS) ●

Red Bud (SCS) ●

Sparta (SCS) ●

Pinckneyville (SCS) ●

Waltonville (SCS) ●

Grayville (SCS) ●

Benton (SCS) ●

Norris City (SCS) ●

Camp Glenn (F) ●

Riverside (SCS) ●

Camp Pomona (F) ●

Eldorado (SCS) ●

Marion (SCS) ●

Camp Kedron (F) ●● Shawneetown (SCS)

Camp Giant City (SP) ●

Camp Stone Fort (SP) ●

Camp Cadiz (F) ●

Camp Hutchins (F) ●

Camp Herod (F) ●

Camp Hicks (F) ●

Camp Union (F) ●

Mill Creek (SCS) ●

Camp Simpson (F) ●

Camp Eddyville (F) ●

Dixon Springs (SCS) ●

Camp Delta (F) ●

Metropolis (SCS) ●

Mounds (SCS) ●

Lola J. Starck

# Appendix 1: Southern Illinois CCC Camps

| CAMP NAME | DESIGNATION | LOCATION | TOWN |
|---|---|---|---|
| **U.S. FOREST SERVICE CAMPS** | | | |
| Camp Glenn | F-1 | T8S R4W Sect.15, , Jackson County | Dry Hill, Murphysboro |
| Camp Pomona | F-2 | T10S R2W Sect. 19, Jackson County | Alto Pass (actually Pomona) |
| Camp Delta | F-3 | T14S R2W Sect. 20, Alexander County | Tamms or McClure |
| Camp Eddyville | F-4 | T12S R6E, Sect. 6 and T11S R6E, S. 31, Pope County | Eddyville |
| Camp Hicks | F-5 | T11S R8E Sect. 30, Hardin County | Herod |
| Camp Kedron | F-6 | T10S R8E Sect. 8?, Gallatin County | near Karber's Ridge, Equality |
| Camp Herod | F-7 | T11S R7E Sect. 9, Pope County | Herod |
| Camp Hutchins | F-8 | T11S R3 W Sect. 34, Union County | Wolf Lake |
| Camp Cadiz | F-9 | T11S R9E, Sect. 8?, Hardin County | Sparks Hill |
| Camp Union | F-10 | T12S R2W Sect. 7, Union County | Jonesboro |
| ? | F-11 | | Gallatin |
| Camp Simpson | F-12 | T12S R4 E Sect. 15 | Simpson, Johnson Co. |
| **SOIL CONSERVATION SERVICE CAMPS** | | | |
| Dixon Springs | SCS-01 | Pope County | Dixon Springs |
| Grayville | SCS-06 | Edwards County | Grayville |
| Shawneetown | SCS-17 | Gallatin County | Shawneetown |
| Riverside | SCS-20 | Jackson County | Murphysboro |
| Mill Creek | SCS-21 | Union County | Anna |
| Benton | SCS-22 | Franklin County | Benton |
| Waterloo | SCS-23 | Monroe County | Waterloo |
| Norris City | SCS-24 | White County | Norris City |
| Marion | SCS-27 | Williamson County | Marion |
| Mounds | SCS-29 | Pulaski County | Mounds |
| Sparta | SCS-34 | Randolph County | Sparta |
| Waltonville | SCS-49 | Jefferson County | Waltonville |
| Metropolis | | Massac County | Metropolis |
| Pinckneyville | PE-66 | Perry County | Du Quoin |
| Red Bud | | Randolph County | Red Bud |
| Eldorado | | Saline County | Eldorado |
| **NATIONAL PARK SERVICE CAMPS** | | | |
| Giant City | SP-11 | Jackson County | Makanda |
| Stone Fort | SP-24, SP-41 | Union County | Makanda |

F: National Forest
SCS: Soil Conservation Service
PE: Private Land Erosion
SP: State Park

Sources: "CCC Camps Approved for Fifth Period (1935) 200-Man Company Units, " State of Illinois, RG 35, National Archives, Washington, DC; "CCC Cards, History Office, Soil Conservation Service, Washington, DC, Made into a List and Map of Civilian Conservation Corps (CCC) Camps, 1934-42": Technical Supervision by the Soil Conservation Service, May 1983, in Kay Rippelmeyer Civilian Conservation Corps Collection, Special Collections Research Center, Morris Library, Southern Illinois University, Carbondale; Monthly Reports of Superintendents of CCC Camps in State and Local Parks, Illinois, RG 35, National Archives; Perry H. Merrill, *Roosevelt's Forest Army: A History of the Civilian Conversation Corps, 1933-1942* (Montpelier, VT: Merrill, 1981).

# Appendix 2: CCC Company #1657 in June 1933

Regular Army Officers
Roehm, John F., Capt. FA, Commanding
Morton, P. M., Second Lt. Cav.

Regular Army Enlisted Officers
Simpson, Odie L., First Sgt. (Acting), 6th Infantry
Rice, Floyd A., Cpl. 6th Infantry
Neeley, Robert., Hq. Co., 6th Infantry

*Enrollees*

| | | | |
|---|---|---|---|
| Altes, Henry E. (cook) | Bloomington | Farney, John | Springfield |
| Amadio, Raymond | Chicago Heights | Felty, Arlie B. (Cook) | Saybrook |
| *Arnold, Hooper (ration)* | | Finley, Floyd T. | Mattoon |
| Ashmore, Charles R. | Alton | Flaminio, Alex | Sherman |
| *Askins, Frank* | | Fleming, George | Glen Ellyn |
| Bailey, Thomas M. | Pawnee | Ford, Joseph | Springfield |
| Balch, William W. | Charleston | Fromback, Everett | Chicago |
| Banks, John R. | Moline | Galloway, Leonard L. (Supply) | Pekin |
| Barra, Tony | Thayer | Gaubatz, LeRoy | Belleville |
| Beard, John | Thayer | Gibbons, Kenneth D. | Rock Island |
| Bergerson, Jack D. | Moline | Gillette, Willard | Riverton |
| Bersin, Chellis A. | Basco | Gossage, Leo E. | Springfield |
| Biscan, Pete P. | Mt. Olive | *Grant, Alec M.* | |
| Blair, Millard W. | Mattoon | Groat, Eugene | Springfield |
| Brandon, Woodrow W. | Bellflower | Halford, Albert | Springfield |
| Broksieck, LeRoy | Rock Island | Hamilton, Raymond | Tallula |
| Burke, Luther P. | Springfield | *Hansen, Sigvold* | |
| Capella, Maurice A. | Springfield | Hardy, Roy D. | Springfield |
| Casteel, James M. | Divernon | *Harper, Allyn E.* | |
| Clauss, Norman | Chicago | *Harton, Alfred L.* | |
| Cobb, Frederic E. | Mattoon | *Haskins, Laurence* | |
| Colclasure, Glen E. | Mechanicsburg | Haskins, William | Moline |
| Cordery, John | Petersburg | Haycraft, Carl | Williamsville |
| Corsaro, James V. | Springfield | Haycraft, John | Williamsville |
| Corsaro, Samuel | Springfield | *Hayes, Porter T.* | |
| Coulson, Thomas | Springfield | Heinen, Richard A. | Springfield |
| *Cox, Carl C. (KP)* | | Henderson, James W. | Sherman |
| Crist, Homer W. | Normal | Herpstreith, Cletus E. | Pawnee |
| *Cronister, Henry J.* | | Hiler, Alfred | Virden |
| Cunningham, Elmer B. | Decatur | *Hill, Arthur J.* | |
| Dammerich, William | Belleville | Hoffman, Frank J. | Decatur |
| Darling, Rex V. | Normal | Hoffstatter, Lloyd L. | Peoria |
| Daugherty, James | Belleville | Homer, Harry | Springfield |
| Davey, Frances W. | Decatur | Huffstedtler, Owen A. | Chatham |
| *Decker, Floyd H.* | | *Hughes, Edward P.* | |
| Dial, John | Springfield | *Hunker, Vard F.* | |
| Dietz, Otto E. | Decatur | Inman, Charles E. | Mattoon |
| Dodd, Charles W. | Loami | Jackson, Homer E. | Decatur |
| Dunbar, Reuben A. | Moline | Jenkins, William E. | Decatur |
| Eastwood, Lyle E. | Towanda | Johnson, Bert | Chicago Heights |
| Emmerson, Clifford L. | Divernon | Jones, George | Peoria |
| Ermling, John | Wheaton | Kimball, Herschel S. | Ashmore |

| | |
|---|---|
| Kirschbaum, Theodore E. | Nauvoo |
| *Knight, Leonard* | |
| Knight, Richard | Bourbon |
| Knittle, Frank D. | Rock Island |
| *Krachik, Emil* | |
| Kreevick, Mat | Mt. Olive |
| Leary, Elston E. | Holder |
| Lempe, Carl L. | St. Louis, Missouri |
| Leonhard, Howard | Chicago |
| Lindstrom, Carl | Moline |
| Littlejohn, George | Divernon |
| Luckhart, Lorenz | Springfield |
| Maring, Nicholas E. | Rock Island |
| *Martin, Woodrow* | |
| McCarty, Frank | Jacksonville |
| McClure, Wayne O. | Bloomington |
| McGrew, Everett | Bloomington |
| McManus, Ernest L. | Peoria |
| McNeill, Charles H. | Bloomington |
| Melton, John | Springfield |
| Michael, Barnard | Springfield |
| Miller, Arthur W. | Bloomington |
| Milligan, William | Decatur |
| Mittershaw, Raymond | Thayer |
| *Moews, Henry M.* | |
| Moorhead, James | Belleville |
| *Mottershaw, Raymond* | |
| Motzer, Jerome A. | Moline |
| Muncy, Claude | Pawnee |
| *Nadler, Emanual* | |
| *Naylor, Charles D.* | |
| Nickols, James | Patterson |
| Novak, Theodore J. | Divernon |
| O'Neill, Samuel F. | Springfield |
| Patrick, Charles L. | Mattoon |
| *Patterson, Charles* | |
| Pickett, Stuart R. (KP) | Springfield |
| Plummer, Earl M. | Colchester |
| Powell, Charles W. | Springfield |
| Pristave, Joe | Springfield |
| Quigley, William/Joe | Pawnee |
| Reed, Earl W. | Pekin |
| Rees, Edwin | Thayer |
| Reinert, Frances | Aurora |
| Rice, Ivan E. | Anna |
| Richmond, William E. | Rock Island |
| Ridell, Clyde D. | Springfield |
| Riedinger, George/Anthony | Springfield |
| Roberts, Frank G. | Springfield |
| Rood, Oliver | Claire City |
| Ruckman, Lawrence E. (KP) | Bloomington |

| | |
|---|---|
| *Runkle, Hugh V.* | |
| Rupe, Holland A. | Palmyr |
| Sackfield, George A. | Rock Island |
| Sandstrom, Nestor C. | Bloomington |
| Schultz, Carl L. | Bloomington |
| *Sencenich, Thomas R.* | |
| Shaw, Orie T. | Mackinaw |
| Shelton, Earl | Belleville |
| Shields, Eugene | Pekin |
| Sigler, William F. | Heyworth |
| Simenella, Joseph | St. Louis, Missouri |
| Simmonds, Ralph | Belleville |
| Smith, Harry | Springfield |
| Smith, William D. | Springfield |
| *Snapp, George W. (first aid)* | |
| Snyder, John | Virden |
| Soloy, John R. | Thayer |
| Sprinkle, Francis G. | Springfield |
| Staley, Charles R. | Chatham |
| Stanley, George | Springfield |
| Sterkowicz, Joseph | Chicago |
| Stutts, Clyde | Belleville |
| Teehan, Charles A. | Rock Island |
| Thompson, Regis J. | West Homestead, Pennsylvania |
| Todd, Robert | Springfield |
| Townsend, Robert L. | Springfield |
| Tuntland, Everett H. (KP) | Buckingham |
| Tyrrell, Walter J. | Mackinaw |
| *Van Runkle, Hugh* | |
| Voliva, James R. | Alton |
| Walters, Harry | Alexander |
| Weinheimer, Harold | Springfield |
| Weinheimer, Wilferd | Springfield |
| White, Baxter | Donaldson |
| Wilson, Thomas T. | Pawnee |
| Winebrinner, William | Wayneville |
| Wisher, Lloyd G. | Moline |
| Wissehr, Arthur | Belleville |
| Zimmerman, Joseph W. | Sidell |

All enrollees were from Illinois unless otherwise stated. Names in italics indicate the enrollee served at Springfield but not at Makanda.

Sources: Floyd Finley, "Alphabetical Roster, 1657th Company CCC, Camp Springfield," June 28, 1933; list of names that accompany a company photo at Camp Stone Fort. Both appear in Giant City State Park Civilian Conservation Corps Collection, Special Collections Research Center, Morris Library, Southern Illinois Unvierstiy Carbondale.

# Appendix 3: Giant City State Park CCC Forestry Personnel and Their Salaries, March 1934

**SP-11**

| | |
|---|---|
| Albin F. Olson, Superintendent | $210 |
| Daniel Brewer, Landscape Foreman | 170 |
| Carrol C. Collier, Cultural Foreman | 170 |
| C. S. Harrell, Erosion Control Foreman | 170 |
| Carl Meyer, Cultural Foreman | 170 |
| Dudley Milburn, Landscape Foreman | 170 |
| A. J. Newlin, Landscape Foreman | 170 |
| Adolph Ruediger, Cultural Foreman | 170 |
| G. W. Thompson, Landscape Foreman | 170 |
| William Unger, Cultural Foreman | 170 |
| Floyd R. Boals, Cleanup Foreman | 150 |
| Charles Sanders, Tool Sharpener | 125 |

**SP-24**

| | |
|---|---|
| Frank N. Dalbey, Assistant Superintendent | 190 |
| Michael J. Howard, Landscape Foreman | 170 |
| J. G. Grant, Cultural Foreman | 160 |
| Edward W. Rupinski, Landscape Foreman | 160 |
| R. E. Kilgore, Cleanup Foreman | 155 |
| W. H. Allen, Miscellaneous/Construction Foreman | 150 |
| Lawrence C. Boyd, Miscellaneous/Construction Foreman | 150 |
| Amos Kelly, Cleanup Foreman | 150 |
| Joseph E. Kenyon, Cleanup Foreman | 150 |
| William Stuemke, Miscellaneous/Construction Foreman | 150 |
| Walter Dahl, Miscellaneous/Construction Foreman | 140 |
| Stanley O. Brooks, Machinist | 135 |
| Jason Lampley, Tool Keeper | 125 |

Source: William Hannon, Camp Inspection Reports, SP-11 and SP-24, March 12, 1934, RG 35, National Archives.

# Appendix 4: CCC Company #692 Roster

**UNITED STATES ARMY OFFICERS (AS OF MARCH 31, 1935)**

Edwin R. Morine, Captain, 579th FA, Commanding — Owosso, Michigan
George D. Markel, 1st Lt., Inf.-Res., Executive Officer — Rockford, Illinois
Jesse A. Bartlett, 2nd Lt., QM-Res., Exchange Officer — Mattoon, Illinois
Earl V. Bishop, MD, Contract Surgeon, Camp Surgeon — Belvidere, Illinois

**NATIONAL PARK SERVICE SUPERVISORY STAFF (AS OF MARCH 31, 1935)**

Adolph G. Ruediger, Project Superintendent — Belleville, Illinois
William H. Murphy, Senior Foreman — Decatur, Illinois
William Stuemke, Senior Foreman — Springfield, Illinois
F. P. Brown, Senior Foreman — Elgin, Illinois
Joseph A. Bangiolo, Foreman — Murphysboro, Illinois
Charles R. Collom, Foreman — Marissa, Illinois
Mark S. Greeley, Foreman — Bristol, Illinois
Elmer A. Klehm, Foreman — Arlington Heights, Illinois
Raymond Hamilton, Machinist — Edgemont, Illinois
George Oliver, Tool Keeper — Tilden, Illinois

## Enrollees

(representing mainly the period October 1934–summer 1935)

| | | | |
|---|---|---|---|
| Ainsworth, Everett | DeKalb | Calbrecht, Joe G. (Senior Foreman) | Moline |
| Akers, Frank T. | Jerseyville | Calvert, Raymond C. | Martinsville |
| Allen, John W. (Leader) | Effingham | Canerdy, Everett | Cobden |
| Allen, William T. | Fairfield | Cankar, John | Belleville |
| Anderson, Edward W. | Chicago | Cannady, Raymond E. | Belleville |
| Ankovitz, Lawrence | | Carlton, Walter | Peoria |
| Atteberry, Kensel R. | Jerseyville | Chambers, Paul E. (Assistant Leader) | Galesburg |
| Auer, Albert | Peoria | Chiesi, Albert | Spring Valley |
| Babbs, James H. | Newton | Christison, James A. | Winchester |
| Barke, Charles W. | Wenona | Clark, Melvin A. | Belleville |
| Bartol, Robert (Assistant Leader) | East St. Louis | Clouse, Gilbert M. | Belleville |
| Bartram, James D. | Peoria | Coan, Robert L. | Henry |
| Bayless, Frank | Peoria | Condie, Adam R. | Spring Valley |
| Benedict, George A. | Belleville | Corzine, Ray | Anna |
| Benn, George | Peoria | Cox, Earl A. | Peoria |
| Benson, Robert B. | Moline | Crawford, Eugene B. | Palestine |
| Bierbaum, Kenneth E. | Marshall | Crawford, Van C. | Flora |
| Billiter, Melvin R. | Litchfield | Crocker, John D. | Palestine |
| Binegar, Daniel A. | Peoria | Culbreth, Cecil V. | White Hall |
| Bloyd, Leslie | DeKalb | Cummins, Glenn | Oblong |
| Boers, Howard F. | Peoria | Curry, Robert A. | Neoga |
| Brewer, Veril (Assistant Leader) | Fairfield | Curtis, Arnold O. | Hamburg |
| Brissman, Grant W. | Rock Island | Davis, Charles L. | Effingham |
| Broadway, Paul | Hurst/Bush | Davis, Milford | |
| Brummett, Paul E. | Nokomis | Dennis, Theodore T. | Peoria |
| Bucanti, Frank | Spring Valley | DeSherlia, Adam H. | Grafton |
| Budisalich, Otmar E. | Peoria | De St. Jean, Elwin W. | Benld |
| Bugger, Clifford | Belleville | Dickey, Earl W. | Newton |
| Burke, Bertrum | Makanda | Doczy, John | Chicago |
| Burlison, John (Assistant Leader) | Goreville | Dunn, John L. | Carlinville |
| Burress, Floyd H. (Leader) | Palestine | Dunnigan, Kermit W. | Flora |
| Bush, George H. (Assistant Leader) | Dixon | Durbin, Steve A. | Nokomis |

| | | | |
|---|---|---|---|
| Eacho, Eugene I. | Belleville | Hunt, H. A. | Makanda |
| Erwin, Winnifred A. | Marshall | Jackson, Charlie E. | Makanda |
| Eubank, Robert F. | Peoria | Janesh, Philip J. | Nokomis |
| Evans, William H. | Winchester | Jeffrey, Kenneth W. (Assistant Leader) | Galena |
| Faeth, Dean (Leader) | Bible Grove | Jeffries, Harry (Assistant Leader) | Palestine |
| Fansler, Roy J. | Wayne City | Jenkins, Frederick W. | Flora |
| Faulkner, Paul E. | Fairfield | Johnson, Charles M. | Fidelity |
| (died of pneumonia while enrolled in CCC) | | Johnson, John | Jonesboro |
| Fellin, James A. | Gillespie | Johnson, Robert E. | Cairo |
| Fenwick, Kenneth S. | Mount Olive | Johnston, Ora E. | Peoria |
| Ferris, Warren I. (Assistant Leader) | Neoga | Jones, Irvin A. | Makanda |
| Fesler, Stanley | Makanda | Jones, Oliver F. (Leader) | Jonesboro |
| Fetsko, Joseph | Nokomis | Kays, John F. | Fairfield |
| Fiedler, Robert L. | Galena | Kays, Kenneth E. | Fairfield |
| Fiocchi, Charles A. (Leader) | Cherry | Keen, Glenn D. | Fairfield |
| Floyd, Harvey H. | Palestine | Kerkes, Mike, Jr. (Leader) | Virden |
| Forbes, Edward M. | Edwards | Kessler, Stanford B. | Nokomis |
| Fowler, Theodore J. | Jonesboro | Kidd, Leon W. | Virden |
| Fox, George R. | Girard | Kircher, Warren I. | Peoria |
| Freeman, Ralph D. | Casey | Kirk, Woodrow R. | Robinson |
| Frey, John G. | Girard | Kneipkamp, Wilfred A. | Belleville |
| Friel, James H. (Assistant Leader) | Amboy | Kollman, Frederick W. (Assistant Leader) | Galena |
| Fry, George F. | Carrollton | Kuegler, Jack | East St. Louis |
| Gaar, Delbert | Thompson | Kupryn, Joseph F. | Chicago |
| Gaffney, Joseph | Peoria | Kuse, George | O'Fallon |
| Gambo, Anthony M. | Standard | Lake, Joseph H. | Effingham |
| Genet, Philip | | Lambert, David E. | Robinson |
| Gerzema, Fred D. | Peoria | Lansberry, Max | Robinson |
| Glenn, Donald R. | Palestine | Leggans, Fred L. | Alto Pass |
| Glover, Glenn A. | Magnolia | Leonhard, Willard W. | Staunton |
| Goodwin, Raymond | Nokomis | Lewis, Delbert | Peoria |
| Grear, Ellis | Jonesboro | Lloyd, Norman P. | Robinson |
| Gregory, James R. | Fairfield | Long, William H. | Pleasant Hill |
| Grieves, George F. | Peoria | Lunn, Melvin W. | Spring Valley |
| Grimes, Porter F. | Beardstown | Malmberg, Benjamin E. | Moline |
| Guennewig, Frank H. (Assistant Leader) | Staunton | Mangum, Lawrence | Peoria |
| Guglielmetti, John | Standard | Manning, Marion A. | Wheeler |
| Guthrie, Roger | Marissa | Mantle, Elden | Belleville |
| Hamlet, John E. | Cairo | Manuel, Walton | Effingham |
| Hangsleben, Arthur | O'Fallon | Maples, Cloice M. (Leader) | Robinson |
| Harris, Dennis T. | Cobden | Marshall, Grant | Arlington Heights |
| Hartline, Edward | Cobden | Masilonus, Theodore A. | Spring Valley |
| Hayes, Charles E. | Robinson | Mason, Kenneth R. | Belleville |
| Healey, Paul J. | Peoria | Mastroianni, Vincent | Chicago |
| Henderson, Ernest | Olive Branch | Mathias, George A. | Mt. Olive |
| Herbert, William | Belleville | May, John (Assistant Leader) | Cherry |
| Hermanson, Carl H. | Peoria | Mayeski, Felix (Assistant Leader) | Spring Valley |
| Hileman, Ebert A. | Anna | McAdam, Walter D. (Assistant Leader) | Chicago |
| Hobbs, Junus L. (Leader) | East St. Louis | McAlister, Ralph D. | Elmwood |
| Hoffman, Anthony E. | Peoria | McBeth, Robert | Hillsboro |
| Holt, Harold E. | Beardstown | McFarland, James M. | Wheeler |
| Horth, John U. | Effingham | McHenry, Charles F. (Assistant Leader) | Flora |
| Hough, Frank W. | Flora | McNair, Raymond A. (Assistant Leader) | Palestine |
| Howe, Harold | Cisne | Mikolased, Adolph | Hillsboro |
| Hoyer, Howard (Assistant Leader) | Savanna | Milan, John S. | Greenup |
| Huling, Al L. | Peoria | Miller, Carl | Makanda |

**APPENDIX 4**

| | | | |
|---|---|---|---|
| Miller, Oda | Jacksonville | Sheaks, Ralph | Greenup |
| Mobley, Peter L. | McNabb | Shelton, Ray | Makanda |
| Moore, Carroll G. | Moline | Shields, Don F. | Flora |
| Moore, Eugene V. | Peoria | Shoemaker, Elmer H. | Peoria |
| Moore, Melvin W. | Fidelity | Short, Lowell | Makanda |
| Morris, Raymond D. | Galena | Skertich, Matthew J. | Gillespie |
| Morrison, Edward T. (Assistant Leader) | Cairo | Smith, Byrl A. | Robinson |
| Munden, William G. | Belleville | Smith, Elmer | Effingham |
| Murtaugh, Stephen C. | Amboy | Smith, Frank B. | Virden |
| Myers, John A. | Amboy | Smith, Glenn | Makanda |
| Nethercott, Robert | Murphysboro | Smith, James E. | Peoria |
| Nichols, Harvey L. | Cairo | Smith, Raymond H. | Amboy |
| Nickel, Emil S. | Peoria | Sprouse, Cletis | Makanda |
| Nunn, Howard | Meredosia | Stansbury, Lynn R. | Roodhouse |
| Ohl, Harold | Belleville | Stauss, Ernest G. | Galena |
| Oldham, Walter | Hopedale | Stewart, Guy O. | Robinson |
| Olszanowski, Sylvester | Spring Valley | Stewart, Walter M. | Greenup |
| Orlandi, Frank | Dalzell | Stieber, Thomas J. | Peoria |
| Otten, Walter | | Stokes, John | Goreville |
| Pacione, Chester J. | Cherry | Stompanato, Carmine | Savanna |
| Page, Louie E. | Alto Pass | Strange, Byrl (Assistant Leader) | Robinson |
| Parker, Alonzo | Anna | Stroupe, Darrell M. | Carlinville |
| Patton, Dennis E. | Neoga | Sutter, Clarence A. | Peoria |
| Pauley, Orrin (Assistant Leader) | Savanna | Teets, Kenneth C. | Palestine |
| Peck, Fred, Jr. | Belleville | Thomas, Everett N. | Jacksonville |
| Persich, Andrew | Peoria | Thompson, Robert | Peoria |
| Pettit, Harold A. | Magnolia | Thompson, Walter B. | Peoria |
| Phillips, Howard C. | Gale | Tidaback, Frank | Peoria |
| Phillips, Wayne | Mt. Carroll | Tieman, Willliam E. | Spring Valley |
| Pleasant, Maurice F. | Robinson | Towell, Wilbur | Peoria |
| Pozzi, Frank W. | Toluca | Tozzi, Nildo V. | Toluca |
| Price, Robert A. | Cairo | Tracy, Elmo G. | Robinson |
| Pudney, Robert C. | Peoria | Turcol, Tom | Benld |
| Purdum, James H. | Flora | Turner, Louie | Alto Pass |
| Raab, Henry | Belleville | Ulrey, Arthur L. | Westfield |
| Rabold, Chester R. | Peoria | Van Houten, LaVern | Peoria |
| Ramsey, Paul L. | Effingham | Vedell, William E. (Leader) | Peoria |
| Reck, John, Jr. | Hillsboro | Vick, Lyle J. | Warren |
| Reives, Leroy | Greenfield | Waitkus, Joe J. | Spring Valley |
| Rider, Ralph O. | Dongola | Wallock, Charles | Spring Valley |
| Roach, David F. | Warren | Walters, James H. | Martinsville |
| Robeen, Harold R. | Michael | Ware, Thomas J. | Virginia |
| Roberts, Hollie A. (Leader) | Anna | Wedlake, William G. | Dixon |
| Rogers, Walter | Makanda | Welty, John | Flora |
| Rose, Ralph | Anna | Wenger, Francis L. | Forrest |
| Rudolph, Dillon S. | Cairo | Westemeier, Arthur E. | Galena |
| Rupalities, John | Spring Valley | Wheaton, Donald R. | Amboy |
| Sage, Ira H. | Peoria | Whisman, Clay R. | Kampsville |
| Scariot, Premo | Hillsboro | White, George O. | White Hall |
| Schabatka, Acel | Peoria | White, Ralph B. | Peoria |
| Schilling, Earl | Belleville | Williams, Gene | Flora |
| Selski, John (Assistant Leader) | Spring Valley | Williams, Thomas L. | Greenup |
| Serby, Marvin | Sandwich | Willyerd, Everett | Jonesboro |
| Seyler, Richard M. (Leader) | Nashville | Wilson, Albert | Cache |
| Shaffner, Guy | Marshall | Woody, Carl M. | Effingham |
| Shaw, Gilbert K. | Flora | Wooldridge, Burland W. | Cairo |

Wys, Robert A.                              Peoria
Wyss, Ben J.                                Peoria
Yanites, John L. (Assistant Leader)         Spring Valley
York, Max F.                                Palestine
Young, Glen B.                              Fairfield
Youngblood, Lloyd W.                        Roodhouse
Yuna, John                                  Nokomis
Zilm, Henry G. (Assistant Leader)           La Rose
Zumwalt, Rhobie L.                          Hamburg

*Sources*: *Company D-692 Civilian Conservation Corps Camp, Stone Fort, DSP-1, Giant City State Park, Makanda, Illinois, Complete Company Roster for Fourth Enrollment Period, October 1, 1934–March 31, 1935*; *Stone-City Weekly*, August–September 1935; Earl Dickey interviews, July 26, 2002, and February 19, 2003; names on photo of Company D-692, Makanda, Illinois, 1935, in Mary J. Schueller, *Soldiers of Poverty*, (Richfield, WI: Rustic, 2006), 109–10.

Appendix 5: Stone-City Weekly, September 25, 1935

| CAMP STONEFORT 692 | STONE-CITY WEEKLY | CAMP GIANT CITY 696 |

VOL. I.  WEDNESDAY, SEPTEMBER 25, 1935  NO. 4

## Projects Completed on Schedule; Workmanship Superior

The projects outlined for state park eleven (Giant City Park), for the period ending September 30, have all been completed or will be completed at the end of the month with the exception of a few park signs and a small amount of guard rails for the park roads.

The unusually fine record made this quarter is due to the whole-hearted cooperation of everyone but it is especially due, according to Superintendent Ruediger, to the industry of the boys whose work for the period has exceeded expectations both in the quantity of work completed and the quality of the workmanship shown on the different jobs.

Skilled workmen are not lacking in the camps. Twenty of the boys who have been working with Mr. Stuemke are now able to go ahead with building construction without supervision using Southern Illinois sandstone as building material. Fifteen of the boys are accomplished carpenters on the rustic type of woodwork found in the park. Ten boys are experts on landscaping and planting, using native shrubs and plants, and five are capable of running survey, both lineal and topographic, on their own responsibility. More will be said about the training possibilities of the CCC camps in a later issue.

A part of the park, which should be better known, lies in the hollow east of Camp Stonefort and the ball diamond. The rustic foot bridges to be found there will make parts of the area easily accessible. The fireplace-type of shelter house in this valley is unusually well made. This area should appeal to those wishing a rather secluded picnic ground.

### VISITORS TO PARK INCREASE

Visitors to Giant City State Park on Sunday, September 15, numbered 1052. This was 235 more than Sunday, September 8. The passing of the summer months seems to make no difference in the number of visitors who are continually enjoying the beauty of Nature as displayed in the park.

As the leaves on the trees, vines and shrubs begin to display themselves in many shades of color, the entire Park takes on the atmosphere of some gala occasion. It is indeed a treat for the visitors and picnickers to see the high rocks seemingly clothed in multi-colored robes.

A hearty welcome is extended to all nature lovers to see the Park in its holiday attire.

## Places of Interest at Giant City Park

The story of Giant City and Stone Fort has appeared in the first three issues of Stone-City Weekly. In this issue the writer will describe briefly some of the park's beauty spots.

One of the most interesting spots is the "Devil's Stand Table." This table is a very peculiar rock formation protruding from the main bluff. It is a tall rock-like candle holder upon which is a large boulder, weighing at least fifty tons.

This rock looks as though it was placed there. It stands about three feet from the main bluff at a height of nearly one hundred feet, with lots of shrubs and trees growing below. One can easily jump from the main bluff to the "table."

Near this Devil's Stand Table is a natural ampi-theatre, located about one hundred feet north. This theatre is similar to a large stage extending about feet in the tall bluff. The rocks have fallen off in large slabs leaving a smooth surface representing the ceiling. These rocks were fallen by earthquakes many years ago.

Overhanging this theatre is a water fall which make the finest view of any place in the park. Shrubs, flowers, ferns and moss, all abound in this spot which is cared for by Mother Nature.

Following the trail onward we come to Hazard Stairs, a set of stairs carved into the sandstone bluff and winding upward. These stairs are well worth the time required to visit them.

To visit the places mentioned here, follow the trail leading north from Giant City picnic grounds. While following this trail one crosses the line adjoining Jackson and Union counties.

In next week's issue of the Stone-City Weekly the writer will tell of more places of interest to visit at Giant City Park.

## CCC Quota Unfilled

Prosperity is back! Nothing shows this more clearly than the enrollment records of the CCC. For the first time in the history of the Corps there is a shortage of applicants. In Illinois, while the quota allowed is 38,300, the present strength is only 22,661. In the entire United States the quota allowed is 600,000 and the present strength is but 430,000 enrollees.

This is due to two major reasons. One is the opening up of thousands of Federally sponsored jobs for the youth of the nation, and the other is the new ruling that only boys from relief families are eligible for CCC enrollment.

## We Need Your Help

It has been our intention to give you absolutely free each issue of the STONE-CITY WEEKLY. This policy has been made possible by the selling of advertising space in our paper. We now find it increasingly difficult to sell our ads at the rate we charge.

As many of you are aware the publication costs of your newspaper is eighteen dollars ($18.00) a week—seventy-two dollars (72) a month. To continue publishing your paper it is now necessary to ask you to subscribe for it. The subscription rate is ten cents for one month for four issues.

Payment of the ten cents will be made on pay day of each month beginning with the September pay day. If you like and want your little paper please help continue it by giving your pledge to subscribe.

Ten cents will mean just one less drink or just a few cigarettes less. In return for this small sacrifice on your part you will be given four issues of your Camp newspaper.

Won't you and your buddy "spare a dime."

### PARK GUESTS

Sunday visitors at Giant City Park were not as many as usual owing to the chilly air and threatening clouds overhead. There were around 500 visitors Sunday, September 8th.

Gerald Helm, former member of Company 696 was a visitor at Giant City Park Sunday. He was accompanied by Margrie Errit, Gladys Helm and Franklin Chrystman, all of Vandalia, Illinois.

Adam R. Condie of Spring Valley, left camp last Wednesday on a transfer from CCC Co. 692 to CCC Co. 1609, located at Starved Rock, Illinois.

Mrs. Koons, shorthand and typing teacher of Co. 696 and Miss Jewell Ferrill of Carbondale were among the park visitors Sunday.

Miss Niama Gore of Harrisburg and Mrs. Leota McFaddin of Carterville were park visitors Sunday. Miss Gore will spend the week with her aunt, Mrs. Charles Gore of Giant City Park.

Lieutenant Adams has returned from Oregon, Wisconsin where he was called by the last illness and death of his mother. The Stone-City Weekly joins Camps 692 and 696 in extending their sympathy to Lieutenant Adams in his irreparable loss.

## Improvements Library Circulation 300 Per Cent

By observing closely the number of boys entering the library it will not be surprising to realize it is fast becoming the most popular spot in camp.

It is easy to understand the reason for this increased popularity when one notes the vast and almost unbelieveable improvement over what was formerly considered the library. From what was considered a drab and uninteresting room, a delightful room has emerged. The ceiling and upper wall of cream and the lower walls of green blend nicely with the natural color of the tables and book racks. The walls and ceiling furnish an excellent background for the clean and neat arrangement of the furniture and book racks.

It is interesting to note that a new filing system has been initiated. This is a great time-saver in that each book has a definite place which gives the shelves a neat and uniform appearance. The shelves are open so that anyone may examine the books before he checks one out.

With such improvements as have been made, plus the additional comfort of new lighting fixtures and smoking stands, the 300 per cent increase in circulation of various magazines is understandable. This increase itself speaks for the worthiness of the improvements.

## Park Vistor Badly Stung by Bees

Sunday, September 8th the little son of Mr. and Mrs. W. B. Lewis of Harrisburg was badly stung by yellow jackets. The parents, with their small son, was following a trail near the scenic Doodle Bug Town. The child, however, stepped out of the trail, stirred the bees and they became furious. Before the child could be taken from the mad bees he received ten stings. He completed his trip onward and after arriving at the picnic grounds was taken to the Camp Infirmary at Co. 696. There he received first aid which helped to cease the burning caused by the yellow jackets.

Mr. and Mrs. Lewis were very interested in the work being done in Giant City Park by the boys of Companies 696 and 692.

Mr. and Mrs. Lewis, accompanied by a group from Harrisburg were escorted through the Lodge and Stone Fort by Charles Gore, park custodian, and Charles Triplett, the park guide.

# STONE-CITY WEEKLY

## THE STAFF

EDITOR-IN-CHIEF, 692................................CARL WOODY
EDITOR-IN-CHIEF, 696................CHARLES TRIPLETT
FEATURE EDITOR..............................PHILIP SMITH
NEWS EDITOR..................................FRED GERZEMA
SPORT EDITOR....................................TONY GHERRA
SPORTS EDITOR............................RAYMOND McNAIR
ASSISTANT SPORTS EDITOR................CHARLES GRUBER
BUSINESS MANAGER................................JOE JINES
ASSISTANT BUSINESS MANAGER........DICK POLONOWSKI
ASSISTANT BUSINESS MANAGER................PAT LIPTON
ADVISORS............MR. EDDY, MR. BRADLEY, MR. DUNSMORE

### SPECIAL WRITERS
LEVIE MILLER, ANDREW PERSICH, WAYNE PHILLIPS,
JOHN RADER, VERNON STANLEY, ROSS LINDHORST.

### REPORTERS
JOE CALBRECHT, FRED KOLLMAN, JAMES WHALEN,
CHAPMAN.

## NOT DRILLS BUT EXERCISES

Not so long ago Captain Thorman, Commanding Officer of Company 696, instituted retreat and we were given a few lessons in squad drills. We wish to take this opportunity to tell the public that we are not being trained for war but only learning to stand to attention, ease and do a few drills which are good exercises.

Lt. Mathews was at Carbondale recently and while there was asked by a man if we were to receive guns before long. Lt. Mathews didn't scarcely know what his questioner meant until he mentioned that the boys were drilled like soldiers.

We are not, so do not believe all you hear. Rumors generally prove to be merely rumors.

## BARRACKS CHIT-CHAT

Of late Joseph Bangiolo has acquired an aversion for felines. Why? He mistook a skunk for a cat.

Pat Murphy, state foreman, is quite a jokester. The other night he scared the state men half out of their wits by tossing fire buckets upon the roof of their barracks.

Mose Hams, second cook at Giant City Camp, seems very popular. Wednesday evenng a carload of girls came here looking for him.

Ralph O. Rider, Jack Dunn, and Fanny Fansler, all of 692, seem to be faring quite well on their gruel diet.

Well, they insisted on having their molars extracted.

John L. Dunn, 692, after submitting to the ridicule of being called a "toothless ole grandpaw," declares that he will now cut quite a figure with the fairer sex since the purchase of his new false teeth.

We have a very fine nurse maid in 696. The chap was seen at a particular place attending the children during a mother's absence.

The boy is known locally as "Fire Chief." Incidentally, we don't mean Mr. Wynn.

Since Veril Brewer, second cook of 692, has clipped all of his hair off he looks and acts like a "tuff guy." He now bears the title of the C Barracks Bully.

Slick "Schnoszola" Wedlake Company 692, thought he was clever until he tried to skip K. P. But his Schnozle got in the way so he still goes over and does his evening chores.

It is thought that Herbert Yates, 692 rookie, should go out for track. It is known that he dashed back to 692 from the fights Thursday night to get his address for his newly found inspiration. He gave it to her for her to write him. T'is best to keep envelopes for ready reference.

Carl Hiller, 696, wanted to know if 692 has cameras to check out. Wonder if he would want them to furnish films to go with them?

The Senior Foreman seems to get a kick out of one of the first cook's new hair cut.

## NEWS ITEMS OF INTEREST

Seven boys from 692 who have been studying under the capable camp Physician, Dr. Bishop, have received their first aid certificates.

These boys feel able to take care of minor injuries by themselves and to give first aid treatment on the job in all injuries. These boys are: Chas. E. Baker, Arthur A. Martin, John H. Betts, Carl Willard, Robert R. Willard, John T. Winkleman, and James B. Osborn.

John "Yugs" Yanites and Frank Pozzie of 692, received their honorable discharge Tuesday. They left camp to accept employment at Spring Valley.

Monthly motion pictures started Tuesday at 692. These pictures are under the auspices of the National Park Service whose offices are in Indianapolis, Ind. George Payne, the operator, opened his monthly shows at 692 with three reels of Daniel Boone, two reels of a Couger Hunt and a Mickey Mouse comedy entitled the Haunted Ship.

We of the Stone-City Weekly staff, regret the goodbyes we gave Reporter Jimmy Whalen of 692 upon receiving his discharge from camp Monday, Sept. 16. He expects to accept employment at Marion. At the same time we welcome Chas. "Bake" Baker who is replacing the vacancy made by Jimmy, to our staff.

### ALAS! NO INFIRMARY

Several days ago a few of the boys of 692 were playing catch in the company street. A missed ball struck one of the company's pets, Ish Kabible. The poor dog, moaning piteously, dragged itself to shelter under the mess hall. The dog glanced once at the infirmary as if imploring aid, but seeing the rocks stacked underneath, knew it was useless. It is believed that a special ward should be placed for the pets of 692.

Van Clea Crawford of 692 was taken to the Base Hospital at Jefferson Barracks, Mo. to undergo an operation for a rupture.

The winter issue, according to Dean Faeth, 692 storekeeper, will be sent to the cleaners this week to be cleaned and issued within the next thirty days.

Lt. Geo. D. Markel, commanding officer of 692, returned late last night from a nine day furlough to his home at Rockford, Ill. Lt. Markel stopped at Fort Sheridan to visit Capt. Edwin R. Morine, 692's former C. O. Capt. Morine sent his best wishes and regards to the entire personnel of 692.

## WEE ONE-DER

Why Porter Leslie stopped going to Carterville every other night?

Why Duck Drake gave up two stripes and went on the road?

Why Will Baker doesn't go in for "Cab Calloway, the second"?

Why the mess steward loiters around the 696 kitchen at night?

If Stecher is getting enough to eat lately?

Why Little Caesar rides in on the milk truck?

What Allbright goes in to town after every night?

Why George Whittaker loves "Dowell Town"?

Who will be on the '35 basketball team?

Why Joe Jines is sometimes called "sweet-lips"?

Why does Kenneth (Scrap-iron) Parris journey with hair so sleek and clothes so clean to Makanda every night?

Who J. M. McFarland sees three nights a week in Murphysboro?

Is that wedding or cow bells we hear over yon hill?

Why "Powerhouse" Magnum challenged "Tuff Guy" Brewer to a grudge fight?

What is the magnetic attraction that draws Ralph (Uncle Ralph) Freeman to Water Valley every Sunday?

Who is the siren that lured Hally Roberts to Anna last Tuesday and Thursday?

What is the identity of the person or persons who are giving 692 the wonderful advertising it is receiving among the girls in Anna? But isn't it expensive to buy ale for the lasses to quaff?

How a certain truck driver felt a week ago Saturday night. Just as the trucks started back to camp his lady friends gathered to watch him gracefully drive away ration truck number 268. Imagine his consternation when the motor died and it was necessary to tow his truck into camp.

If it's true that Veril Brewer promised to buy the Murphysboro girls beer if they would call him Assistant Leader Veril instead of just Brewer?

Why John Betts, 692, "B" barracks, is known to have the loudest mouth in the camp?

Who Pearl is whom Estel Jackson, 692, talks about in his sleep?

Who the gallant gentlemen of 692 were that kicked a hole through the door of "B" barracks and later marched up to the stringer and admitted it so that the whole barracks wouldn't be confined to camp?

If Herbert Klinck and Virgil Ward, 692, will go out for football this season?

# SPORTS NEWS

## Sparta Wins Sub-District No. 2 Championship

On Thursday, September 19, Camp Giant City and Camp Sparta locked horns to decide the championship of Sub-District No. Two. The two teams were tied for first place, each having 13 wins against two losses. The game was played on the Anna State Hospital diamond.

In this crucial game Camp Giant City was defeated by a score of 6 to 1. Sparta enjoyed a 6 to 1 lead in the sixth inning. They then held the Giant City team to three hits for the rest of the game.

| Sparta | AB | H | R | E |
|---|---|---|---|---|
| Davis, 1b | 4 | 2 | 1 | 0 |
| Stefani, 2 b | 5 | 3 | 0 | 0 |
| Geerearts, cf | 3 | 1 | 1 | 0 |
| Allen c | 5 | 2 | 0 | 0 |
| Diangelo, lf | 5 | 0 | 0 | 0 |
| Stimac, p | 4 | 1 | 1 | 0 |
| Magdich, ss | 5 | 0 | 1 | 7 |
| Metcalf, rf | 5 | 0 | 0 | 0 |
| Lewis, 3b | 4 | 1 | 2 | 0 |
| *Goyack | 1 | 0 | 0 | 0 |

*Batted for Geerearts in eighth.

| Giant City | AB | H | R | E |
|---|---|---|---|---|
| Sims, ss | 4 | 0 | 0 | 3 |
| Crisler, rf | 4 | 0 | 0 | 2 |
| Baker, cf | 4 | 1 | 0 | 0 |
| Vancil, c | 4 | 1 | 0 | 1 |
| Jines, 3b | 2 | 0 | 1 | 1 |
| Nicholson, lf | 3 | 1 | 0 | 0 |
| Drake, 2b | 2 | 1 | 0 | 0 |
| D. Polonowski, 1b | 3 | 2 | 0 | 2 |
| C. Polonowski, p | 2 | 0 | 0 | 0 |
| P. Julius, p | 1 | 0 | 0 | 0 |

|  | R | H | E |
|---|---|---|---|
| Sparta ......000 110 040 | 6 | 10 | 1 |
| Giant City 000 000 100—1 | 6 | 9 | |

Winning pitcher, Stimac; losing pitcher, C. Polonowski. Two base hits, Baker; three base hits, Stimac; home runs, none; strike outs, Stimac 18, C. Polonowski 10, P. Julius 1; base off balls, Stimac 2, C. Polonowski 1, P. Julius 1.

### CORRECTIONS

The name of Adolph G. Ruediger, project superintendent was omitted from the Camp staff in the issue of last week. Mr. Ruediger has been at his present post for the past twenty-seven months.

Arnel B. Adams, Assistant Sub-District Commander is a First Lieutenant, Quartermaster Reserve.

## Murphy Defeated 6-5, G. City in 2nd Place in League

Chances of winning the District baseball league looked somewhat brighter Sunday when the local boys defeated Murphysboro in a hard fought battle by a score of 6 to 5.

Murphysboro led 3 to 1 until the seventh inning when a four-run rally put the Giant City boys out in front 5 to 3. Nicholson started the fireworks by doubling to center. Baker, next man up, got on by an error and both runners advanced on Drake's hot grounder to short. D. Polonowski, first baseman, hit the first ball pitched to deep left field. It was good for a triple and tied up the game.

C. Polonowski struck out for the second out. Sims, lead off man, walked and Chrisler, the next hitter, singled through short, scoring two runs. Jones then grounded out to retire the side.

C. Polonowski held the Murphysboro boys until the ninth when two runs were pushed across, but Shepard, Murphysboro's catcher, hit into a fast double play to end the game. Polonowski, newly acquired twirler, showed good form by allowing six hits and striking out seven. He also starred at the plate by getting a single and a triple.

Krisfaluzy did the stick work for Murphysboro by tripling in the ninth, driving in four of Murphysboro' runs.

The results of the game put Giant City in second place in the Second Sub-District Baseball league and will result in a play-off if Sparta loses to Camp Delta. Results of the game were as follows:

### Score by Innings

|  | 1 | 2 | 3 | 4 | 5 | 6 | 7 | 8 | 9 |
|---|---|---|---|---|---|---|---|---|---|
| Murphy | 0 | 1 | 0 | 2 | 0 | 0 | 0 | 0 | 2 |
| G. City | 0 | 1 | 0 | 0 | 0 | 0 | 4 | 1 | x |

Two base hits, Nicholson. Hudson; three base hits, D. Polonowski, C. Polonowski; losing pitcher, Abbott.

New signs have been placed in the Park prohibiting hunting and trapping. The signs are about 12 by fourteen inches and are of metal. They were erected by Charles Triplett.

## Camp Mounds Trims Giant City 3-0

On Sunday, September 8. Camp Giant City was the recipient of a crushing defeat by Camp Mounds to the tune of a 3-0 score. Had Giant City have won the team would have had a chance to play Sparta for the championship of the Twenty-Second Sub-District, the winner of which will compete for a trip to Chicago.

Giant City's route by Mounds was a complete upset. The Mounds team got to the Giant City pitcher, Costa, in the second inning and outplayed Giant City thence forward. Up to this game Costa had pitched winning ball all season. Julius was sent in to try and save the game but his entrance was too late.

By losing this game Giant City was virtually eliminated from the championship race. The Mounds pitcher held the Giant City team to four hits. He pitched splendid ball from start to finish, allowing only one runner, Baker, to reach third base. Baker, outfielder, stole from first to second to third base.

Mounds secured three runs on five hits—enough to cinch the game. Giant City struck out consistently. Julius, relief pitcher, held Mounds to two hits in seven innings.

The attendance was less than 200.

### Summary:

| Giant City | AB | R | H | E | PO |
|---|---|---|---|---|---|
| Jines, 3b. | 4 | 0 | 0 | 0 | 3 |
| Drake, 2b. | 3 | 0 | 0 | 0 | 5 |
| Sims, ss. | 3 | 0 | 0 | 0 | 2 |
| Vancil, c. | 3 | 0 | 1 | 0 | 6 |
| Polonowski, 1b. | 2 | 0 | 0 | 0 | 12 |
| Crisler, rf. | 3 | 0 | 1 | 0 | 0 |
| Nicholson, lf. | 3 | 0 | 1 | 1 | 2 |
| Baker, cf. | 3 | 0 | 1 | 0 | 1 |
| Costa, p. | 0 | 0 | 0 | 0 | 0 |
| Julius, p. | 3 | 0 | 0 | 0 | 2 |
|  | 28 | 0 | 4 | 1 | 34 |

Polonowski batted for Drake in ninth.

| Mounds | AB | R | H | E | PO |
|---|---|---|---|---|---|
| Biance, 2b. | 4 | 0 | 0 | 0 | 1 |
| Bell, ss. | 4 | 0 | 1 | 1 | 2 |
| Paveletich, lf. | 3 | 0 | 0 | 0 | 2 |
| Funk, p. | 4 | 0 | 1 | 0 | 4 |
| Kasnar, c. | 3 | 0 | 0 | 0 | 8 |
| McDowell, 1b. | 4 | 1 | 1 | 0 | 10 |
| Zajc, 3b. | 3 | 1 | 2 | 0 | 2 |
| Bruna, cf. | 2 | 1 | 1 | 0 | 2 |
| Melton, rf. | 3 | 0 | 1 | 0 | 1 |
|  | 30 | 3 | 7 | 1 | 32 |

|  | R | H | E |
|---|---|---|---|
| Giant City | 0 | 4 | 1 |
| Mounds | 3 | 7 | 1 |

## Clothes Make The CCC Boy

The Army uses the acme of simplicity in fitting uniforms to the CCC boy. There are only two sizes officially recognized by the quartermaster tailors—large and larger.

The shirts begin with size seventeen and go upward and outward. They resemble overcoats rather than shirts. One rookie ran his head through the sleeve recently and was none the wiser.

The breeches, too, are built in the same august fashion. It is rumored that one enrollee got lost in his breeches and was thirty minutes finding a way out of the woolen labyrinth.

And so through the outfit! Raincoats would make rather leaky tents. Caps are made only for men with Gargantuan heads. Shoes are composed of whole steer hides. "Feet" Kosma created quite a sensation in camp by once compadining of a shoe pinching his foot.

The only things that fit are the neckties and shoe-strings. The neckties are wrapped about the neck three times before tying. The strings are laced up the shoes, back down the shoes and looped six times quite loosely about the ankles.

The enrollee, dressd in his new-issue clothes, can only be describep as an overloaded clothes drape. Giant scarecrows in comparison appear better turned out.

To all outcries against this crass indifference to size as practiced by the Army the Supply Sergeant's reply is "the CCC camps breed men!"

### CAT LOSES ALL NINE LIVES

Judge Lt. Markel passed the death sentence upon a cat recently. The execution was administered under the able hands of Dr. Bishop. In lieu of the customary rope a liberal amount of ether was used as an agent of destruction.

The remains were claimed by Robert Fielder and funeral services and interment were conducted under his full charge.

# Appendix 6: CCC Company #696 Roster from 1937 Official Annual

**COMPANY # 696 COMMANDING OFFICERS**

Major (then Capt.) Walter S. Wood
Capt. (then Lieut.) Walter Urbach
Capt. Arnel B. Adams
Capt. Ben Thorman
Capt. Harold H. Capers

**COMPANY # 696 TECHNICAL PERSONNEL**

Biggs, J. J. (Superintendent)
Denny, R. H.
Hirschenberger, M. J.
Roehl, A. E.
Sanders, C.
Brewer, D. H.
Newlin, A. J.
Meyer, C. F.

---

## Enrollees

Alexander, George (waiter)
Allen, G.
Anderson, Albert (carpenter)
Angleton, Harley
Baker, William
Ball, S.
Baltimore, B.
Barker, William (construction)
Barr, John
Beaver, C.
Benefield, K.
Bennett, Fred H.
Berry, C.
Berry, Vernon (carpenter)
Biggs., Vern
Bishop, D.
Bittle, D.
Blaase, Donald S.
Blessing, F.
Blessing, Jack (carpenter-musician)
Boals, Floyd R.
Bodcker, William
Bodkin, Oscar
Bradley, Edward (carpenter)
Bradley, Gilbert
Bradley, R.
Bradley, W.
Bradshaw, A.
Brandon, Woodrow W.
Brooks, James
Burke, Bertrum
Burnett, Kenneth J.
Burns, C.
Callis, W.
Campbell, J.
Campbell, V.
Carroll, T.
Caterino, Vincent (rock mason)
Cauble, H.
Chapman, Leon (cook)

Cheek, C.
Claxton, Lee
Clayton, John
Cook, E.
Corbett, W.
Costa, E.
Cover, John
Cox, Clinton (carpenter)
Coy, R.
Crisler, Ellis (electrical worker)
Cronin, Louis
Crowe, Everett
Davidson, R.
Davis, Kenneth (rock mason)
Davison, Dale
Dial, Lewis (auto-service)
Dudas, S.
Dunlap, Alex (cook)
Dunlap, Sandy
Dunn, L.
Dunning, A.
Fairhart, Brandon E.
Edwards, Bob (laborer)
Eschmann, Robert (waiter)
Eubanks, L.
Evans, M.
Farthing, Stanley
Finley, Floyd T.
Fiocchi, Charles
Fitz, J.
Fortner, Bill
Foster, James (truck driver)
Frazier, Barto
Fries, R.
Fuiten, Charles H.
Furlow, Raymond
Gerl, Edward (blacksmith)
Godsil, James (musician, waiter)
Gottschammer, Art
Gould, G.

Griffin, Russell (auto-mechanic)
Griggs, M.
Guenther, Clifford J. (carpenter)
Hagler, Carl
Harmon, Harold (auto-mechanic)
Harris, George
Harris, Joseph
Harrison, Otis
Hawk, Kenneth
Hazelwood, H.
Heater, T.
Helms, Gerald
Henderson, D.
Hicks, Authanile
Hileman, H.
Hindman, T.
Hobbs, W.
Hogan, T.
Holbrook, Adrian
Hood, Eugene
Humm, Boniface
Humm, Christopher
Humm, Joseph
Humme, Lewis
Johnson, W.
Jones, D.
Kendrick, J.
Kirsh, Joe
Koros, J.
Krisfalusy, S.
Lamb, Jim
Lauder, G.
Lawrence, Waldo
Lence, W.
Leonard, D.
Leonhard Howard O.
Lester, Johnson
Lezu, S.
Lindhurst, Ross (forester-nursery man)
Lindsey, Albert (truck-driver, barber)

Lindsey, Everett
Long, C.
Lucas, W.
Lyster, M. D.
Malone, M.
Martin, John (blacksmith)
Mathias, Victor (carpenter)
Matlock, W.
McCandless, Lyle D.
McDaniel, L.
McGhee, W.
Miller, Howard (carpenter)
Miller, W.
Mills, R.
Mitchell, Edward (tool man)
Mitchell, Eugene
Morefield, J.
Morgan, E.
Morgan, William
Morphis, Cliff
Mowery, Frank
Myers, R.
Myers, Townsend (truck-driver)
Nethercott, Robert (construction, photography)
Newlon, D.
Ossig, Roy (rock mason, waiter)
Padgett, L. (first aid, musician)
Patterson, Stanley (truck driver)
Pearce, C.
Penrod, Ronald (rock mason)
Peterson, E.
Pinkston, Conway

Pledger, M.
Polonowski, A.
Pulcher, Gilbert (carpenter)
Rayle, Lynn Sr.
Raynor, George
Reames, Alvin (rock mason)
Rendleman, Donald (rock mason)
Reynolds, J.
Rice, Ivan
Richmond, Hubert (laborer)
Rix, Harold
Robinson, R.
Rodgers, Fred (rock mason)
Ross, Harry (truck driver)
Rowatt, V.
Rumsey, Lester
Rushing, C.
Salvo, Angelo (rock mason)
Sanders, C.
Sanders, F.
Sauls, Goa
Sawin, Francis (caterpillar tractor man)
Schnaare, Raymond
Schwall, Ray
Scott, Elmer T.
Scott, H.
Simmons, Harold (rock mason)
Simpson, Paul (plumber-welder)
Sims, W.
Skertich, Matthew J.
Slack, Arthur (mechanic)
Smiley, Thomas (janitor)
Smith, W.

Stanley, Kenneth (waiter, cook)
Stanley, Troy (rock mason)
Stecher, Rudolph (rock mason)
Stokes, W.
Stutz, Lloyd
Sumner, Howard (laborer)
Sumner, Walter
Sweazy, Ralph (truck driver)
Thomas, D.
Tinsley, E.
Toler, A.
Treece, Ray
Triplett, Charles (rock mason, photographer)
Watson, H.
Westbrooks, A.
White, Weldon (waiter, musician)
Whitecotton, D.
Wilmoth, J.
Wrench, Harry M.
Wright, James
Yancy, L.
Youngblood, E.
Zimmerman, C.

Sources: *Official Annual: Civilian Conservation Corps, Jefferson Barracks CCC District, Sixth Corps Area, 1937* (U.S. Government). *Giant City News*, September 15, 1937. The names with a CCC job in parentheses are those men who left Camp Giant City to look for work in September 1937.

# Appendix 7: Company #696, CCC Camp Giant City, SP-11, Makanda, Illinois, February 27, 1940

**COMPANY # 696 OFFICERS**

William G. Lefferts, Company Commander
Arthur W. Fox, Subaltern
Dr. Ellis R. Crandle, Civilian Physician
Ernest Plambeck, Camp Educational Advisor
Thomas P. Bermingham, Area Chaplain

**PROJECT STAFF**

Stirling [Sterling] S. Jones, Project Superintendent
Sumner M. Anderson, Geologist
Carl F. Meyer, Engineer
Arnold E. Roehl, Landscape Architect
Andrew J. Newlin, Foreman
William L. Perker, Foreman
Floyd R. Boals, Mechanic
Charles Sanders, Toolkeeper

*Enrollees*

Aaron, James L.
Akin, John R.
Allen, Martin D.
Anderson, Escol E.
Anneuser, John L.
Ashley, Eugene T.
Atkinson, Wayne
Banaszek, Felix
Bayers, Henry J. (Commissary Clerk)
Bidwell, Logan J.
Bird, Robert E.
Blair, Chas. K.
Blus, Frank S.
Boner, Harlen H.
Bowman, Howard
Burbes, Wm. E. (Radio Operator)
Burch, Robert
Burnett, Kenneth J. (Assistant Leader/ Baker)
Byer, Virgil J.
Cantrell, Neil M. (Assistant Leader)
Carlisle, Wayne P.
Casper, Adolphus L.
Casper, James F.
Cerny, Robert E.
Cheek, George R.
Clark, Harry L.
Clemens, John M.
Clevenger, Noble L.
Coleman, Paul A.
Congleton, Fred R.
Connelly, Eugene C.
Cox, Clinton, P. A. (Leader)
Cox, Glenn C.
Craft, Alvin S.
Craig, Paul M.
Crain, Robert J.
Crain, Woodrow P.
Crider, Franklin T.

Cropper, Herbert M.
Curattalo, James C.
Daffron, James O.
Dardeen, Wilfred H.
Davison, Allen D.
De Giacinto, Bruno (Leader/Mess Std.)
De Rouse, Joseph J.
Deaton, Kenneth
Dorsey, Dale H.
Dudas, William (Assistant Leader/ 2nd Cook)
Duncan, Wayne H.
Edmonds, Manly G.
Evans, Meredith S.
Fillback, Robert H.
Finley, Robert E.
Fisher, Kenneth R.
Fitz, Joseph, P.A. (Leader/Clerk)
Forsec, Robert N.
Fowler, Edward J.
Fowler, Joseph D.
Frazee, Martin R.
Frazier, Barto
Friedline, Robert N.
Fultz, Earl H.
Fultz, Forest E.
George, Dwight J.
Goodwin, Jean L.
Gottschammer, Arthur C.
Haffley, Joe W.
Hagler, Carl I. (Leader/Cabinet Maker)
Hall, Andrew N.
Hancock, Ralph R. (Inspection Clerk)
Hansil, Joseph J.
Harmon, Harold F. (Mechanic/ Leader)
Harrell, Armand V.

Harrell, Clemouth
Harrell, Edwin
Harris, Joseph W.
Harris, Wm. E. (Leader)
Harrison, Otis G.
Helvey, Raymond L.
Henard, James R.
Henderson, Ben F.
Herron, Robert W.
Higginbotham, Roy
Higginson, James M.
Hill, Charles E.
Hill, Christopher H.
Hines, Loren W.
Hodges, Thomas F. (Assistant Leader/ 2nd Cook)
Hood, Allen L. (Bugler)
Hood, Eugene W.
Hope, Julius T. (Assistant Leader)
Hougland, Murel D.
Humm, Boniface (Leader/1st Cook)
Irwin, John C.
Johnson, Dalton R.
Johnson, William W. (Leader/1st Cook)
Jones, Allen L.
Juenger, Russel H.
Keller, Clyde J.
Kimmel, Leroy C.
Lacy, Robert D.
Lacy, William C.
Lawrence, Waldo L. (Assistant Leader)
Layton, Morris E. (Assistant Leader)
Lence, Dennis E.
Lence, Robert L.
Lentz, William
Lindsey, Arthur J.
Litton, Willie

Lowry, Delmar L.
Maxwell, Howard
McBride, Joe L.
McCollum, Franklin L.
McDonald, Walter H. (Assistant
    Leader/Supply)
McRaven, Benj. F.
Melton, Melvin F.
Mercer, Lawrence D.
Miles, Otis H.
Miller, Harold C.
Mills, Fred H. (Leader/Company
    Clerk)
Mines, Norman O.
Mistoler, Louis
Mitchell, Anthony P.
Montgomery, Chas. L.
Murphy, Logan T.
Neber, William E. (Army Night
    Guard)
Nederbrook, Roy C.
Needles, Jack D.
Nickens, Kenneth E.
O Bryan, John W.
Odum, Glen W.
Owen, Dale
Owen, Wm. E.
Owens, Everett E.
Owens, Richard C.
Pace, Robert M.
Paris, F. (Assistant Army Clerk)
Parker, Edward L.
Parker, Louis C.
Patton, George E.

Payne, Robert (Bathhouse)
Pelker, Raymond J.
Perkey, Louis L.
Pflasterer, Philip J.
Pierce, Willis J.
Prewitt, Ralph
Purdue, Dewey C.
Queen, Charles H.
Queen, Thomas A.
Raines, Oscar L. (Officers' Orderly)
Raymond, Johnny
Reed, Edgar Jr.
Reidelberger, Melvin
Renaud, Marceau
Riley, Don A.
Roberts, Winton L.
Robertson, Almond V. ( SeniorLeader)
Robertson, Oran A.
Rodgers, E. G. (Assistant 1st Aid
    Orderly)
Rogers, Elmer C.
Ross, Bertram W.
Rumsey, Lester E.
Rushing, Harlis, Jr.
Saksa, Vincent J.
Satterfield, John W.
Segafredo, Rico M. (Assistant Leader)
Shockley, Roy D. (Assistant N.P.S.
    Clerk)
Shoemaker, Frederick D. (Assistant
    Leader/Carpenter)
Shubert, Raymond H.
Slaby, Wm. G.
Smith, Houston R.

Sprinkle, Robert L.
Stewart, John O.
Stone, Robert C.
Stotts, Wm. W.
Sumner, James W.
Taylor Wm. L. Jr.
Taylor, Milburn C. (Assistant Leader/
    Canteen)
Terry, Lewis
Thomson, Clifford L.
Tiindall, John J. (Assistant Leader)
Tindall, J. H. (Official Car Driver)
Treece, John R. (Assistant Leader/
    Truck Driver)
Treece, Ray W.
Turner, James R.
Turner, Paul H. (Assistant Leader/
    First Aid)
Venegoni, Louie
Webb, Hollie
Webb, Travis, Jr.
Wilson, Carrol L. (Assistant Leader/
    Assistant Ed. Adv.)
Woodbridge, Charles R. (Mainte-
    nance)
Wrolen, George H.
Yates, John W. ( Assistant Leader)

Source: Taken from photo composite
of entire company, "696th Company
CCC Camp Giant City, SP-11 (Ill.)
Makanda, Illinois." Photo by Spencer
and Wyck, Detroit, Michigan, February 27, 1940.

# Notes

**INTRODUCTION**

1. Mohlenbrock, *Giant City State Park*, 3–4.

2. Ibid., 14–20.

3. *1878 History and 1907 Atlas of Jackson County, Illinois*, 100 (hereafter *1878 Jackson County History*).

4. Thompson, "Pioneer Days and Early Settlers."

5. Also see Herbert Russell's introduction to Mary Tracy Earle's *Flag on the Hilltop*, xi; and Mabel Thompson Rauch's *Vinnie and the Flag Tree*. The caves and physical geography of the Makanda area are important elements to the themes and action in both these books. Legends tell of Civil War deserters using the caves as hideouts. Earle's book is the story of the Thompson brothers, T. W. and Albert, who with two friends raised the Union flag on Banner Hill, their farm near Makanda, during the Civil War in support of the Union cause and in defiance of sympathizers and those belonging to the Knights of the Golden Circle. Nearly the entire first half of the novel takes place in the caves around Giant City, where a deserting soldier hides and secret meetings are held. Alec Ford, Doc Ford, and T. D. portray characters much like the Thompsons. The villains, however, are varied, and as Herb Russell writes, Earle "captures the spirit of ambivalence among the contending forces in a southern Illinois border county." Rauch's book, *Vinnie and the Flag-Tree*, is a juvenile novel that tells the tale of Makanda-area families during the Civil War, both Union soldiers, such as the Thompson brothers, and their neighbors, whose son fights on the Confederate side and who support the southern cause. The heroine is young Vinnie, who works as a nurse in the Cairo hospital and marries Theodore Thompson. Some of the action takes place in the caves and rock overhangs of the surrounding area and in Pine Hills to the west. In secret, southern sympathizers meet to plan destruction of the railroad supply line running through Makanda and the killing of Union soldiers. Rauch uses such real Union county family names as Thompson, Rendleman, Hileman, and Hartline and depicts John A. Logan and his wife as regional heroes.

6. "Zane Grey Recent Giant City Visitor, Is Belief."

7. *1878 Jackson County History*, 100. The Vancil barn was located on the northwest quarter of section 35 in Makanda township and was built ca. 1840–50. The spectacular 44-by-24-foot double crib barn with one room on each side of a central passageway was wide enough to drive through with a team and wagon, and all under a common roof. The barn was deconstructed and taken from Giant City State Park in July 1981, under some vocal but insufficient public protest, to be reconstructed at the Lincoln Log Cabin Historic Site near Charleston, Illinois. Bob Kristoff, Giant City State Park superintendent at that time, said that the Conservation Department moved the cabin "because the park is not a historic site and because it believed the structure would be more at home in Charleston." It has never been rumored that

Kristoff fought to keep the cabin or for that matter any of the historic legacies of the park. See Keith Sculle, "Lincoln Log Cabin State Historic Site," 7–9; photo and story in *Southern Illinoisan*, July 17, 1981, n.p.

8. Brieschke, *Notes on Makanda*, 47–49.

9. Ibid., 19, 26, 59.

10. *Official Annual: Civilian Conservation Corps, Jefferson Barracks CCC District, Sixth Corps Area, 1937*, 51 (hereafter *CCC 1937 Annual*).

11. Ward and Sculle, "National Register of Historic Places Inventory Form."

12. Jenny Skufca, site interpreter, Giant City State Park, e-mail correspondence with author, Aug. 30, 2007. Beginning with company rosters supplied by the author to Skufca, the visitor center staff began collecting names of visitors who said they were CCC alumni who had worked at the park. Each roster that is exhibited as an appendix in this book is the list for only that company at that time period. Many enrollees came and went, so each six months might reflect new names. Although Skufca left the park in 2009, she said that the park will continue to create a full list of names of all those who have proven service in the CCC at Giant City State Park.

**1. THE LAND AND ITS PEOPLE**

1. "Glacial History"; Harris, Horrell, and Irwin, *Exploring the Land and Rocks of Southern Illinois*; Raymond Wiggers, *Geology Underfoot in Illinois*, 8–9. The latter source states that the Illinoian glacier occurred 300,000 to 125,000 years ago.

2. Butler, Wagner, DelCastello, Herndon, and Parker, *Giant City Stone Fort*, 210–13.

3. Newsome, *Historical Sketches of Jackson County, Illinois*, 115.

4. Thus, the town of Boskeydell was formed two miles south of Carbondale. From the Boskeydell quarry came some of the stone for Southern Illinois Normal University's Old Main building as well as for Carbondale's First Baptist and First Presbyterian churches and the state capitol in Springfield. Boskeydell thrived between 1855 and 1930, reaching its population peak in the 1890s. See Sneed, *Ghost Towns of Southern Illinois*, 72–73.

5. See *South Pass Revisited* about Cobden's history. Also in Union County, the town of Alto Pass was established as a railroad station on the Narrow Gauge line connecting Murphysboro with points south.

6. *1878 Jackson County History*, 101; Rosson, "Makanda Township."

7. Brieschke, *Notes on Makanda*, 31.

8. Adams, *Transformation of Rural Life*, 46–47. Also see *South Pass Revisited* for an explanation of the differing cultures and political leanings between the Union County residents in the townships of Casper (Cobden) and Rich, just

south of the park property, which developed when New Englanders moved into the profitable regions of southern Illinois during the latter decades of the nineteenth century.

9. Rosson, "Makanda Township"; *1878 Jackson County History*, 100; and Brieschke, *Notes on Makanda*, quoting from L. C. Ferrell, Illinois Central Railroad clerk, 104–5, and from *Jonesboro Gazette* articles from 1877 and 1888, 105–8.

10. *Makanda News*, February 15, 1896, 1.

11. Soady, "Making of the Shawnee," 5–6.

12. Adams, *Transformation of Rural Life*, 108–22.

13. *Barton Free Press* (Carbondale, IL), July 7, 1888, and July 14, 1888; Brieschke, *Notes on Makanda*, 47; *1878 Jackson County History*, 101.

14. Mulcaster also worked to establish recognition of the Cherokee Trail of Tears through southern Illinois, and he advocated for Brownsville in Jackson County to become a state park. See John G. Mulcaster Scrapbook in John W. Allen Papers, 76.3.F1., vol. 23. Hal Trovillion of Herrin published the *Egyptian Republican* in the 1930s. On the newspaper's stationery, he describes the paper as "the only strictly Republican partisan publication in southern Illinois, circulating among Republican office holders, committeemen and party workers in Senatorial Districts, 42, 44, 46, 48, 49, 50, and 51st, covering also the 22, 23, 24, and 25 Congressional Districts, embracing the 33 most southern counties known as Egypt, and dealing with the political, economic, and social progress of the community."

15. Taylor, "How Illinois Got Its First State Park."

16. Hal Hassen (chief archaeologist, Illinois Department of Natural Resources), e-mail correspondence with Jenny Skufca and with author, February 23, 2007; Jenny Skufca, e-mail correspondence with author, June 13, 2007.

17. "Giant City Park Booster Praises Park: Makanda Citizen and Park Devotee Thanks All Who Aided," *Carbondale Free Press*, December 29, 1928.

18. Mulcaster, "Rock Formations in Giant City Park Near Makanda, Ill."

19. John G. Mulcaster to H. H. Cleaveland, April 19, 1929, in Giant City Visitor Center Manuscript Collection (hereafter GCVC).

20. "Giant City Appointment Causes Stir."

21. Ralph Corzine, job application and letters in GCVC; Willis Rendleman to H. H. Cleaveland, June 29, 1929, GCVC.

22. Letters and public petition to H. H. Cleaveland, February 7 and 16, 1929, GCVC.

23. Ralph Corzine to H. H. Cleaveland, November 21 and October 25, 1929, GCVC.

24. "Giant City Appointment Causes Stir."

25. "Mulcaster Says Park Interest to Be on Payroll."

26. G. Lockard, R. K. Loomis, M. C. Lockard, and E. W. Newman to H. H. Cleaveland, July 12, 1929; Adams, "Years Ago in Union County."

27. J. G. Mulcaster to H. H. Cleaveland, April 19, 1929; H. H. Cleaveland to Rodney Brandon, Director, Department of Public Welfare, November 27, 1929; H. H. Cleaveland to John

G. Mulcaster, January 3, 1930, all in GCVC; "County Paying Rock Haulage for Road to State Park." This article says that the Jackson County Highway Committee appropriated $1,000 for the freightage charges to carry gravel from Menard Penitentiary to Makanda in order to gravel from Route 2 through Makanda to the park. It mentions that convict labor will "load, unload, and spread the gravel," but this doesn't seem to be what happened.

28. H. H. Cleaveland to Rodney Brandon, Director, Department of Public Welfare, November 27 and December 28, 1929; Dr. Hagebush, Managing Officer, Anna State Hospital, to Rodney Brandon, December 17, 1929; H. H. Cleaveland to Ralph Corzine, August 22, 1930; H. H. Cleaveland to John G. Mulcaster (a letter of thanks for his perseverance in getting the gravel spread by Anna State Hospital patients), January 3, 1930, all in GCVC; "Insane Men Only Hauling Stone and Not Working."

29. Bailey West (Makanda postmaster) to Governor Louis L. Emmerson, June 26, 1929, GCVC.

30. Bailey West to H. H. Cleveland [*sic*], June 25, 1929; Bailey West to Governor Louis L. Emmerson, June 26, 1929; Gusta Smith (Makanda constable), notarized statement, June 29, 1929, all in GCVC.

31. Elbert Waller to Director H. H. Cleaveland, Illinois Department of Public Works, July 8, 1929, GCVC; "'Giant City' Boomed for State Park," newspaper clipping ca. 1928, in box 12, John W. Allen Papers. The article says that because of its "daunting chasms," Makanda was "euchred" out of the State Road [in 1919, State Route 2 was built to the west of town, along smoother terrain, partially to avoid flooding], so now this park will help to make amends."

32. "Giant City in Winter."

33. "'Giant City' Boomed for State Park."

34. Ralph Corzine to H. H. Cleaveland, June 7, 1930, GCVC.

35. Edgar Roberts to Mr. Cleveland [*sic*], July 19, 1930, and H. H. Cleaveland's response to Ralph Corzine, July 23, 1930, GCVC.

36. H. H. Cleaveland to Ralph Corzine, September 9, 1930, GCVC.

37. Don Moles (Illinois Department of Natural Resources' Division of Realty), telephone interview, June 14, 2007. Moles stated that during the initial land purchases, those before 1940, there were no lands taken under eminent domain. Eminent domain was used in later decades to acquire some land.

38. Ralph Corzine to H. H. Cleaveland, August 23 and 28, 1930, GCVC; *Carbondale Free Press*, mid-August 1930; Frank Hopkins to Governor Louis Emmerson, June 8, 1931, GCVC.

## 2. THE CCC COMES TO SOUTHERN ILLINOIS

1. *Illinois Blue Book 1927–1928*, 486.

2. Meltzer, *Brother, Can You Spare a Dime?* 121–23.

3. Franklin Delano Roosevelt, inauguration speech, January 20, 1937, as quoted in Smith, *FDR*, 376. For depic-

tions of the personal tragedies made common during the Great Depression, see chapter 16, "What the Depression Did to People," in Ellis, *A Nation in Torment*. This is one of the best overall books about the Depression era and its profound effect on individuals and the American people as a whole.

4. Adams, *Transformation of Rural Life*, 132–43; Conrad and Jones, "Town Life in Southern Illinois During the Great Depression," 121–38; Meltzer, *Brother, Can You Spare a Dime?* 121–23.

5. *Illinois Blue Book 1935*, 459.

6. *Murphysboro Daily Independent*, June 5, 1934.

7. Thelma L. Baker, interview, May 1979; Homer and Viola Minton, interview, October 5, 1979.

8. Meltzer, *Brother, Can You Spare a Dime?* 49.

9. Pomona Township Records, 1920s and 1930s, Jackson County Historical Society.

10. Maurer, "Unemployment in Illinois during the Great Depression," 123–24; "End of State Unemployment Relief Scheme."

11. "10,088 Families Transferred to Work Relief Jobs."

12. *Illinois Blue Book 1930*, 845.

13. Soady, "Making of the Shawnee," 6–9.

14. Lacy, *Soil Soldiers*, 17–18; Smith, *FDR*, 319–20.

15. Steen, *U.S. Forest Service*, 214.

16. Maurer, "Unemployment in Illinois during the Great Depression," 121.

17. Cohen, *Tree Army*, 6.

18. Kenney, "Remembering Kent Keller." Also see Keller, "What Has Been Done for the 25th District of Illinois with $122,000,000 and Egypt's Future," 6.

19. Burns, *Roosevelt*, 169.

20. As reprinted in Cohen, *Tree Army*, 9.

21. Ibid., 7.

22. Salmond, *Civilian Conservation Corps*, 14. This is the best overall review and analysis of the Civilian Conservation Corps.

23. Lacy, *Soil Soldiers*, 28–29.

24. Salmond, *Civilian Conservation Corps*, 18–20; Richardson, "Was There Politics in the Civilian Conservation Corps?" 13.

25. Salmond, *Civilian Conservation Corps*, 23.

26. Ibid., 35.

27. Ibid., 35–36.

28. *CCC 1937 Annual*; Kay Rippelmeyer Collection.

29. Anderson, "Tough Babes in the Woods," 7.

30. Cohen, *Tree Army*, 63–64.

31. Fechner, "Objectives and Results of the Civilian Conservation Corps Program," 8.

32. "CCC: Least Criticized New Deal Unit."

33. As quoted in Salmond, *Civilian Conservation Corps*, 57.

34. Cohen, *Tree Army*, 6–7. Also see articles in *Murphysboro Daily Independent* about the "Reforestation Army," June 12 and 16, 1933.

35. Adams, *Transformation of Rural Life*, 160.

## 3. CCC COMPANIES #696 AND #1657 AND THEIR CAMPS, GIANT CITY AND STONE FORT

1. George Oliver, interview, August 31, 1987.

2. Fechner, "Objectives and Results of the Civilian Conservation Corps Program," 8–9; McEntee, *Now They Are Men*, 16–17.

3. Narrative Supplementary Report, Camp SP-11, March 31, 1936, RG 79, National Archives. According to Mary Schueller, whose father, Mike Kerkes, was a leader in Company #696, the advance group came in a truck convoy from Jefferson Barracks to Camp Giant City. See Schueller, *Soldiers of Poverty*, 66.

4. Six Month Summary Report, ECW #11, Giant City State Park, June–December 1933, RG 79, National Archives.

5. Narrative Report to Accompany Monthly Progress Report for September, ECW Camp #11, September 30, 1933, RG 79, National Archives (hereafter Narrative Report, September 30, 1933); Narrative Report to Accompany Monthly Progress Report, ECW #11, October 31, 1933, RG 79, National Archives (hereafter Narrative Report, October 31, 1933).

6. Salmond, *Civilian Conservation Corps*, 59–60; Oliver interview.

7. Narrative Report, September 30, 1933; Oliver interview.

8. "Giant City Woods Army Likes Peaches." The southern Illinois newspapers and the *Chicago Daily Tribune* referred to the CCC as the "Forest Army" or "Forester Army" in June and July 1933, but by August they referred to it as the "Conservation Corps." See *Chicago Daily Tribune*: "Call for 3,125 Vets from Chicago Area for Forester Army"; "237,984 Men Are Now Enrolled in U.S. Forest Army"; "Roosevelt Puts Forest Army on Higher Pay"; "Possibilities of the Conservation Corps."

9. Schueller, *Soldiers of Poverty*, 88–89.

10. Narrative Reports, September 30 and October 31, 1933.

11. Ibid.; Narrative Report to Accompany Monthly Progress Report, ECW #11, November 30, 1933, RG 79, National Archives (hereafter Narrative Report, November 30, 1933); Six Month Summary Report, June–December 1933. Schueller, *Soldiers of Poverty*, in the chapter "Hewed to the Line," 116–25, describes the work of the hewing department at Giant City in which her father, Mike Kerkes, was designated lead carpenter.

12. Six Month Summary Report, June–December 1933.

13. Narrative Reports, September 30 and October 31, 1933.

14. Ibid.

15. Narrative Report, November 30, 1933.

16. Ibid.

17. "Reforestation Concentration Camps Sought." By September 1933, eleven CCC camps had been established in Illinois state parks (at Springfield, Starved Rock, Pere Marquette, Mississippi Palisades, Skokie Lagoon, and Giant City), and five camps were set up along the Illinois and Michigan Canal. See "Illinois To Have 26 Conservation Winter Camps."

18. See CCC Giant City State Park Narrative Reports, 1935–1940, National Archives.

19. "More Men to CCC Camps."

20. Six Month Summary Report, June–December 1933; "Forestry Army Chiefs Praise Enthusiasm of Rural Recruits."

21. *Spirit of 57* (a monthly publication edited and published by the members of CCC Company #1657, editor-in-chief Captain C. G. Whitney) 1.1 (July 1934): 3; Floyd Finley, "Information About Company 1657 CCC 1933 and 1934," two-page reminiscence written June 22, 1984, for the author. Finley was the company clerk for #1657.

22. Finley reminiscence; Finley interview, September 24, 1987.

23. Finley interview.

24. *CCC 1937 Annual.*

25. "Co. #1657 Salutes Departing Captain with Farewell Party and Dynamite." Guy Whitney worked as an internal auditor for Marshall Field's when he left the CCC.

26. *Spirit of 57*, 3; Finley interview. Camp Stone Fort was first numbered Illinois State Park SP-24 in the CCC system; later, when Company #692 came to Giant City, its number became SP-41. Camp Giant City was SP-11.

27. Narrative Report, ECW #11 and #24, Giant City State Park, Makanda, Illinois, December 30, 1933, RG 79, National Archives.

28. William P. Hannon, Camp Inspection Reports for SP-11 and SP-24, both March 12, 1934, RG 35, National Archives; Joseph Zimmerman, written correspondence with author.

29. Finley interview; *Spirit of 57*, 4; "Ode to Lieutenant Paul W. Nieman," lyrics typed on original stationery of Company 1657, given to author by Floyd Finley, September 24, 1987.

30. Finley interview; Finley reminiscence.

31. *Spirit of 57*, 16.

32. "Show Us the Way to Cotton Hill," lyrics typed on Company #1657 stationery, given to author by Floyd Finley, September 24, 1987.

33. *Spirit of 57*, 4–7.

34. Jim Watkins, interview, February 18, 2005.

35. Oliver interview.

36. Ibid.

37. Perkins, "FDR Was 'A Little Left of Center,'" 384–85.

### 4. WORK PROJECTS

1. Albin Olson, Monthly Report, ECW Camps #11 and #24, Giant City State Park, Makanda, Illinois, January 31, 1934, RG 79, National Archives (hereafter Olson, Monthly Report, [date]).

2. Ibid.

3. Ibid.; Olson, Monthly Reports, February 28 and March 31, 1934.

4. Oliver interview.

5. Brieschke and Rackerby, "Stone Forts of Illinois," 5–9; Butler, Wagner, DelCastello, Herndon, and Parker, *Giant City Stone Fort*; Jon Muller as quoted by Jane Adams, "Mystery of Stone Fort Remains."

6. Mulcaster, "Old Stone Fort," and "Prehistoric Forts of Southern Illinois, Called Egypt," typed manuscript in John G. Mulcaster Collection, box 2, folder 1.

7. Olson, Monthly Report, March 31, 1934.

8. Ibid.

9. French, "Stone Fort near Makanda, Jackson County, Illinois," 582–84.

10. Olson, Monthly Report, March 31, 1934; "Indian Relics at Stonefort."

11. Olson, Monthly Report, March 31, 1934.

12. Ibid.; John G. Mulcaster to Director Robert Kingery, December 11, 1934, GCVC. Mulcaster wanted an exhibit space or museum at Giant City State Park. He mentioned the possibility of including the Indian relic collection of Irvin Peithman and the animal, insect, and bird collections of George H. Center of Du Quoin. Peithman had also written to Kingery, November 26, 1934, asking if a building for the Indian artifacts would be erected at Giant City and also advocating for himself if someone were to be hired in a job position there.

13. Brieschke, *Notes on Makanda*, 40, 45–46.

14. "Jackson County," box 3, George Washington Smith Papers.

15. Butler, Wagner, DelCastello, Herndon, and Parker, *Giant City Stone Fort*.

16. Olson, Monthly Reports, February 28 and March 31, 1934.

17. Ibid., January 31 and February 28, 1934.

18. Ibid.

19. Albin Olson, Camp Report, ECW Camp #11, CCC Co. #696, April 30, 1934, RG 79, National Archives.

20. Albin Olson, Camp Report, ECW Camp #11, June 30, 1934, RG 79, National Archives.

21. Albin Olson, Semi-monthly Report of Progress of Work at Giant City State Park Project, CCC Co. #696, Makanda, Illinois, July 1–15, 1934, RG 79, National Archives.

22. Ibid.

23. Ibid.

24. Kenneth Hawk, interview, September 9, 1987.

25. Olson, Camp Report, June 30, 1934.

26. "Story about the Grasshopper and Ants," about Kent Keller's visit to CCC Camp Giant City, in Kay Rippelmeyer Collection.

27. Kenney, "Remembering Kent Keller," 147–53. Kent Keller attended SINU and taught school in Nevada before returning to southern Illinois to establish a high school in Ava, becoming its first principal. He again attended SINU to complete requirements for a bachelor's degree in the classics. He attended Heidelberg University in Germany for a year, then returned to Ava to publish the *Ava Register*.

28. Ibid.; Smith, *FDR*, 312.

29. "Story about the Grasshopper and Ants."

30. Kenney, "Remembering Kent Keller," 150–52.

31. Ibid.

## 5. LODGE CONSTRUCTION AND ARRIVAL OF CCC COMPANY #692

1. Booten, "State Park Architecture Harmonizes With Scenery."

2. From notes taken by author from records in Giant City State Park superintendent's office, 1984.

3. Ward and Sculle, "National Register of Historic Places Inventory, Nomination Form," United States Department of the Interior, National Park Service, 1984, Item #8, 2. This form states that Giant City's lodge is made of limestone, but it is not. It is sandstone.

4. The lodges at Giant City, Pere Marquette, and Black Hawk are primarily made of stone. Starved Rock's lodge is a mixture of stone, logs, and wood shingles, while White Pines' lodge is built of unhewn pine logs. See section on Giant City in Ward and Sculle, "National Register of Historic Places Inventory, Nomination Form," n.p.

5. Oliver interview; Olson, Camp Report, June 30, 1934.

6. Albin Olson, Camp Report, ECW #11, July 31, 1934, RG 79, National Archives (hereafter Olson, Camp Report, July 31, 1934).

7. *Company D-692 Civilian Conservation Corps Camp, Stone Fort, DSP-1, Giant City State Park, Makanda, Illinois, Complete Company Roster for Fourth Enrollment Period, October 1, 1934–March 31, 1935* (hereafter Camp Stone Fort, Company Roster), pamphlet that also includes "History of D-692nd Company," in Giant City State Park Civilian Conservation Corps Collection (MSS 280). See appendix 4 for Company #692 company roster.

8. Earl Dickey, interview, July 26, 2002.

9. Camp Stone Fort, Company Roster.

10. Ibid. In September 1934, Lieutenant Urbach was promoted to Acting Assistant Adjutant General of the Sixth Corps Area and Lieutenant George D. Markel assumed command of Company #692 at Giant City.

11. Oliver interview.

12. Camp Stone Fort, Company Roster; Oliver interview.

13. Albin Olson, Camp Report, ECW Camp #11, September 30 and November 30, 1934, RG 79, National Archives; Schueller, *Soldiers of Poverty*, 144.

14. See numerous articles in the *Murphysboro Daily Independent*, May–June 1934, about high temperatures and drought.

15. Albin Olson and F. P. Britson, Monthly Camp Reports, ECW #696, Giant City State Park, July 31, 1934–May 1935, RG 79, National Archives.

16. Albin Olson, Camp Report, ECW #696, August 31, 1934, RG 79, National Archives.

17. Lynn Rayle, written correspondence with author, March 17, 1989.

18. Scott Vancil, interview, November 9, 1987.

19. Albin Olson, Camp Reports, Giant City SP-11, October 31 and November 30, 1934, RG 79, National Archives.

20. Olson, Camp Report, November 30, 1934.

21. F. P. Britson, Camp Report, SP-11, December 1934 and January 1935, RG 79, National Archives; William P. Hannon,

Camp Inspection Report, Camp Stone Fort, DSP-1, Co. D-692, January 16, 1935, RG 79, National Archives.

22. Hawk interview; William P. Hannon, Camp Inspection Report, Company #696, January 16, 1935, RG 79, National Archives.

23. Hawk interview.

24. Ibid.

25. Ibid.

26. Vancil interview.

27. Ibid.

28. F. P. Britson, Camp Report, SP-11, December 1934 and January 1935.

29. Rayle correspondence; Hannon, Camp Inspection Report, Company #696, January 16, 1935. This report mentions that "shatter-proof goggles are in possession of the army and the technical service."

30. F. P. Britson, Monthly Reports, SP-11, February and March 1935, RG 79, National Archives (hereafter Britson, Camp Report, February and March 1935).

31. Hawk interview.

32. Britson, Camp Report, February and March 1935.

33. Thomas, "Makanda Floods," 95.

34. Oliver interview; F. P. Britson, "Camp SP-11 Narrative Report of Activities of Camp during Months of June and July," RG 79, National Archives.

35. F. P. Britson, "Status Report," part of Camp Report, Giant City Camp SP-11, CCC Company #696, April and May 1935, RG 79, National Archives; Dickey interview, July 26, 2002.

36. Britson, Status Report, April and May 1935.

37. Ibid.

38. C. C. Lindsey to Robert Feckner [sic], November 20, 1934.

39. J. J. McEntee, Assistant Director of CCC, to Col. Earl North, Assistant Secretary of War, and to F. A. Silcox, Chief Forest Service, and to A. B. Cammorer, National Park Service, November 26, 1934; Kent Keller to Robert Feckner [sic], November 22, 1934, all in National Archives. (Copies are in the Giant City State Park Civilian Conservation Corps Collection.)

40. William P. Hannon to J. J. McEntee, November 29, 1934, National Archives.

41. Carter Jenkins to "Gentleman" at Second District Office, State Park Conservation Work, December 10, 1934, National Archives.

42. E. O. Desobry to the Adjutant General, December 19, 1934, National Archives.

43. C. F. Thompson to Regional Forester, December 19, 1934, National Archives.

44. Dickey interview, July 26, 2002.

45. A. G. Ruediger, Monthly Narrative Report—August and September (1935), Giant City SP-11, Makanda, Illinois, RG 79, National Archives.

46. "CCC Improving Giant City State Park for Visitors," *St. Louis Post-Dispatch*, May 6, 1935; Brieschke, *Notes on Makanda*, 91; John G. Mulcaster Scrapbook in John W.

Allen Papers; *Carbondale Free Press*, February 3, 1937; and Mulcaster's biography notes by Barbara Burr Hubbs in folder 1 of John G. Mulcaster Collection.

### 6. CAMP LIFE

1. "CCC Will Operate 55 Illinois Camps in Next 3 Months"; "237,984 Men Are Now Enrolled in U.S. Forest Army"; Perry Merrill, *Roosevelt's Forest Army*, 125.

2. As quoted in Salmond, *Civilian Conservation Corps*, 57; Smith, *FDR*, 359.

3. Zimmerman correspondence.

4. F. P. Britson, Camp Report, SP-11, December 1934 and January 1935, National Archives.

5. William P. Hannon, Camp Inspection Report, January 16, 1935; Hawk interview.

6. Dickey interview, July 26, 2002.

7. Hannon, Camp Inspection Report, January 16, 1935.

8. "Forestry Army Chiefs Praise Enthusiasm of Rural Recruits."

9. Dickey interviews, July 26, 2002, and February 19, 2003; Oliver interview. According to Earl Dickey, Pop Johnson had a long career in the restaurant business in southern Illinois. After cooking at several CCC camps, he had a popular food stand under the bleachers at Riverside Park, Murphysboro, in his later years.

10. Hawk interview.

11. Ibid.

12. Ibid.

13. Dickey interview, July 26, 2002.

14. "Clothes Make the CCC Boy."

15. Hawk interview; Finley interview.

16. Dickey interview, July 26, 2002.

17. Hawk interview.

18. Vancil interview.

19. Hawk interview.

20. "Forestry Army Chiefs Praise Enthusiasm of Rural Recruits."

21. Oliver interview.

22. Hawk interview.

23. Vancil interview.

24. Hawk interview; Rayle correspondence; Dickey interviews, July 26, 2002, and February 19, 2003.

25. Rayle correspondence; Dickey interviews, July 26, 2002, and February 19, 2003; Finley interview.

26. Hawk interview.

27. William Hannon, Camp Inspection Report, January 16, 1935.

28. Rayle correspondence.

29. Dickey interview, February 19, 2003.

30. Hawk interview.

31. Andrew Esposito, interview, March 26, 1979.

32. Dickey interview, July 26, 2002.

33. Dickey interviews, July 26, 2002, and February 19, 2003.

34. Dickey interview, July 26, 2002.

35. Hawk interview.

36. Baker interview; Hawk interview.

37. George H. Luker, Superintendent of National Parks, to Director Robert Kingery, December 21, 1934, GCVC.

38. Carter Jenkins, report to Charles Casey, November 18, 1936, GCVC.

39. Local businesses that sold goods and services to Giant City camps and that were listed in camp reports include Maloney Shoe Repair, Egyptian Lumber Co., Yourtee-Roberts Sand Co., Chas. Easterly Lumber Co., Egyptian Powder Co., Valentine Hardware Co., Anna Quarries, Alpha Portland Cement, Union County Lumber Co., H. H. Halliday Sand Co., Stotlar Lumber Yard, Sligo Iron Store Co., Boren Plumbing and Electric Co., Fred Roberts Motor Corp., Rapp Tire Co., Rogers Auto Supply, Thompson's Machine Shop, and Hamilton Tractor and Equipment Co.

40. F. P. Britson, Camp Report, Giant City Camp SP-11, April and May 1935, RG 79, National Archives.

41. F. P. Britson, Narrative Report of Activities of Camp during Months of June and July [1935]; Albin Olson, Fifth Period Summary Report, Giant City SP-11, April 1–October 1, 1935, National Archives.

42. Untitled article, *Murphysboro Daily Independent*, May 1, 1935.

43. "Giant City Park Awaits Visitors," *Herrin News*, May 9, 1935.

44. *Stone-City Weekly*, September 4, 1935, 1; Dickey interview, July 26, 2002.

45. *Stone-City Weekly*, August 28, September 4, September 11, and September 25, 1935.

46. Businesses that advertised in the *Stone-City Weekly* included Chas. Easterly Lumber, Clelands and Hoffman's Clothing, Louis Wolff Plumbing and Heating, Oak Grove Dairy Farm, Green Tavern, the Shlitz Night Club, Rhinegold Tavern, Sims Café, Blue Moon, Stumble Inn, Hill Produce Co., Bradley Bros. Nursery, New Era Dairy, McGuire's Fruit Farm, Green Mill Ice Cream Co., Leon W. Smith Service Station, the Bungalow Inn, H. W. Patterson (dentist), H. and M. Clothing Store, Mallard Tavern, Star Tavern, Dunk's Place, Doerr's Drug Store, Blankenship Automobiles, Koenig Hardware Store, Elite Barber Shop, Hirsch Clothing, Wolf Shoe Store, Egyptian Lumber Co., Brown and Colombo, Grady Music Store, Walters and Eddings Furnaces and Sheet Metal, and Kroger.

47. "We Need Your Help." "Brother, Can You Spare a Dime?" was a popular song in the 1930s, along with "Solidarity Forever" and Woody Guthrie's answer to "God Bless America," which was "This Land Is Your Land." The staff of the *Stone-City Weekly* by September 11, 1935, included Carl [or Carol] Woody (editor), Charles Triplett (editor), Philip Smith, Fred Gerzema, Tony Gherra, Raymond McNair, Charles Gruber, Joe Jines, Dick Polonowski, Pat Lipton, Levie Miller, Andrew Persich, Wayne Phillips, John Rader, Vernon Stanley, Ross Lindhorst, Joe Calbrecht, Fred Kollman, and James Whalen. The newspaper's advisors were John M. Eddy, the camp's educational advisor; Mr. Bradley; and Mr. Dunsmore.

48. "Projects Completed on Schedule; Workmanship Superior." From 1936 to 1938, Camp Giant City printed a CCC newspaper called, at different times, *Giant City Minne-graph*, *M-graph*, *Giant City Goliath*, and *Giant City News*.

49. SINU was accredited as a teachers' college in 1931. SINU became SIU in 1947.

50. "Various Departments to Offer Classes for Men of the CCC"; Zimmerman correspondence.

51. Finley interview; Hannon, Camp Inspection Report SP-11, March 12, 1934.

52. Hawk interview.

53. Lacy, *Soil Soldiers*, 66. In 1935, the number of CCC camps in the country reached a peak of 2,652.

54. "CCC Quota Unfilled."

55. Oliver interview.

56. Albin Olson, Narrative Report, Giant City SP-11, October and November 1935, RG 79, National Archives.

57. Camp Stone Fort, Company Roster; Schueller, *Soldiers of Poverty*, 151.

58. Earl Dickey, letter to Juanita Ernest, November 4, 1935; *CCC 1937 Annual*, 47.

59. Albin Olson, Narrative Report, Giant City, SP-11, February and March 1936, RG 79, National Archives.

60. William P. Hannon, Camp Inspection Report, SP-11, February 27, 1936, RG 79, National Archives.

61. Ibid.

62. Olson, Narrative Report, Giant City, February and March 1936.

63. Vancil interview.

64. Albin Olson, Narrative Report, Giant City SP #11, June–July 1936, RG 79, National Archives.

65. Ibid.

66. Ibid.; Thomas Bermingham, "Lodge Dedication Occasion for Homecoming, July 31, 1936," report included in Olson, Narrative Report, Giant City, June–July 1936; Hugh Roach, "Seventh Period Summary Report," Giant City SP-11, September 30, 1936.

67. Roach, "Seventh Period Summary Report"; "Horner Praises CCC in Dedication Speech at Grant [*sic*] City Park."

68. William P. Hannon, Camp Inspection Report, November 10, 1936, Giant City SP #11, RG 79, National Archives.

69. Smith, *FDR*, 367–68.

## 7. THE LAST YEARS OF THE CCC AND ITS LEGACIES

1. Hawk interview.

2. Matthew Skertich, correspondence with author, September 2, 1987.

3. Ibid.; see Appendix 6 for the names of men who left the CCC in September 1937.

4. Mary Schueller, correspondence with author, February 4, 2003, and March 7, 2003.

5. Dickey interview, February 19, 2003.

6. Fechner, "Objectives and Results of the Civilian Conservation Corps Program."

7. Salmond, *Civilian Conservation Corps*, 104–5; Richardson, "Was There Politics in the Civilian Conservation Corps?" 13–14.

8. Salmond, *Civilian Conservation Corps*, 110–12; Hawk interview.

9. Salmond, *Civilian Conservation Corps*, 110–12.

10. McEntee, *Now They Are Men*, 52.

11. John J. Biggs, "Proposal," January 11, 1937, RG 79, National Archives.

12. In 1937, of the 44,671 new CCC enrollees throughout the country, about 70 percent of them were nineteen or younger. Only about 8 percent of that portion had finished high school. "44,671 Youths Accepted for Camps, First Job for Many."

13. Harry Collier, Camp Inspection Report, July 25, 1938, RG 35, National Archives.

14. Merrill, *Roosevelt's Forest Army*, 68–69.

15. Farmer, "History of the Shawnee National Forest, 1933–Present [1938]," portion of Atlas 10, p. 27.

16. *CCC 1937 Annual*, 20, 51.

17. "CCC."

18. "Says New Deal Going Into Red Millions Daily."

19. Salmond, *Civilian Conservation Corps*, 201.

20. Perkins, "FDR Was 'A Little Left of Center,'" 385; "Pacifists Begin Sniping at Army Training for CCC"; Salmond, *Civilian Conservation Corps*, 193; "Not Drills but Exercises."

21. Salmond, *Civilian Conservation Corps*, 114.

22. Harold G. Chafey, Supplemental Report [to Camp Inspection Report], Camp SP-11, Company #696, Makanda, Illinois, March 27, 1939, RG 35, National Archives. In October 1938, the following men from Co. #696 transferred to Co. #1625 and moved to Golconda, Nevada: Marion Benbrook, Clifford Booten, Nolan Cornett, Charles Dunn, James Highland, Victor Just, Harry Mathews, Robert Smith, Afton Toler, and Keith York. Among the newcomers to Co. #696 were the following men: Loren Anderson, Paul Bird, Bill Blackwell, Judson Boyle, John Brown, Kenneth Burnett, Robert Chism, Robert Finley, Eugene George, Raymond Graf, Christopher Hill, Allen Hood, Harold Horner, Walter Hutchings, Amos Jones, Leroy Kimmel, Dale Koenegestein, Harry Koonce, Hugh McCaughan, Roy Mederbreck, Lawrence Mercer, William Odom, Philip Pflasterer, Roy Ragland, John Russell, Raymond Schnaare, Paul Shaw, Loren Spencer, Charles Stroud, Robert Sutterfield, and John Tindal. See *Giant City News*, October 1938.

23. Harold G. Chafey, Camp Inspection Reports, Camp SP-11, Company #696, March 27, 1939, and January 10, 1940, RG 35, National Archives.

24. "The History of Giant City Lodge," a ten-page Xerox, deposited by author in Giant City State Park Civilian Conservation Corps Collection; Wayman Presley to Hon. F. Lynden Smith, Director of Public Works and Buildings, Springfield, Illinois, June 22, 1939, GCVC. In this letter, Presley refers to southernmost Illinois as "Little Egypt." During this same time and for nearly a hundred years previously, more educated southern Illinoisans, such as Daniel H.

Brush, George W. Smith, Paul Angle, Baker Brownell, John W. Allen, and Barbara Burr Hubbs, as well as Will Griffith, founder of the Greater Egypt Association, and publisher Hal Trovillion, always referred to the area as "Egypt," never "Little Egypt." "Little Egypt" was the name of the scantily clad "hootchy-kootchy" dancer who became notorious after the Chicago 1893 World's Fair. The regional magazine *Egyptian Key* fulminated against defiling the longstanding nickname "Egypt" in the way that Presley was consistently doing to promote his tourism business. See *Egyptian Key* 3.4 (September 1951): 48.

25. "The History of Giant City Lodge," 5.

26. Report from R. M. Johnson, Department Inspector, to Mr. D. B. Littrell, Field Supervisor of National Park Service, November 29, 1940 (report prepared by Richard E. Bishop), GCVC.

27. Esposito interview; Chafey, Camp Inspection Report, March 27, 1939.

28. McEntee, *Now They Are Men*.

29. Cohen, *Tree Army*, 144.

30. Harold G. Chafey, Camp Inspection Report, Camp SP-11, Company #696, January 22, 1941, RG 35, National Archives.

31. Ibid. A typical daily menu such as that of January 17, 1941, featured for breakfast fresh grapefruit, dry cereal, milk, pork links, pineapple fritters, butter, syrup, and coffee. For lunch was cold salmon, combined salad, mashed potatoes, chopped onions, butter, coffee, and banana cake. The dinner menu included soup, scalloped ham with potatoes, buttered beets, spinach with boiled eggs, cabbage-celery salad, butter, coffee, and butterscotch pudding.

32. Harold G. Chafey, Camp Inspection Reports, Camp SP-11, Company #696, March 17 and November 18, 1941, RG 35, National Archives.

33. Harold G. Chafey, Camp Inspection Report, Camp SP-11, Company #696, March 25, 1942, RG 35, National Archives.

34. Hopkins, "War on Distress," 151–58; Lacy, *Soil Soldiers*, 209.

35. Cohen, *Tree Army*, 145.

36. Records from National Archives in Kay Rippelmeyer Collection; "3 Illinois CCC Park Camps to Be Discontinued."

37. "Gov. Green Gives 4-H Clubs Right to Use CCC Camps"; "U.S. Takes Over CCC Camps at Illinois Parks"; Roscoe Pulliam to George W. Williams, Superintendent of Parks and Memorials, May 14, 1942, GCVC. Pulliam wrote about SINU taking over use of barracks for Boy Scouts or SINU student organizations, referring to some CCC barracks that were previously removed from the park to SINU campus. However, Pulliam indicated that the university didn't want to take over responsibility for the remaining barracks at the park unless they could also be removed onto SINU property.

38. A. R. Kugler to Bond Blackman, February 21, 1942, GCVC. The WPA did not have as good a reputation as the CCC. The men of the CCC were separated from the general public in camps, whereas the WPA workers lived in their homes, alongside regular workers, which caused more public tension. In July 1939, five thousand WPA employees in Madison and St. Clair counties in Illinois walked off their jobs in protest against an extended work week. Their walkout triggered similar ones across the country, plus threats by the American Federation of Labor to unionize the WPA.

39. Cohen, *Tree Army*, 88–90; Lacy, *Soil Soldiers*, 139.

40. From an excerpt of James J. McEntee's "Final Report of the Civilian Conservation Corps"; Cohen, *Tree Army*, appendix.

41. Cohen, *Tree Army*, 147–55.

42. Fechner, "My Hopes for the CCC," 10.

43. Lacy, *Soil Soldiers*, 209.

44. As quoted from a 1938 article in the *St. Louis Post-Dispatch*, April 4, 1999, A6; Dickey interview, July 26, 2002.

45. Vancil interview.

46. Hawk interview.

47. Oliver interview.

48. Dickey interview, July 26, 2002.

49. Dickey interview, July 26, 2002, and correspondence with Juanita Earnest, November 10, 1935.

50. "Crowds Swarm over Illinois' Park System."

# Bibliography

## NEWSPAPERS AND PERIODICALS

*American Forests*
*Barton Free Press* (Carbondale, IL)
*Carbondale (IL) Free Press*
*Carbondale (IL) Herald*
*Chicago Tribune*
*Du Quoin (IL) Daily News*
*Egyptian* (Southern Illinois Normal University)
*Egyptian Key* (Herrin, IL)
*Egyptian Republican* (Herrin, IL)
*Farmer and Fruit Grower* (Anna, IL)
*Forest History*
*Giant City Goliath* (CCC Co. #696)
*Giant City News* (CCC Co. #696)
*Herrin (IL) News*
*ICarbs* (Special Collections, Morris Library, Southern Illinois University Carbondale)
*Life*
*Literary Digest*
*Makanda (IL) News*
*Monday's Pub* (Anna, IL)
*Murphysboro (IL) Daily Independent*
*Southern Illinoisan* (Carbondale, IL)
*The Spirit of 57* (monthly publication, CCC Company #1657)
*St. Louis Post-Dispatch*
*Stone-City Weekly* (CCC Companies #692 and #696)
*Today*

## INTERVIEWS AND CORRESPONDENCE WITH AUTHOR

Baker, Thelma Fuller. Interview, May 1979.
Bodeker, William. Interview, August 27, 1987.
Dickey, Earl. Interviews, July 26, 2002, February 19, 2003, and March 12, 2003.
Esposito, Andrew. Interview, March 26, 1979.
Finley, Floyd. Interview, September 24, 1987.
———. Written reminiscence, June 22, 1984.
Hassen, Hal. E-mail correspondence, 2007.
Hawk, Kenneth. Interview, September 9, 1987.
Minton, Homer, and Viola Minton. Interviews, October 5, 1979, and January 16, 1980.
Oliver, George. Interview, August 31, 1987.
Rayle, Lynn. Letter correspondence, March 17, 1989.
Schueller, Mary J. E-mail correspondence, 2003.
Skertich, Matthew. Letter correspondence, September 2, 1987.
Skufca, Jenny. E-mail correspondence, 2006–7.
Vancil, Scott. Interview, November 9, 1987.
Watkins, Jim. Interview, February 18, 2005.
Zimmerman, Joseph. Letter correspondence, n.d.

## COLLECTIONS, PAPERS, AND REPORTS

Allen, John W., Papers. Special Collections Research Center, Morris Library, Southern Illinois University Carbondale.

Giant City State Park Civilian Conservation Corps Collection (MSS 280), Special Collections Research Center, Morris Library, Southern Illinois University Carbondale. Includes Emergency Conservation Work (ECW) and Civilian Conservation Corps (CCC) Narrative Reports, Camp Reports, Monthly Reports, Semi-monthly Reports, Status Reports, Summary Reports, Inspection Reports, and Proposals for Camps SP-11, SP-24, and SP-41, 1933 to 1941, authored by Thomas Bermingham, John J. Biggs, H. P. Britson, Harold G. Chafey, Harry Collier, William P. Hannon, Albin Olson, Hugh Roach, and A. G. Ruediger, originally found in RG 79 and RG 35, National Archives, Washington, DC.

Giant City Visitor Center Manuscript Collection, Giant City State Park, Makanda, Illinois. Includes correspondence from John J. Biggs, Bond Blackman, Rodney Brandon, H. H. Cleaveland, Ralph Corzine, Governor Louis Emmerson, Charles Gore, O. J. Hagebush, Frank Hopkins, Ray Hubbs, Carter Jenkins, Robert Klingery, A. R. Kugler, Charles Lamer, H. H. Lamer, George Luker, John G. Mulcaster, Irvin Peithman, Wayman Presley, Roscoe Pulliam, Willis Rendleman, Edgar Roberts, Elbert Waller, Bailey H. West, and George W. Williams.

Mulcaster, John G., Collection. Special Collections Research Center, Morris Library, Southern Illinois University Carbondale.

Pomona Township Records. Jackson County Historical Society, Murphysboro, Illinois.

Rippelmeyer, Kay, Collection. Special Collections Research Center, Morris Library, Southern Illinois University Carbondale.

Smith, George Washington, Papers. Special Collections Research Center, Morris Library, Southern Illinois University Carbondale.

## ARTICLES AND BOOKS

Adams, Jane. "Mystery of Stone Fort Remains." *Monday's Pub*, August 29, 1983.
———. *The Transformation of Rural Life: Southern Illinois, 1890–1990.* Chapel Hill: University of North Carolina Press, 1994.
———. "Years Ago in Union County." *Monday's Pub*, February 28, 1983, 4.
Anderson, Sherwood. "Tough Babes in the Woods." *Today*, February 10, 1934, 6–7, 22.
Booten, Joseph F. "State Park Architecture Harmonizes with Scenery." *Illinois Public Works* 3.2 (1945): 18–23.
Brieschke, Walt L., ed. *Notes on Makanda.* Makanda, IL: self-published, 1983.

Brieschke, Walt L., and Frank Rackerby. "The Stone Forts of Illinois." In *Notes on Makanda*, edited by Walter L. Brieschke. Makanda, IL: self-published, 1983. 5–9.

Burns, James MacGregor. *Roosevelt: The Lion and the Fox, 1882–1940*. Vol. 1. New York: Harcourt Brace Jovanovich, 1956.

Butler, Brian M., Mark J. Wagner, Brian D. DelCastello, Richard L. Herndon, and Kathryn E. Parker. *The Giant City Stone Fort (11J-35), Jackson County, Illinois*. Technical Report 02–2. Center for Archaeological Investigations, Southern Illinois University Carbondale, May 2002.

"Call for 3,125 Vets from Chicago Area for Forester Army." *Chicago Tribune*, June 4, 1933, 20.

"CCC." *Life*, June 6, 1938, 58–59.

"CCC Camps Approved for Fifth Period (1935) 200-Man Company Units." State of Illinois, RG 35, National Archives, Washington, DC.

"CCC Improving Giant City State Park for Visitors." *St. Louis Post-Dispatch*, May 6, 1935.

"CCC: Least Criticized New Deal Unit." *Literary Digest*, April 18, 1936, 48.

"CCC Quota Unfilled." *Stone-City Weekly*, September 25, 1935, 1.

"CCC Will Operate 55 Illinois Camps in Next 3 Months." *Chicago Tribune*, September 11, 1937, 11.

"Clothes Make the CCC Boy." *Stone-City Weekly*, September 25, 1935, 3, col. 4.

"Co. #1657 Salutes Departing Captain with Farewell Party and Dynamite." Springfield area newspaper, date unknown.

Cohen, Stan. *The Tree Army: A Pictorial History of the Conservation Corps, 1933–1942*. Missoula, MT: Pictorial Histories, 1980.

*Company D-692 Civilian Conservation Corps Camp, Stone Fort, DSP-1, Giant City State Park, Makanda, Illinois, Complete Company Roster for Fourth Enrollment Period, October 1, 1934–March 31, 1935*. Pamphlet printed about CCC Company #692 in 1935. In Giant City State Park Civilian Conservation Corps Collection (MSS 280), Special Collections Research Center, Morris Library, Southern Illinois University Carbondale.

Conrad, David E., and Glen M. Jones. "Town Life in Southern Illinois during the Great Depression." *ICarbs* 1.2 (Spring–Summer 1974): 121–40.

"County Paying Rock Haulage for Road to State Park." Undated newspaper article, in John W. Allen Papers, box 12.

"Crowds Swarm over Illinois' Park System." *Chicago Tribune*, June 6, 1948, C16.

Earle, Mary Tracy. *The Flag on the Hilltop*. Carbondale: Southern Illinois University Press, 1989.

*1878 History and 1907 Atlas of Jackson County, Illinois*. Reproductions by Jackson County Historical Society.

Ellis, Edward Robb. *A Nation in Torment: The Great American Depression, 1929–1939*. New York: Coward-McCann, 1970.

"End of State Unemployment Relief Scheme—Plan Forecast to Have Federal Government Take Complete Charge." *Murphysboro Daily Independent*, September 7, 1934, 1.

Farmer, Leonard. "History of the Shawnee National Forest, 1933–Present [1938]." Portion of Atlas 10, Forest Supervisor's Office, Harrisburg, IL.

Fechner, Robert. "My Hopes for the CCC." *American Forests* 45.1 (1939): 10–12, 30.

———. "Objectives and Results of the Civilian Conservation Corps Program." U.S. Government Documents, 1938. Morris Library, Southern Illinois University Carbondale.

"Forestry Army Chiefs Praise Enthusiasm of Rural Recruits." *Chicago Tribune*, July 26, 1933, 5.

"44,671 Youths Accepted for Camps, First Job for Many." *Chicago Tribune*, April 25, 1937, 23.

French, George H. "A Stone Fort near Makanda, Jackson County, Illinois." In *Annual Report of the Smithsonian Institution for 1881*. Washington, DC: GPO, 1883, 582–84.

"Giant City Appointment Causes Stir: Desired Custodianship Goes to Union County Man. Makanda Sore." *Murphysboro Daily Independent*, July 3, 1929.

"Giant City in Winter." Undated newspaper article, ca. 1927, in John W. Allen Papers, box 12.

"Giant City Park Awaits Visitors." *Herrin News*, May 9, 1935.

"Giant City Woods Army Likes Peaches." *Murphysboro Daily Independent*, July 1, 1933.

"Gov. Green Gives 4-H Clubs Right to Use CCC Camps." *Chicago Tribune*, January 8, 1943, 9.

Harris, Stanley E., C. William Horrell, and Daniel Irwin. *Exploring the Land and Rocks of Southern Illinois: A Geological Guide*. Carbondale: Southern Illinois University Press, 1977.

Hopkins, Harry. "The War on Distress." Reprinted in *New Deal Thought*, edited by Howard Zinn. New York: Bobbs Merrill, 1966. 151–58.

"Horner Praises CCC in Dedication Speech at Grant [*sic*] City Park." *Chicago Tribune*, August 31, 1936.

Howell, Glenn. *CCC Boys Remember: A Pictorial History of the Civilian Conservation Corps*. Medford, OR: 1976.

*Illinois Blue Book, 1927–1928*. State of Illinois.

*Illinois Blue Book, 1930*. State of Illinois

*Illinois Blue Book, 1935*. State of Illinois.

"Illinois to Have 26 Conservation Winter Camps." *Chicago Tribune*, September 13, 1933, 22.

"Indian Relics at Stonefort." *Stone-City Weekly*, August 28, 1935, 1.

"Insane Men Only Hauling Stone and Not Working." *Egyptian Republican*, January 1930. In John Mulcaster Scrapbook in John W. Allen Papers, 76.3.F1, vol. 23.

Iowa Aerial Surveys. Jackson County, Illinois, aerial photograph, 1938. BGQ-4-30, 10-21-38. 9 x 9 inches; scale 1:20,000. Washington, DC: US Department of Agriculture, 1938.

Keller, Kent. "What Has Been Done for the 25th District of Illinois with $122,000,000 and Egypt's Future." Monograph. Christopher, IL: Everett Alldridge, 1940.

Kenney, David. "Remembering Kent Keller." Section of an unpublished memoir, "A Gathering of Riches." 2002.

"Labor of Love: Murphysboro Man Helped Cut Stones for Giant City Lodge." *Southern Illinoisan*, September 4, 1985, A-8.

Lacy, Leslie Alexander. *The Soil Soldiers: The Civilian Conservation Corps in the Great Depression*. Radnor, PA: Chilton, 1976.

Maurer, David J. "Unemployment in Illinois during the Great Depression." In *Essays in Illinois History*, edited by Donald Tingley. Carbondale: Southern Illinois University Press, 1968. 120–32.

McEntee, James J. "Final Report of the Civilian Conservation Corps." 1942. National Archives, Washington, DC.

———. *Now They Are Men*. Washington, DC: National Home Library Foundation, 1940.

Meltzer, Milton. *Brother, Can You Spare a Dime? The Great Depression, 1929–1933*. New York: Knopf, 1969.

Merrill, Perry H. *Roosevelt's Forest Army: A History of the Civilian Conservation Corps, 1933–1942*. Montpelier, VT: Merrill, 1981.

Mohlenbrock, Robert. *Giant City State Park: An Illustrated Handbook*. Carbondale, IL: Robert Mohlenbrock, n.d.

"More Men to CCC Camps." *Murphysboro Daily Independent*, December 5, 1933.

Mulcaster, John G. "Old Stone Fort." *Egyptian Republican*, n.d.

———. "Rock Formations in Giant City Park Near Makanda, Ill." As reported from a speech given by John Mulcaster and quoted in *Du Quoin Daily News*, June 15, 1935.

———. Scrapbook in John W. Allen Papers, 76.3.F1, vol. 23.

"Mulcaster Says Park Interest to Be on Payroll." *Murphysboro Daily Independent*, July 3, 1929.

Newsome, Edmund. *Historical Sketches of Jackson County, Illinois*. Carbondale, IL: E. Newsome, 1894.

"Not Drills but Exercises." *Stone-City Weekly*, September 25, 1935, 2.

*Official Annual: Civilian Conservation Corps, Jefferson Barracks CCC District, Sixth Corps Area, 1937*. U.S. Government.

"Pacifists Begin Sniping at Army Training for CCC." *Chicago Tribune*, March 5, 1939, 13.

Perkins, Francis. "FDR Was 'A Little Left of Center.'" In *New Deal Thought*, edited by Howard Zinn. New York: Bobbs Merrill, 1966.

"Possibilities of the Conservation Corps." *Chicago Tribune*, August 27, 1933, 14.

"Projects Completed on Schedule; Workmanship Superior." *Stone-City Weekly*, September 25, 1935, 1.

Rauch, Mabel Thompson. *Vinnie and the Flag Tree*. New York: Duell, Sloan, and Pearce, 1959.

"Reforestation Concentration Camps Sought." *Murphysboro Daily Independent*, August 30, 1933, 1.

Richardson, Elmo R. "Was There Politics in the Civilian Conservation Corps?" *Forest History* 16 (July 1972): 13–21.

"Roosevelt Puts Forest Army on Higher Pay." *Chicago Tribune*, July 16, 1933, 7.

Russell, Herbert. Introduction to *The Flag on the Hilltop*, by Mary Tracy Earle. Carbondale: Southern Illinois University Press, 1989. vii–xxiv.

Salmond, John A. *The Civilian Conservation Corps, 1933–1942: A New Deal Case Study*. Durham, NC: Duke University Press, 1967.

"Says New Deal Going into Red Millions Daily." *Chicago Tribune*, October 8, 1934, 8.

Schueller, Mary J. *Soldiers of Poverty*. Richfield, WI: Rustic, 2006.

Sculle, Keith. "Lincoln Log Cabin State Historic Site." *Illinois Magazine*, March–April 1983, 7–9.

Smith, Jean Edward. *FDR*. New York: Random 2007.

Sneed, Glenn. *Ghost Towns of Southern Illinois*. Johnston City, IL: AERP.

Soady, Fred. "The Making of the Shawnee." Reprint from *Forest History* 9.2 (July 1965).

*South Pass Revisited*. Cobden, IL: Union County Historical and Genealogical Society, 2007.

State of Illinois. "Glacial History." Guide leaflet, Makanda Area, State Geological Survey Division, 1971.

Steen, Harold K. *The U.S. Forest Service: A History*. Seattle: University of Washington Press, 1976.

"A Story about the Grasshopper and Ants." Unnamed newspaper, ca. July 25, 1934.

Taylor, Richard S. "How Illinois Got Its First State Park." *Historic Illinois* 4.1 (1981): 4–5, 13.

"10,088 Families Transferred to Work Relief Jobs." *Murphysboro Daily Independent*, May 17, 1934, 1, col. 3.

Thomas, James W. "Makanda Floods." Reprinted in *Notes on Makanda*, edited by Walter L. Brieschke. Makanda, IL: self published, 1983. 95.

Thompson, Theodore W. "Pioneer Days and Early Settlers in and around Makanda." *Farmer and Fruit Grower* (Anna, IL), first printed sometime during the 1890s, later copied in the *Carbondale Herald*, May 13, 1899.

"3 Illinois CCC Park Camps to Be Discontinued." *Chicago Tribune*, April 29, 1934, 6.

"237,984 Men Are Now Enrolled in U.S. Forest Army." *Chicago Tribune*, June 22, 1933, 11.

"U.S. Takes Over CCC Camps at Illinois Parks." *Chicago Tribune*, September 16, 1942, 2.

"Various Departments to Offer Classes for Men of the CCC." *Egyptian*, November 22, 1933, 1.

Ward, Michael, and Keith Sculle. "National Register of Historic Places Inventory Nomination Form." United States Department of the Interior, National Park Service, October 1984.

"We Need Your Help." *Stone-City Weekly*, September 25, 1935, 1.

Wiggers, Raymond. *Geology Underfoot in Illinois*. Missoula, MT: Mountain Press, 1997.

"Zane Grey Recent Giant City Visitor, Is Belief." Undated newspaper article, ca. 1928, in John W. Allen Papers, box 12.

Zinn, Howard, ed. *New Deal Thought*. New York: Bobbs Merrill, 1966.

# Index

Page numbers in italics refer to illustrations.

Myers, John A., *138–39*
Myers, T., *156*
Myers., R., *156*

national forests, 27, 162
national forest system, 168
National Guard, 155
National Natural Landmark, 1
National Youth Administration, 26
native Americans, 2, 11, 65–67
Neal, David, 13
Neber, William, 160
Nethercott R. *138–39*, *156*
Neville, J. Wesley, 19
New Deal, 26, 30, 58, 144; legacies of, 168; programs, 114, 146; progressives in, 162; workforce relief agencies created during, 148
Newlin, Andrew Jackson, *37*, *42*, 68, 161
Newlon, D., *156*
Newlon, John W., *84*
Newman, E. W., 20
New Salem State Park, 17
Newsome, Edmund, 12
Nichols, Harvey L., *138–39*
Nickel, Emil S., *138–39*
North Pass (Makanda), 12
Nunn, Howard, *129*, *130*, *138–39*

O'Brien, Mr. (educational advisor), *130*
Odom, William, 193n22
*Official Annual of the Jefferson Barracks District (1937)*, 7
Ogilini's Bakery, 94
Ohl, Harold, *138–39*
Oldham, Walter, *138–39*
Oliver, George, 33, *33*, 37–38, 57–58, 63, 79, 83, *84–85*, 106–7, 118, 126–27, 137, *138–39*, 166, *167*
Olson, Albin F. (CCC superintendent), 33–34, 37, 63, 65, 75, 83, 86, 132, 137, 141–42, 144
Olszanowski, Sylvester, *138–39*
orchards, 6, 13, 15, 18–19, 25, 57, 131
Orlandi, Frank, *138–39*
Ossig, R., *156*
Otten, Walter, 130
Owens, George, 66
Ozark Hills, 2

Pacione, Chester J., *138–39*
Padgett, L., *156*
Paris, F., 160
Parker, William L., 160
Patterson, G. G., 18
Patterson, S., *156*
Pauley, Orrin, 82, 137, *138–39*
Payne, Robert, 160
Peak, Thomas, 18
Pearce, C., *156*

Peck, Fred Jr., *138–39*
Penrod, R., *156*
Percel, *96*
Pere Marquette (Piasa Bluff) St. Park, 17, 29, 79, 163
Perkins, Francis (secretary of labor), 157
Persich, Andrew, *138–39*, 192n47
Peterson, E., *156*
Pettit, Harold A., *138–39*
Pflasterer, Philip, 193n22
Phillips, Howard C., *138–39*
Phillips, Wayne, *138–39*, 192n47
picnic table construction, *75*
Pinckneyville, IL, 94
Plambeck, Ernest, 160
Pledger, M., *156*
Plumbers Local #160, 110
Polencheck, Marguerite, 148
Polonowski, A., *156*
Polonowski, Dick, 192n47
Pomona, IL, 15, 25
Pomona Natural Bridge, 2
Pomona township, 15
Pope County, IL, 29; geography of, 11
Post Creek cutoff, 166
Pragaldin, Charles V., 161
Prairie Farms, 94
Pray, Irene, 147
Presley, Wayman, 158,193n24
Prohibition, 25
Public Works Administration, 26
Pudney, Robert C., *138–39*
Pulaski County, IL, geography, 11
Pulcher, G., *156*
Purdum, James H., *138–39*

quarries, 12, 80, *88*, 95, 107–8
quarry, Chester, 21, 90

Raab, Henry, *138–39*
Rabold, Chester, *130*, *138–39*
Rader, John, 192n47
Ragland, Roy, 193n22
railroads in southern Illinois, 12, 15
Raines, Oscar L., 160
Rawls, Homer, 82
Raws, Mike, 82
Rayle, Lynn, 87, *88–89*, 99, 127–28
Reames, A., *156*
Reed, John, 22
reforestation, 27, 137, 147
Reforestation Army, 32
Reforestation Camp, 41
Rendleman family, 15
Rendleman School, 2
Rendleman, D., *156*
Rendleman, Jerome F., 19, 24

**Kay Rippelmeyer** is newly retired from her work as a lecturer, researcher, and academic advisor in the College of Liberal Arts at Southern Illinois University Carbondale. A program liaison for the Illinois Humanities Council, she has researched southern Illinois history for more than thirty years and has lectured widely on the Civilian Conservation Corps and river work in southern Illinois.

 *A Shawnee Book*

*Also available in this series . . .*